1

Grammar in Context

4TH EDITION

SANDRA N. ELBAUM

HEINLE
CENGAGE Learning

Australia • Brazil • Japan • Korea • Mexico • Singapore • Spain • United Kingdom • United States

HEINLE
CENGAGE Learning

Grammar in Context 1, Fourth Edition
SANDRA N. ELBAUM

Publisher, Adult & Academic, ESL: James W. Brown

Senior Acquisitions Editor, Adult & Academic, ESL: Sherrise Roehr

Director of Product Development: Anita Raducanu

Director of Marketing: Amy Mabley

Marketing Manager: Laura Needham

Senior Print Buyer: Mary Beth Hennebury

Development Editor: Charlotte Sturdy

Compositor: Nesbitt Graphics, Inc.

Project Manager: Lois Lombardo

Photo Researcher: Connie Gardner

Illustrators: Ralph Canaday, James Edwards, Larry Frederick, and Brock Nichol

Interior Designer: Jerilyn Bockorick

Cover Designer: Joseph Sherman

Cover Image: Brooklyn Bridge, New York by Julian Barrow/Private Collection/Bridgeman Art Library

> For product information and technology assistance, contact us at
> **Cengage Learning Customer & Sales Support, 1-800-354-9706**
> For permission to use material from this text or product, submit all requests online at **cengage.com/permissions**
> Further permissions questions can be emailed to **permissionrequest@cengage.com**

Library of Congress Control Number: 2004118367

ISBN-13: 978-1-4130-0736-7

ISBN-10: 1-4130-0736-8

ISE ISBN-13: 978-1-4130-1394-8

ISE ISBN-10: 1-4130-1394-5

Heinle
25 Thomson Place
Boston, MA 02210
USA

Cengage Learning is a leading provider of customized learning solutions with office locations around the globe, including Singapore, the United Kingdom, Australia, Mexico, Brazil, and Japan. Locate your local office at: **international.cengage.com/region**

Cengage Learning products are represented in Canada by Nelson Education, Ltd.

Visit **elt.heinle.com**

Visit our corporate website at **cengage.com**

Printed in the United States of America
7 8 9 10 11 12   12 11 10 09

Contents

Lesson 5   131

Lesson 6   159

Lesson 9   **263**

Lesson 13   377

Lesson 14   401

Appendices

In memory of
Herman and Ethel Elbaum

Acknowledgments

Many thanks to Dennis Hogan, Jim Brown, Sherrise Roehr, Yeny Kim, and Sally Giangrande from Thomson Heinle for their ongoing support of the *Grammar in Context* series. I would especially like to thank my editor, Charlotte Sturdy, for her keen eye to detail and invaluable suggestions.

And many thanks to my students at Truman College, who have increased my understanding of my own language and taught me to see life from another point of view. By sharing their observations, questions, and life stories, they have enriched my life enormously—*Sandra N. Elbaum*

Heinle would like to thank the following people for their contributions:

Marki Alexander
Oklahoma State
  University
Stillwater, OK

Joan M. Amore
Triton College
River Grove, IL

**Edina Pingleton
Bagley**
Nassau Community
  College
Garden City, NY

Judith A. G. Benka
Normandale Community
  College
Bloomington, MN

**Judith Book-
Ehrlichman**
Bergen Community
  College
Paramus, NJ

Lyn Buchheit
Community College of
  Philadelphia
Philadelphia, PA

Charlotte M. Calobrisi
Northern Virginia
  Community College
Annandale, VA

Sarah A. Carpenter
Normandale Community
  College
Bloomington, MN

Jeanette Clement
Duquesne University
Pittsburgh, PA

Allis Cole
Shoreline Community
  College
Shoreline, WA

**Jacqueline M.
Cunningham**
Triton College
River Grove, IL

Lisa DePaoli
Sierra College
Rocklin, CA

Maha Edlbi
Sierra College
Rocklin, CA

Rhonda J. Farley
Cosumnes River College
Sacramento, CA

Jennifer Farnell
University of Connecticut
American Language
  Program
Stamford, CT

**Abigail-Marie
Fiattarone**
Mesa Community College
Mesa, AZ

Marcia Gethin-Jones
University of Connecticut
American Language
  Program
Storrs, CT

Linda Harlow
Santa Rosa Junior
  College
Santa Rosa, CA

Suha R. Hattab
Triton College
River Grove, IL

Bill Keniston
Normandale Community
  College
Bloomington, MN

Walton King
Arkansas State
  University
Jonesboro, AR

Kathleen Krokar
Truman College
Chicago, IL

John Larkin
NVCC-Community and
  Workforce
  Development
Annandale, VA

Michael Larsen
American River College
Sacramento, CA

Bea C. Lawn
Gavilan College
Gilroy, CA

Rob Lee
Pasadena City College
Pasadena, CA

**Oranit
Limmaneeprasert**
American River College
Sacramento, CA

Gennell Lockwood
Shoreline Community
  College
Shoreline, WA

Linda Louie
Highline Community
  College
Des Moines, WA

Melanie A. Majeski
Naugatuck Valley
  Community College
Waterbury, CT

Maria Marin
De Anza College
Cupertino, CA

Karen Miceli
Cosumnes River College
Sacramento, CA

Jeanie Pavichevich
Triton College
River Grove, IL

Herbert Pierson
St. John's University
New York City, NY

Dina Poggi
De Anza College
Cupertino, CA

Mark Rau
American River College
Sacramento, CA

John W. Roberts
Shoreline Community
  College
Shoreline, WA

Azize R. Ruttler
Bergen Community
  College
Paramus, NJ

Ann Salzmann
University of Illinois,
Urbana, IL

Eva Teagarden
Yuba College
Marysville, CA

Susan Wilson
San Jose City College
San Jose, CA

Martha Yeager-Tobar
Cerritos College
Norwalk, CA

A word from the author

It seems that I was born to be an ESL teacher. My parents immigrated to the U.S. from Poland as adults and were confused not only by the English language but by American culture as well. Born in the U.S., I often had the task as a child to explain the intricacies of the language and allay my parents' fears about the culture. It is no wonder to me that I became an ESL teacher, and later, an ESL writer who focuses on explanations of American culture in order to illustrate grammar. My life growing up in an immigrant neighborhood was very similar to the lives of my students, so I have a feel for what confuses them and what they need to know about American life.

ESL teachers often find themselves explaining confusing customs and providing practical information about life in the U.S. Often, teachers are a student's only source of information about American life. With **Grammar in Context, Fourth Edition,** I enjoy sharing my experiences with you.

Grammar in Context, Fourth Edition connects grammar with American cultural context, providing learners of English with a useful and meaningful skill and knowledge base. Students learn the grammar necessary to communicate verbally and in writing, and learn how American culture plays a role in language, beliefs, and everyday situations.

Enjoy the new edition of **Grammar in Context!**

Sandra N. Elbaum

Grammar in Context

Students learn more, remember more, and use language more effectively when they learn grammar in context.

Learning a language through meaningful themes and practicing it in a contextualized setting promote both linguistic and cognitive development. In **Grammar in Context**, grammar is presented in interesting and culturally informative readings, and the language and context are subsequently practiced throughout the chapter.

New to this edition

- **New and updated readings** on current American topics such as Instant Messaging and eBay.
- **Updated grammar charts** that now include essential language notes.
- **Updated exercises and activities** that provide contextualized practice using a variety of exercise types, as well as additional practice for more difficult structures.
- **New lower-level *Grammar in Context Basic*** for beginning level students.
- **New wrap-around Teacher's Annotated Edition** with page-by-page, point-of-use teaching suggestions.
- **Expanded Assessment CD-ROM** with ExamView ® Pro Test Generator now contains more questions types and assessment options to easily allow teachers to create tests and quizzes.

Distinctive Features of *Grammar in Context*

Students are prepared for academic assignments and everyday language tasks.

Discussions, readings, compositions, and exercises involving higher-level critical thinking skills develop overall language and communication skills.

Students expand their knowledge of American topics and culture.

The readings in **Grammar in Context** help students gain insight into and enrich their knowledge of American culture and history. Students gain ample exposure to the practicalities of American life, such as writing a résumé, dealing with telemarketers, and junk mail, and getting student internships. Their new knowledge helps them adapt to everyday life in the U.S.

Students learn to use their new skills to communicate.

The exercises and Expansion Activities in **Grammar in Context** help students learn English while practicing their writing and speaking skills. Students work together in pairs and groups to find more information about topics, to make presentations, to play games, and to role-play. Their confidence in using English increases, as does their ability to communicate effectively.

Welcome to **Grammar in Context, Fourth Edition**

Students learn more, remember more, and use language more effectively when they learn grammar in context.

Grammar in Context, Fourth Edition connects grammar with rich, American cultural context, providing learners of English with a useful and meaningful skill and knowledge base.

An **Audio Program** allows students to hear the readings and dialogs, and provides an opportunity to practice their listening skills.

Readings on American topics such as Instant Messaging, eBay, and The AIDS Ride present and illustrate the grammatical structure in an informative and meaningful context.

Grammar charts offer clear explanations and provide contextualized examples of the structure.

Language Notes refine students' understanding of the target structure.

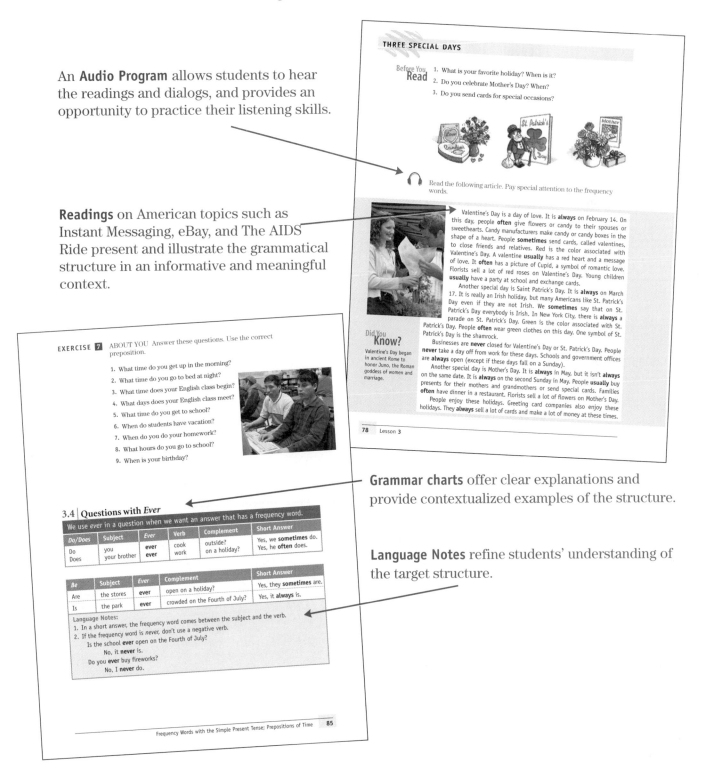

THREE SPECIAL DAYS

Before You Read
1. What is your favorite holiday? When is it?
2. Do you celebrate Mother's Day? When?
3. Do you send cards for special occasions?

Read the following article. Pay special attention to the frequency words.

Valentine's Day is a day of love. It is **always** on February 14. On this day, people **often** give flowers or candy to their spouses or sweethearts. Candy manufacturers make candy or candy boxes in the shape of a heart. People **sometimes** send cards, called valentines, to close friends and relatives. Red is the color associated with Valentine's Day. A valentine **usually** has a red heart and a message of love. It **often** has a picture of Cupid, a symbol of romantic love. Florists sell a lot of red roses on Valentine's Day. Young children **usually** have a party at school and exchange cards.

Another special day is Saint Patrick's Day. It is **always** on March 17. It is really an Irish holiday, but many Americans like St. Patrick's Day even if they are not Irish. We **sometimes** say that on St. Patrick's Day everybody is Irish. In New York City, there is **always** a parade on St. Patrick's Day. Green is the color associated with St. Patrick's Day. People **often** wear green clothes on this day. One symbol of St. Patrick's Day is the shamrock.

Did You Know?
Valentine's Day began in ancient Rome to honor Juno, the Roman goddess of women and marriage.

Businesses are **never** closed for Valentine's Day or St. Patrick's Day. People **never** take a day off from work for these days. Schools and government offices are **always** open (except if these days fall on a Sunday).

Another special day is Mother's Day. It is **always** in May, but it isn't **always** on the same date. It is **always** on the second Sunday in May. People **usually** buy presents for their mothers and grandmothers or send special cards. Families **often** have dinner in a restaurant. Florists sell a lot of flowers on Mother's Day.

People enjoy these holidays. Greeting card companies also enjoy these holidays. They **always** sell a lot of cards and make a lot of money at these times.

78   Lesson 3

EXERCISE 7   ABOUT YOU Answer these questions. Use the correct preposition.

1. What time do you get up in the morning?
2. What time do you go to bed at night?
3. What time does your English class begin?
4. What days does your English class meet?
5. What time do you get to school?
6. When do students have vacation?
7. When do you do your homework?
8. What hours do you go to school?
9. When is your birthday?

3.4 | Questions with *Ever*

We use *ever* in a question when we want an answer that has a frequency word.

Do/Does	Subject	Ever	Verb	Complement	Short Answer
Do	you	ever	cook	outside?	Yes, we **sometimes** do.
Does	your brother	ever	work	on a holiday?	Yes, he **often** does.

Be	Subject	Ever	Complement	Short Answer
Are	the stores	ever	open on a holiday?	Yes, they **sometimes** are.
Is	the park	ever	crowded on the Fourth of July?	Yes, it **always** is.

Language Notes:
1. In a short answer, the frequency word comes between the subject and the verb.
2. If the frequency word is *never*, don't use a negative verb.
    Is the school **ever** open on the Fourth of July?
        No, it **never** is.
    Do you **ever** buy fireworks?
        No, I **never** do.

Frequency Words with the Simple Present Tense; Prepositions of Time   85

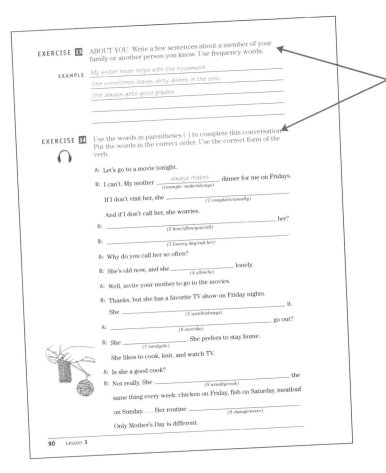

EXERCISE **13** ABOUT YOU Write a few sentences about a member of your family or another person you know. Use frequency words.

EXAMPLE My sister never helps with the housework.

She sometimes leaves dirty dishes in the sink.

She always gets good grades.

_____

_____

EXERCISE **14** Use the words in parentheses ( ) to complete this conversation. Put the words in the correct order. Use the correct form of the verb.

A: Let's go to a movie tonight.

B: I can't. My mother ___always makes___ dinner for me on Fridays.
                    (example: make/always)

If I don't visit her, she _____.
                          (1 complain/usually)

And if I don't call her, she worries.

A: _____ her?
            (2 how/often/you/call)

B: _____ .
            (3 I/every day/call her)

A: Why do you call her so often?

B: She's old now, and she _____ lonely.
                          (4 often/be)

A: Well, invite your mother to go to the movies.

B: Thanks, but she has a favorite TV show on Friday nights.

She _____ it.
        (5 watch/always)

A: _____ go out?
        (6 ever/she)

B: She _____ . She prefers to stay home.
        (7 rarely/do)

She likes to cook, knit, and watch TV.

A: Is she a good cook?

B: Not really. She _____ the
                    (8 usually/cook)

same thing every week: chicken on Friday, fish on Saturday, meatloaf

on Sunday. . . . Her routine _____ .
                            (9 change/never)

Only Mother's Day is different.

A variety of contextualized activities keeps the classroom lively and targets different learning styles.

A **Summary** provides the lesson's essential grammar in an easy-to-reference format.

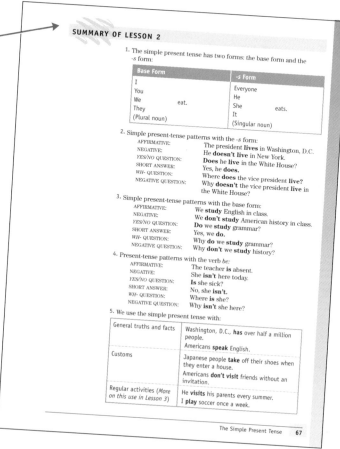

SUMMARY OF LESSON 2

1. The simple present tense has two forms: the base form and the -s form:

Base Form		-s Form	
I		Everyone	
You		He	
We	eat.	She	eats.
They		It	
(Plural noun)		(Singular noun)	

2. Simple present-tense patterns with the -s form:

AFFIRMATIVE: The president **lives** in Washington, D.C.
NEGATIVE: He **doesn't live** in New York.
YES/NO QUESTION: **Does** he **live** in the White House?
SHORT ANSWER: Yes, he **does.**
WH- QUESTION: Where **does** the vice president **live?**
NEGATIVE QUESTION: Why **doesn't** the vice president **live** in the White House?

3. Simple present-tense patterns with the base form:

AFFIRMATIVE: We **study** English in class.
NEGATIVE: We **don't study** American history in class.
YES/NO QUESTION: **Do** we **study** grammar?
SHORT ANSWER: Yes, we **do.**
WH- QUESTION: Why **do** we **study** grammar?
NEGATIVE QUESTION: Why **don't** we **study** history?

4. Present-tense patterns with the verb be:

AFFIRMATIVE: The teacher **is** absent.
NEGATIVE: She **isn't** here today.
YES/NO QUESTION: **Is** she sick?
SHORT ANSWER: No, she **isn't.**
WH- QUESTION: Where **is** she?
NEGATIVE QUESTION: Why **isn't** she here?

5. We use the simple present tense with:

General truths and facts	Washington, D.C., **has** over half a million people.
	Americans **speak** English.
Customs	Japanese people **take** off their shoes when they enter a house.
	Americans **don't visit** friends without an invitation.
Regular activities (More on this use in Lesson 3)	He **visits** his parents every summer.
	I **play** soccer once a week.

The Simple Present Tense **67**

Editing Advice gives students pre-writing practice by alerting them to common errors.

Test/Review at the end of each lesson provides a chance to review and/or assess the grammar from the lesson.

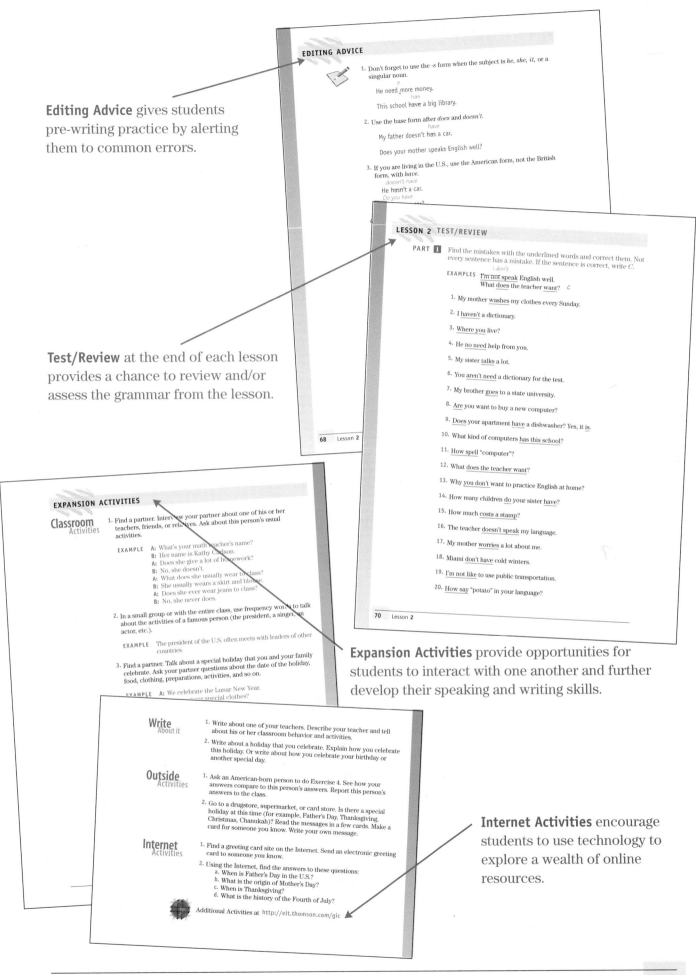

EDITING ADVICE

1. Don't forget to use the -s form when the subject is *he, she, it,* or a singular noun.

   He need more money.

   This school have a big library.

2. Use the base form after *does* and *doesn't*.

   My father doesn't has a car.

   Does your mother speaks English well?

3. If you are living in the U.S., use the American form, not the British form, with *have*.

   He hasn't a car.

   Do you have

LESSON 2 TEST/REVIEW

PART I Find the mistakes with the underlined words and correct them. Not every sentence has a mistake. If the sentence is correct, write *C*.

EXAMPLES I'm not speak English well.
          What does the teacher want? c

1. My mother washes my clothes every Sunday.
2. I haven't a dictionary.
3. Where you live?
4. He no need help from you.
5. My sister talks a lot.
6. You aren't need a dictionary for the test.
7. My brother goes to a state university.
8. Are you want to buy a new computer?
9. Does your apartment have a dishwasher? Yes, it is.
10. What kind of computers has this school?
11. How spell "computer"?
12. What does the teacher want?
13. Why you don't want to practice English at home?
14. How many children do your sister have?
15. How much costs a stamp?
16. The teacher doesn't speak my language.
17. My mother worries a lot about me.
18. Miami don't have cold winters.
19. I'm not like to use public transportation.
20. How say "potato" in your language?

68   Lesson 2

70   Lesson 2

EXPANSION ACTIVITIES

Classroom Activities

1. Find a partner. Interview your partner about one of his or her teachers, friends, or relatives. Ask about this person's usual activities.

   EXAMPLE A: What's your math teacher's name?
            B: Her name is Kathy Carlson.
            A: Does she give a lot of homework?
            B: No, she doesn't.
            A: What does she usually wear to class?
            B: She usually wears a skirt and blouse.
            A: Does she ever wear jeans to class?
            B: No, she never does.

2. In a small group or with the entire class, use frequency words to talk about the activities of a famous person (the president, a singer, an actor, etc.).

   EXAMPLE The president of the U.S. often meets with leaders of other countries.

3. Find a partner. Talk about a special holiday that you and your family celebrate. Ask your partner questions about the date of the holiday, food, clothing, preparations, activities, and so on.

   EXAMPLE A: We celebrate the Lunar New Year.
            special clothes?

Write About it

1. Write about one of your teachers. Describe your teacher and tell about his or her classroom behavior and activities.

2. Write about a holiday that you celebrate. Explain how you celebrate this holiday. Or write about how you celebrate your birthday or another special day.

Outside Activities

1. Ask an American-born person to do Exercise 4. See how your answers compare to this person's answers. Report this person's answers to the class.

2. Go to a drugstore, supermarket, or card store. Is there a special holiday at this time (for example, Father's Day, Thanksgiving, Christmas, Chanukah)? Read the messages in a few cards. Make a card for someone you know. Write your own message.

Internet Activities

1. Find a greeting card site on the Internet. Send an electronic greeting card to someone you know.

2. Using the Internet, find the answers to these questions:
   a. When is Father's Day in the U.S.?
   b. What is the origin of Mother's Day?
   c. When is Thanksgiving?
   d. What is the history of the Fourth of July?

   Additional Activities at http://elt.thomson.com/gic

Expansion Activities provide opportunities for students to interact with one another and further develop their speaking and writing skills.

Internet Activities encourage students to use technology to explore a wealth of online resources.

Welcome to *Grammar in Context*   **xvii**

Grammar in Context Student Book Supplements

Audio Program
- Audio CDs and Audio Tapes allow students to listen to every reading in the book as well as selected dialogs.

More Grammar Practice Workbooks
- Workbooks can be used with *Grammar in Context* or any skills text to learn and review the essential grammar.
- Great for in-class practice or homework.
- Includes practice on all grammar points in *Grammar in Context*.

Teacher's Annotated Edition
- New component offers page-by-page answers and teaching suggestions.

Assessment CD-ROM with ExamView® Pro Test Generator
- Test Generator allows teachers to create tests and quizzes quickly and easily.

Interactive CD-ROM
- CD-ROM allows for supplemental interactive practice on grammar points from *Grammar in Context*.

Split Editions
- Split Editions provide options for short courses.

Instructional Video/DVD
- Video/DVD offers teaching suggestions and advice on how to use *Grammar in Context*.

Web Site
- Web site gives access to additional activities and promotes the use of the Internet.

GRAMMAR

The Present Tense of the Verb *Be*
Prepositions of Place
This, That, These, Those

CONTEXT: College Life

Community College Life in the U.S.
Letter from College
Instant Message from a Student in the U.S.
In the School Cafeteria

Before You Read

Circle *T* for True or *F* for False and discuss your answers.

1. Most of the students in my class are immigrants.   **T   F**

2. My school is in a convenient[1] location.   **T   F**

 Read the following article. Pay special attention to *is* and *are*.

A community college (or two-year college) **is** a good place to begin your education in the U.S. The tuition **is** usually cheaper than at a university. Because a community college **is** often smaller than a university, foreign students **are** often more comfortable. They **are** closer to their professors and get more attention.

Truman College **is** a typical community college. It **is** one of seven City Colleges of Chicago. It **is** a two-year college on the north side of Chicago. It **is** near public transportation—buses and trains—so it **is** convenient for everyone. For students with a car, parking **is** free. Credit classes **are** $70 per credit hour. Adult education classes **are** free.

Truman College **is** an international school. Many of the students **are** from other countries and **are** in ESL courses. Some of the students **are** immigrants. Some of the students **are** international students. International students **are** in the U.S. only to study. Tuition for international students **is** much higher.

Many of the students have jobs, so evening and weekend classes **are** convenient for these students. Some students have small children, so Truman has a child-care center.

The semester **is** 16 weeks long. Summer semester **is** eight weeks long. Students **are** free to choose their own classes.

[1]Something that is *convenient* is easy for you. A convenient location is near your house or near public transportation. Convenient classes are at a time that is good for you.

Read the following student composition. Pay special attention to *is*, *am*, *are*.

> My name **is** Rolando Lopez. I **am** from Guatemala. I **am** a student at Truman College. My major **is** engineering. I **am** married, and I work during the day. My classes **are** at night and on Saturdays. The college **is** a good place for me to start my education in the U.S. because the tuition **is** low and the attention to students **is** very high. My plan **is** to take 60 credit hours here and then go to a four-year college, such as the University of Illinois. I like it here because the teachers **are** friendly and helpful and the students from other countries **are** interesting.

1.1 | Forms of *Be*

Examples			Explanation
Subject	Form of *Be*	Complement	Use *am* with *I*.
I	**am**	a college student.	
My teacher He Truman It My wife She	**is**	an American. friendly. a City College. in Chicago. a student. busy.	Use *is* with *he*, *she*, *it*, and singular subjects (*teacher*, *wife*, *college*).
We You The students They	**are**	students. the teacher. from all over the world. immigrants.	Use *are* with *we*, *you*, *they*, and plural subjects.

EXERCISE 1   Fill in the blanks with *is*, *are*, or *am*.

EXAMPLE   My name _____*is*_____ Rolando Lopez.

1. I _____ from Guatemala.

2. My wife _____ from Mexico.

3. My wife and I _____ students.

4. The University of Illinois _____ a four-year college.

5. My classmates _____ from many different countries.

6. We _____ immigrants.

7. The professors at my college _____ friendly and helpful.

8. My major _____ engineering.

9. The semester _____ 16 weeks long.

1.2 | Uses of *Be*

Examples	Explanation
The college is **good**. Evening classes are **convenient** for me. The tuition is **low**. The teachers are very **friendly**.	Use a form of *be* with a description of the subject.
Truman College is **a community college**. The University of Illinois is **a four-year college**.	Use a form of *be* with a classification or definition of the subject.
Truman College is **in Chicago**. Chicago is **in Illinois**. The college is **near public transportation**.	Use a form of *be* with the location of the subject.
I am **from Guatemala**. My wife is **from Mexico**.	Use a form of *be* with the place of origin of the subject.
I am **24 years old**. My teacher is **about 40 years old**.	Use a form of *be* with the age of the subject.
It is **cold** in Chicago in the winter. It is **warm** in Guatemala all year.	Use *is* with weather. The subject is *it*.
It is **6 o'clock** now. It is **late**.	Use *is* with time. The subject is *it*.

EXERCISE 2   Fill in the blanks to make true statements.

EXAMPLE   Chicago is _____*in Illinois*_____.
                              (location)

1. Chicago is a _____. Illinois is a state.
                    (classification)

2. My college is _____ public transportation.
                       (location)

3. The teacher is about _____ years old.
                               (age)

4. The teacher is from _____.
                          (place of origin)

5. It is _____ now.
             (time)

6. It is _____ today.
            (weather)

7. This city is _____.
                   (description)

1.3 | Word Order with *Be*

Examples			Explanation
Subject	***Be***	**Complement**	• The subject is first. The subject tells who or what we are talking about.
I	am	from Guatemala.	• The verb (*am, is, are*) is second.
Guatemala	is	in Central America.	• The complement is third. The complement finishes, or completes, the sentence with a location, classification, description, etc.
It	is	a small country.	
Spanish	is	my native language.	
You	are	from Vietnam.	
It	is	in Asia.	

EXERCISE 3 Put the words in the correct order to make a statement.
Use a capital letter at the beginning and a period at the end.

EXAMPLE a two-year college / my college / is _My college is a two-year college._

1. am / I / a student _____

2. my parents / in Guatemala / are _____

3. high / is / tuition at a four-year college _____

4. is / convenient / my college _____

5. my teacher / is / 40 years old _____

6. is / from New York / my teacher _____

7. eight weeks long / the summer semester / is _____

8. Rolando / married / is _____

The Present Tense of the Verb *Be*; Preposition of Place; *This, That, These, Those*   **5**

1.4 | The Subject

Examples	Explanation
I am from Guatemala. **You** are an American citizen. **It** is warm in Guatemala. **We** are happy in the U.S.	The subject pronouns are: *I, you, he, she, it, we, they.*
Chicago is very big. **It** is in Illinois. **My wife** is a student. **She** is from Mexico. **My teacher** is American. **She** is a native speaker of English. **My parents** are in Guatemala. **They** are happy. **My wife and I** are in the U.S. **We** are in Chicago.	• Subject pronouns (*it, she, he, we*) can take the place of nouns (*Chicago, sister, father, friend, I*) • A noun can be singular (*my father*) or plural (*my parents*). A plural noun usually ends in *s.* • When the subject is "another person and I," put the other person before *I.* **Note:** In conversation you sometimes hear "me and my wife" in the subject position. This is very informal.
My classmates are from many countries. **They** are immigrants. **English and math** are my favorite subjects. **They** are useful subjects.	We use *they* for plural people and things.
The U.S. is a big country. **It** is in North America.	*The United States* (*the U.S.*) is a singular noun. Use *the* before United States or U.S.
You are a good teacher. **You** are good students.	*You* can be a singular or plural subject.
It is cold in Chicago in the winter. **It** is 6 o'clock now.	Use *it* to talk about time and weather.

EXERCISE **4**   Fill in the blanks with the correct pronoun.

EXAMPLE   Nicaragua and Guatemala are countries. _____*They*_____ are in
Central America.

1. My wife and I are students. _____ are at Truman
College.

2. Guatemala is a small country. _____ is south of
Mexico.

3. Some of the students in my class are international

students. _____ are from China, Japan, and Spain.

4. _____ am a busy person.

5. English is a hard language. _____ is necessary in the U.S.

6. Adult classes at my college are free. _____ are for ESL students.

7. My book is new. _____ is *Grammar in Context.*

8. My parents are in Guatemala. _____ are old.

9. My teacher is a nice woman. _____ is from Boston.

10. My classmates and I are interested in American life. _____ are new in this country.

LETTER FROM COLLEGE

Before You Read

Circle *T* for True or *F* for False and discuss your answers.

1. The students in this class are from the same country.   T   F

2. Most of the students in this class are the same age.   T   F

Read the following letter. Pay special attention to contractions with *am*, *is*, *are.*

United States

Atlantic Ocean

Gulf of Mexico

Puerto Rico

Dear Ola,

College **is** so different here. Students in my class **are** all ages. **We're** 22—**that's** a normal age for college students back home. But some students here **are** in their 50s or 60s. One man in my class **is** 74. **He's** from Korea. This **is** very strange for me, but it **is** interesting too. Some students **are** married. Most students have jobs, so **we're** all very busy.

The students **are** from all over the world. One student **is** from Puerto Rico. Her native language **is** Spanish, but Puerto Rico **isn't** a foreign country and it **isn't** a state of the U.S. It **is** a special territory. It **is** a small island near the U.S.

(continued)

The Present Tense of the Verb *Be*; Preposition of Place; *This, That, These, Those*   **7**

The classrooms **are** different here too. **They're** big and comfortable. But the desks **are** so small. Another strange thing **is** this: The desks **are** in a circle, not in rows.

In our country, **education's** free. But here **it's** so expensive. At my college, the **tuition's** $125 per credit hour. And books **are** expensive too.

The teacher's young and informal. **He's** about my age. His **name's** Rich Weiss, and **he's** very friendly. **We're** always welcome in his office after class. But English **is** so hard. **It's** not hard to read English, but **it's** hard to understand American speech.

I'm in Minneapolis. **It's** in the northern part of the U.S. **It's** very cold here in the winter. But the summers **are** warm and sunny.

Tell me about your life. **Are** you happy with your college classes? **What's** your major now? **How's** the weather? **What's** your favorite class this semester? How are your teachers? **Are** they strict?

Take care,
Maya

1.5 | Contractions with *Be*

Examples		Explanation
I am	**I'm** in Minneapolis.	We can make a **contraction** with a subject pronoun and *am, is,* and *are*. We take out the first letter of *am, is, are* and put an apostrophe (') in its place. We usually use a contraction when we speak. We sometimes write a contraction in informal writing.
You are	**You're** a student of English.	
She is	**She's** a young teacher.	
He is	**He's** 75 years old.	
It is	**It's** cold in winter.	
We are	**We're** so busy.	
They are	**They're** big.	
The United States is a big country. College is different here. English is the language of the U.S. Rich is my English teacher.		We don't make a contraction with *is* if the noun ends in these sounds: *s, z, g, sh,* or *ch*.
Books are expensive. **The classrooms are** big.		We don't make a contraction with a plural noun and *are*.

EXERCISE 5 Fill in the blanks with the correct form of *be* (*am*, *is*, *are*). Make a contraction whenever possible. Not every sentence can have a contraction.

EXAMPLE The United States ____is____ a big country. It____'s____ between Canada and Mexico.

1. Puerto Rico _____ an island. Puerto Ricans _____ American citizens.

2. English _____ the main language of the U.S. Spanish and English _____ the languages of Puerto Rico.

3. My classmates and I _____ immigrants. We _____ in the U.S.

4. Maya _____ in Minneapolis. She _____ at a city college there.

5. Minneapolis _____ a big city. It _____ in the northern part of the U.S.

6. The teacher _____ informal. He _____ friendly.

7. The students _____ from all over the world. They _____ nice people.

8. The classroom _____ on the first floor. It _____ big.

EXERCISE 6 Fill in the blanks. Make a contraction whenever possible. Not every sentence can have a contraction.

I ___'m_____ a student of English at Truman College. _____'m
    (example)   *(1)*

happy in the U.S. My teacher _____ American. His
                                (2)

name _____ Charles Madison. Charles _____ an
        (3)   *(4)*

experienced teacher. _____ patient with foreign students.
                        (5)

My class _____ big. _____ interesting. All the students
            (6)   *(7)*

_____ immigrants, but we _____ from many different
   (8)   *(9)*

countries. Five students _____ from Asia. One woman _____
                            (10)   *(11)*

from Poland. _____ from Warsaw, the capital of Poland. Many
                (12)

students _____ from Mexico.
            (13)

We _____ ready to learn English, but English _____ a
        (14)   (15)

difficult language. I sometimes tell Charles, "You _____ a very kind
                                                      (16)

teacher." Charles says, "_____ all good students, and I _____
                            (17)   (18)

happy to teach you English."

1.6 | *Be* with Descriptions

Examples	Explanation
Subject *Be* (*Very*) **Adjective** My teacher is **young.** The desks are *very* **small.** The weather is **cold** in winter.	After a form of *be*, we can use a word that describes the subject. Descriptive words are **adjectives.** *Very* can come before an adjective.
The school is **big.** The classrooms are **big.**	Descriptive adjectives have no plural form. *Wrong:* The classrooms are bigs.
Some of my classmates are **married.** My class is **interesting.** I'm **interested** in American life.	Some words that end with *–ed* and *–ing* are adjectives: *married, divorced, worried, tired, interested, interesting, bored, boring.*
It's **cold.** I'm **thirsty.** We're **afraid.**	We use a form of *be* with physical or mental conditions: *hungry, thirsty, cold, hot, tired, happy,* etc.

EXERCISE **7**   Complete each statement with a subject and the correct form of *be*. Write a contraction wherever possible. Make a *true* statement. Use both singular and plural subjects.

EXAMPLES   <u>My parents are</u> intelligent.   <u>The teacher's very</u> patient.

1. _____ expensive.
2. _____ cheap.
3. _____ new.
4. _____ big.
5. _____ wonderful.
6. _____ difficult.
7. _____ beautiful.
8. _____ famous.

EXERCISE **8**   Write a form of *be* and an adjective to describe each of the following nouns. You may work with a partner.

EXAMPLES   This classroom <u>is clean.</u>

New York City <u>is interesting.</u>

1. The teacher _____
2. This city _____
3. This college _____
4. Today's weather _____
5. Americans _____
6. American food _____
7. The students in this class _____

1.7 | *Be* with Definitions

Examples				Explanation
Singular Subject	**Be**	**A/An**	**Singular Noun**	We use a noun after a form of *be* to classify or define the subject.
I	**am**	a	student.	Use *a* or *an* before the definition of a singular noun. Use *a* before a consonant sound. Use *an* before a vowel sound. (The vowels are *a, e, i, o, u*.)
You	**are**	a	teacher.	
Puerto Rico	**is**	an	island.	
Plural Subject	**Be**		**Plural Noun**	Don't use *a* or *an* before the definition of a plural noun.
You and I	**are**		students.	*Wrong: You and I are a students.*
They	**are**		Americans.	
Subject	**Be**	**(A)**	**Adjective** **Noun**	We can include an adjective as part of the definition.
Chicago	is	a	**big** city.	
We	are		**good** students.	

EXERCISE 9 Fill in the blanks with a form of *be* and a definition of the subject. You may add an adjective. Be careful to add *a* or *an* for singular nouns.

EXAMPLE California _is a state._ _____

1. Canada _____

2. Chicago _____

3. Blue _____

4. Wednesday _____

5. The Pacific and the Atlantic _____

6. White and green _____

7. January and February _____

EXERCISE 10 Add an adjective to each statement. Be careful to use *a* before a consonant and *an* before a vowel sound.

EXAMPLE July 4 is a holiday.
         July 4 is an important holiday.

1. August is a month.   4. I'm a student.

2. Puerto Rico is an island.   5. Los Angeles and Chicago are cities.

3. A rose is a flower.   6. John is a name.

EXERCISE 11 Fill in the blanks with the correct form of *be*. Add *a* or *an* for singular nouns only. Don't use an article with plural nouns.

EXAMPLES The U.S. ___*is a*___ big country.

          The U.S. and Canada ___*are*___ big countries.

1. English and Spanish _____ languages.

2. England and Spain _____ countries.

3. The University of Illinois _____ state university.

4. It _____ old university.

5. Chicago _____ interesting city.

6. Chicago and Minneapolis _____ big cities.

7. I _____ student.

8. You _____ English teacher.

9. Some students _____ immigrants.

EXERCISE 12 Complete each statement. Give a subject and the correct form of *be*. Add *a* or *an* for singular nouns only. Don't use an article with plural nouns. You may work with a partner.

EXAMPLES <u>Russia is a</u> big country.

<u>Canada and Brazil are</u> big countries.

1. _____ nice person.

2. _____ expensive item.

3. _____ American holiday.

4. _____ warm months.

5. _____ big cities.

6. _____ famous people.

(NOTE: *people* is plural)

7. _____ American cars.

EXERCISE 13 Fill in the blanks to talk about this city. Make true statements. Remember to add *a* or *an* for a singular noun. You may work with a partner.

EXAMPLES <u>Chez Paul is an</u> expensive restaurant in this city.

<u>January and February are</u> cold months in this city.

1. _____ popular tourist attraction.

2. _____ big stores.

3. _____ beautiful months.

4. _____ beautiful park.

5. _____ inexpensive restaurant.

6. _____ busy streets.

7. _____ good college.

EXERCISE 14 Fill in the blanks to make true statements about the U.S. or another country.

EXAMPLES <u>Rock music is</u> popular <u>in the U.S.</u>

<u>Politicians are</u> rich <u>in my native country.</u>

1. _____ the biggest city _____.

2. _____ the language(s) _____.

3. _____ a popular sport _____.

4. _____ a common last name _____.

5. _____ a beautiful place _____.

1.8 | Prepositions

We use prepositions to show location and origin.

Preposition	Examples
On	The book is **on** the table. The cafeteria is **on** the first floor.
At (a general area)	I am **at** school. My brother is **at** home. They are **at** work.
In (a complete or partial enclosure)	The students are **in** the classroom. The wastebasket is **in** the corner.
In front of	The blackboard is **in front of** the students.
In back of / Behind	The teacher is **in back of** the desk. The blackboard is **behind** the teacher.
Between	The empty desk is **between** the two students.
Over / Above	The exit sign is **over** the door. The clock is **above** the exit sign.
Below / Under	The textbook is **below** the desk. The dictionary is **under** the textbook.
By / Near / Close to	The pencil sharpener is **by** the window. The pencil sharpener is **near** the window. The pencil sharpener is **close to** the window.
Next to	The light switch is **next to** the door.
Far from	Los Angeles is **far from** New York.

(continued)

Preposition	Examples
Across from	Room 202 is **across from** Room 203.
In (a city)	The White House is **in** Washington, D.C.
On (a street)	The White House is **on** Pennsylvania Avenue.
At (an address)	The White House is **at** 1600 Pennsylvania Avenue.
From	Mario is **from** Brazil. He is **from** São Paulo.

EXERCISE [15] ABOUT YOU Use a form of *be* and a preposition to tell the location of these things or people in your classroom or school.

EXAMPLE   My dictionary
My dictionary is in my book bag.

1. My classroom   5. The parking lot

2. I   6. The teacher

3. The library   7. We

4. The cafeteria   8. My books

1.9 | Negative Statements with *Be*

Examples	Explanation
I am **not** married. Peter is **not** at home. We are **not** doctors.	We put *not* after a form of *be* to make a negative statement.
I'm not late. English **isn't** my native language. My friends **aren't** here now.	We can make contractions for the negative.

Language Note: There is only one contraction of *I am not*. There are two negative contractions for all the other combinations. Study the negative contractions:

I am not	I'm not	—
you are not	you're not	you aren't
he is not	he's not	he isn't
she is not	she's not	she isn't
it is not	it's not	it isn't
we are not	we're not	we aren't
they are not	they're not	they aren't
Tom is not	Tom's not	Tom isn't

EXERCISE 16 Fill in the blanks with a pronoun and a negative verb. Practice using both negative forms.

EXAMPLE The classroom is clean and big.

_____*It isn't*_____ dirty. _____*It's not*_____ small.

1. We're in the classroom.

   _____ in the library. _____ in the cafeteria.

2. Today's a weekday.

   _____ Saturday. _____ Sunday.

3. I'm a student. _____ a teacher.

4. The students are busy.

   _____ lazy. _____ tired.

5. You're on time.

   _____ early. _____ late.

6. My classmates and I are in an English class.

   _____ in the cafeteria. _____ in the library.

EXERCISE 17 ABOUT YOU Fill in the blanks with a form of *be* to make a true affirmative statement or negative statement.

EXAMPLES I ___*am*___ busy on Saturdays.

My English class ___*isn't*___ in the morning.

1. My class _____ small.

2. The students _____ all the same age.

3. The students _____ from many countries.

4. Books in the U.S. _____ expensive.

5. The teacher _____ from my native country.

6. The seats in this class _____ in a circle.

7. I _____ a full-time student.

8. My classes _____ easy.

9. We _____ in the computer room now.

EXERCISE 18 True or False. Tell if you think the following statements are true or false. Discuss your opinions.

	True	False
1. English is easy for me.		
2. English is easy for children.		
3. American teachers are very strict.[2]		
4. This school is in a nice area.		
5. This course is expensive.		
6. All Americans are rich.		
7. Baseball is popular in the U.S.		
8. January and February are nice months.		

EXERCISE 19 ABOUT YOU If you are from another country, tell your classmates about life there. Fill in the blanks with a form of *be* to make an affirmative or negative statement.

EXAMPLES   I ____'m____ from the capital city.

I ____'m not____ from a small town.

1. I _____ happy with the government of my country.

2. I _____ from the capital city.

3. American cars _____ common in my country.

4. Teachers _____ strict.

5. Most people _____ rich.

6. Gas _____ cheap.

7. Apartments _____ expensive.

8. Bicycles _____ a popular form of transportation.

9. Public transportation _____ good.

10. A college education _____ free.

11. The president (prime minister) _____ a woman.

12. My hometown _____ in the mountains.

13. My hometown _____ very big.

14. It _____ very cold in the winter in my hometown.

15. Cell phones _____ popular in my country.

[2]A *strict* teacher has a lot of rules.

EXERCISE 20   Use the words in parentheses ( ) to change each sentence into a negative statement.

EXAMPLE   My teacher is American. (Canadian)

He isn't Canadian. _____

1. Los Angeles and Chicago are cities. (states)

   _____

2. I'm from Mexico. (the U.S.)

   _____

3. The U.S. is a big country. (Cuba)

   _____

4. We're in class now. (in the library)

   _____

5. You're an English teacher. (a math teacher)

   _____

6. Chicago and Springfield are in Illinois. (Miami)

   _____

7. January is a cold month. (July and August)

   _____

EXERCISE 21   ABOUT YOU Fill in the blanks with the affirmative or negative of the verb *be* to make a true paragraph.

My name _____*is*_____ _____. I _____ from an
         (example)   *(your name)*   *(1)*

English-speaking country. I _____ a student at City College.
                    (2)

I _____ in my English class now. The class _____
  (3)   *(4)*

big. My teacher _____ a man. He/She _____ very
          (5)   *(6)*

young. The classroom _____ very nice. It _____ clean.
               (7)   *(8)*

My classmates _____ all very young students. We _____
        (9)   *(10)*

all from the same country. We _____ all immigrants.
                  (11)

INSTANT MESSAGE FROM A STUDENT IN THE U.S.

Before You Read

1. Is your family in this city?

2. Do you communicate with your family and friends by e-mail?

Read the following instant message between Mohammad (MHD), a student in the U.S., and his brother, Ali (AL27), back home. Pay special attention to questions.

AL27: Hi, Mohammad.
MHD: Hi, Ali. **How are you?**
AL27: I'm fine.
MHD: **Where are you now?**
AL27: I'm in the college computer lab. **Are you at home?**
MHD: Yes, I am. It's late.

AL27: It's 4:15 p.m. here. **What time is it there?**
MHD: It's 1:15 a.m. here.
AL27: **Why are you still up[3]?**
MHD: I'm not sleepy.
AL27: **Why aren't you sleepy?**
MHD: I'm nervous about my test tomorrow.
AL27: **Why are you nervous?**
MHD: Because my class is very hard.
AL27: **How's college life in the U.S.? Is it very different from here?**
MHD: Yes, it is. But it's exciting for me. My new classmates are so interesting. They're from many countries and are all ages. One man in my class is very old.
AL27: **How old is he?**
MHD: He's 75.
AL27: **Are you serious?**
MHD: Of course, I'm serious. He's an interesting man and a great student.

AL27: **Where's** he from?
MHD: Korea.
AL27: All my classmates are young.
MHD: **Where are Mom and Dad?**
AL27: They're at work.
MHD: **Are they worried about me?**

(continued)

[3]To *be up* means to be awake.

AL27: A little.

MHD: **Why?**

AL27: Because there's so much freedom in the U.S.

MHD: Tell them I'm a good student. I'm on the dean's list.

AL27: **What's that?**

MHD: It's a list of students with a high grade point average.

AL27: That's great. Bye for now.

MHD: Bye.

1.10 | *Be* in *Yes/No* Questions and Short Answers

Compare statements, *yes/no* questions, and short answers.

Statement	*Yes/No* Question	Short Answer	Explanation
I am a student.	**Am I** a good student?	Yes, you are.	• In a *yes/no* question, we put *am, is, are* before the subject.
You are in bed.	**Are you** sleepy?	No, I'm not.	
He is old.	**Is he** a good student?	Yes, he is.	• We usually answer a *yes/no* question with a short answer. A short answer contains a pronoun. We don't use a contraction for a short *yes* answer. We usually use a contraction for a short *no* answer.
She is from Africa.	**Is she** from Nigeria?	No, she isn't.	
It is cold today.	**Is it** windy?	Yes, it is.	
We are here.	**Are we** late?	No, you aren't.	
They are worried.	**Are they** angry?	No, they aren't.	

Pronunciation Note: We usually end a *yes/no* question with rising intonation. Listen to your teacher pronounce the questions above.

EXERCISE 22 Answer the questions based on the last reading (the instant message).

EXAMPLES Is Ali in the U.S.?
No, he isn't.

Is Mohammad in the U.S.?
Yes, he is.

1. Are Ali's parents at work?

2. Are they worried about Mohammad?

3. Is Mohammad a good student?

4. Is it the same time in the U.S. and in Mohammad's native country?

5. Is Ali at home?

6. Are all the students in Mohammad's class from the same country?

7. Is Mohammad tired?

EXERCISE 23 ABOUT YOU Close your book. The teacher will ask you some questions. Answer with a true short answer. If the answer is negative, you may add more information.

EXAMPLE Is your book new?
Yes, it is. OR No, it isn't. It's a used book.

1. Is your hometown big?
2. Is Spanish your native language?
3. Is English hard for you?
4. Are you a citizen of the U.S.?
5. Is my pronunciation clear to you?
6. Am I a strict teacher?
7. Are all of you from the same country?
8. Are all of you the same age?

EXERCISE 24 Ask questions about this school and class with the words given. Another student will answer. Use the correct form of *be*.

EXAMPLE school / big
A: Is this school big?
B: Yes, it is.

1. it / near public transportation
2. the cafeteria / on this floor
3. it / open now
4. the library / in this building
5. it / closed now
6. this course / free
7. the textbooks / free
8. the teacher / strict
9. this room / clean
10. it / big

EXERCISE 25 Ask questions about the U.S. with the words given. Another student will answer. If no one knows the answer, ask the teacher.

EXAMPLE movie stars / rich
A: Are American movie stars rich?
B: Yes, they are. They're very rich.

1. a high school education / free
2. college books / free
3. medical care / free
4. doctors / rich
5. blue jeans / popular
6. houses / expensive
7. Americans / friendly
8. Japanese cars / popular
9. fast-food restaurants / popular
10. movie tickets / cheap

1.11 | *Wh-* Questions with *Be*

Examples				Explanation
*Wh-*Word	*Be*	Subject	Complement	A *wh-* question asks for information.
Where	**are**	Mom and Dad?		
Why	**are**	they	worried?	
How old	**is**	the teacher?		
Where	**is**	he	from?	
Why	**aren't**	you	sleepy?	

Question Words

Question	Answer	Meaning of Question Word
Who is your teacher? **Who** are those people?	My teacher is Rich Weiss. They're my parents.	Who = person
What is your classmate's name? **What** is that?	His name is Park. It's a cell phone.	What = thing
When is your test? **When** is the class over?	It's on Friday. It's over at 10 o'clock.	When = time
Why are they worried? **Why** aren't you in bed?	They're worried because you're alone. I'm not in bed because I'm not tired.	Why = reason
Where is your classmate from? **Where** are Mom and Dad now?	He's from Korea. They're at work.	Where = place
How is your life in the U.S.? **How** are you?	It's great! I'm fine.	How = description or health

Language Notes:
1. The *wh-* word + *is* can form a contraction: *who's, what's, when's, where's, how's, why's*
   We can't make a contraction for *which is*.
   We can't make a written contraction for a *wh-* word + *are*.
2. We usually end a *wh-* question with falling intonation. Listen to your teacher say the questions in the above boxes.

EXERCISE 26   Fill in the blanks with the correct question word and a form of *be*.

EXAMPLE   _____*What's*_____ your name?
My name is Frank.

1. _____ Los Angeles?
   It's in California.

2. _____ your birthday?
   It's in June.

3. _____ your teacher?
   My teacher is Martha Simms.

4. _____ a rose?
   A rose is a flower.

5. _____ you late?
   I'm late because of traffic.

6. _____ your sisters and brothers?
   They're in my country.

7. _____ you?
   I'm fine. And you?

8. _____ the teacher's office?
   It's on the second floor.

9. _____ the restrooms?
   The restrooms are at the end of the hall.

10. _____ Labor Day in the U.S.?
    It's in September.

11. _____ we here?
    We're here because we want to learn English.

EXERCISE 27   Test your knowledge. Circle the correct answer to the following questions. The answers are at the end of the exercise. You may work with a partner.

1. Where's Dallas?
   a. in California   **b.** in Texas   **c.** in Illinois

2. When is American Independence Day?
   a. July 4   **b.** May 31   **c.** December 25

3. It's 8 a.m. in New York. What time is it in Los Angeles?
   a. 11 a.m.   **b.** 5 a.m.   **c.** 10 a.m.

4. On what day is Thanksgiving?
   a. on Friday   **b.** on Sunday   **c.** on Thursday

5. Which one of these is the name of a Great Lake?
    a. Mississippi   **b.** Missouri   **c.** Michigan

6. Where is the Statue of Liberty?
    a. in San Francisco   **b.** in New York City   **c.** in Los Angeles

7. What is the first day of summer?
    a. June 1   **b.** June 21   **c.** June 30

8. When is Labor Day in the U.S.?
    a. in May   **b.** in June   **c.** in September

9. What's the biggest state?
    a. Alaska   **b.** Texas   **c.** New York

Answers: 1b, 2a, 3b, 4c, 5c, 6b, 7b, 8c, 9a,

The United States of America

AL	Alabama	HI	Hawaii	MA	Massachusetts	NM	New Mexico	SD	South Dakota
AK	Alaska	ID	Idaho	MI	Michigan	NY	New York	TN	Tennessee
AZ	Arizona	IL	Illinois	MN	Minnesota	NC	North Carolina	TX	Texas
AR	Arkansas	IN	Indiana	MS	Mississippi	ND	North Dakota	UT	Utah
CA	California	IA	Iowa	MO	Missouri	OH	Ohio	VT	Vermont
CO	Colorado	KS	Kansas	MT	Montana	OK	Oklahoma	VA	Virginia
CT	Connecticut	KY	Kentucky	NE	Nebraska	OR	Oregon	WA	Washington
DE	Delaware	LA	Louisiana	NV	Nevada	PA	Pennsylvania	WV	West Virginia
FL	Florida	ME	Maine	NH	New Hampshire	RI	Rhode Island	WI	Wisconsin
GA	Georgia	MD	Maryland	NJ	New Jersey	SC	South Carolina	WY	Wyoming
								DC*	District of Columbia

*The District of Columbia is not a state. Washington, D.C., is the capital of the United States.
Note: Washington, D.C., and Washington state are not the same.

For a map with major U.S. cities, see Appendix K.

1.12 | Comparing Statements and Questions with *Be*

Affirmative Statements and Questions

Wh-Word	Be	Subject	Be	Complement	Short Answer
		Mom and Dad	are	out.	
	Are	they		at the store?	No, they aren't.
Where	are	they?			
		It	is	late.	
	Is	it		1 a.m.?	No, it isn't.
What time	is	it?			

Negative Statements and Questions

Wh-Word	Be + n't	Subject	Be + n't	Complement
		You	aren't	in bed.
Why	aren't	you		sleepy?
		He	isn't	in the U.S.
Why	isn't	he		with his parents?

EXERCISE **28** Respond to each statement with a question.

EXAMPLE Mom and Dad are not here. Where _____*are they?*_____

1. Mom and Dad are worried about you. Why _____

2. I'm not sleepy. Why _____

3. My teacher is great. Who _____

4. My classes are early. When _____

5. My roommate's name is hard to pronounce.
   What _____

6. My cell phone isn't on. Why _____

7. Mom isn't in the kitchen. Where _____

The Present Tense of the Verb *Be*; Preposition of Place; *This, That, These, Those*   **25**

1.13 | Questions with *What* and *How*

Examples	Explanation

What is a verb?
  It's an action word.
What is the Dean's List?
  It's a list of the best students.
	What can ask for a definition.

What nationality is the teacher?
  She's American.
What day is today?
  It's Friday.
What time is it?
  It's 4:15 p.m.
What color is the dictionary?
  It's yellow.
What kind of book is this?
  It's a grammar book.
	A noun can follow *what:*
	• *what nationality*
	• *what day*
	• *what time*
	• *what color*
	• *what kind (of)*
	• *what month*

How is your new class?
  It's great.
How is the weather today?
  It's cool.
	We can use *how* to ask for a description.
	
	We use *how* to ask about the weather.

How old is your brother?
  He's 16 (years old).
How tall are you?
  I'm 5 feet, 3 inches tall.
How long is this course?
  It's 16 weeks long.
How long is the table?
  It's 3 feet long.
How much is the college tuition?
  It's $75 per credit hour.
	An adjective or adverb can follow *how:*
	• *how old*
	• *how tall*
	• *how long*
	• *how much*
	• *how big*
	• *how fast*

Usage Notes:
1. For height, Americans use feet (') and inches (").
   He's 5 feet, 8 inches tall. OR He's five-eight. OR He's 5'8".[4]
2. *How are you?* is often just a way to say hello. People usually answer, "Fine, thanks. How are you?"

---

[4]See Appendix G for conversion from feet and inches to centimeters and meters.

EXERCISE 29 Fill in the blanks to complete the questions.

EXAMPLE How ___old are___ your parents? They're in their 50s.

1. What _____ it? It's 3 o'clock.

2. What _____ car _____ that?
   That's a Japanese car.

3. What _____ words _____ *tall, old,*
   new, and *good?* They're adjectives.

4. What _____ your new car? It's dark blue.

5. How _____? My son is 10 years old.

6. How _____? My brother is 6 feet tall.

7. How _____? I'm 25 years old.

8. How _____? That car is $10,000.

9. How _____? The movie is 2 ½ hours long.

EXERCISE 30 ABOUT YOU Fill in the blanks to make true statements about
yourself. Then find a partner from a different country, if possible,
and interview your partner by asking questions with the words in
parentheses ( ).

EXAMPLE I'm from ___Bosnia___. (Where)

A: I'm from Bosnia. Where are you from?
B: I'm from Taiwan.

1. My name is _____. (What)

2. I'm from _____. (Where)

3. The president / prime minister of my country is _____

   _____. (Who)

4. The flag from my country is _____. (What colors)

5. My country is in _____. (Where)
   _____(continent or region)_____

6. I'm _____ feet, _____ inches tall. (How tall)

7. My birthday is in _____. (When)
   _____(month)_____

8. My favorite TV show is _____. (What)

The Present Tense of the Verb *Be;* Preposition of Place; *This, That, These, Those*   **27**

EXERCISE 31 Complete the following phone conversation between Cindy (C) and Maria (M).

C: Hello?

M: Hi, Cindy. This is Maria.

C: Hi, Maria. _____How are you_____?
                    (example)

M: I'm fine.

C: _____ your first day of class?
        (1)

M: Yes, it is. I'm at school now, but I'm not in class.

C: Why _____ in class?
            (2)

M: Because it's break time now.

C: How _____ the break?
            (3)

M: It's 10 minutes long.

C: How _____ ?
            (4)

M: My English class is great. My classmates are very interesting.

C: Where _____ from?
              (5)

M: They're from all over the world.

C: _____ American?
        (6)

M: Yes. My teacher is American. What time _____?
                                                (7)

C: It's 3:35.

M: Oh, I'm late.

C: Let's get together soon. _____ free this weekend?
                                  (8)

M: I'm free on Saturday afternoon.

C: I have a class on Saturday.

M: When _____ free?
              (9)

C: How about Sunday afternoon?

M: Sunday's fine. Talk to you later.

Before You Read

1. Do you like American food?

2. Do you eat in the school cafeteria?

Read the following conversation between an American (A) student and his Chinese (C) roommate. Pay special attention to *this, that, these, those.*

A: Is **this** your first time in an American college?

C: Yes, it is.

A: Let me show you around the cafeteria. **This** is the cafeteria for students. **That's** the cafeteria for teachers. The vending machines are in **that** room. When the food service is closed, **that** room is always open.

C: The food is in a machine?

A: Yes. And **that's** the change machine. **This** is the line for hot food.

C: What are **those?**

A: They're tacos.

C: Tacos? What are tacos?

A: They're Mexican food.

C: What's **that?**

A: It's pizza. It's Italian food.

C: What's **this?**

A: It's chop suey. It's a Chinese dish.

C: I'm from China, and I'm sure **this** is not a Chinese dish. Where's the American food in America?

A: This *is* American food—Mexican, Italian, Chinese—it's all American food.

C: Where are the chopsticks?

A: Uh . . . chopsticks? **Those** are the forks and knives, but there are no chopsticks here.

1.14 | *This, That, These, Those*

Examples	Explanation
Singular **This** is pizza. **Plural** **These** are tacos.	Use *this* and *these* to identify near objects and people.
Singular **That** is the change machine. **Plural** **Those** are forks and knives.	Use *that* and *those* to identify far objects and people.
This is pizza. **It's** an Italian food. **Those** are knives and forks. **They're** clean. **That's** my teacher. **She's** a nice woman.	After we identify a noun, we can use subject pronouns.
That room is for the teachers. **Those forks** are clean.	A noun can follow *this, that, these, those*.

Language Note: Only *that is* can form a contraction in writing: **That's** the change machine.

EXERCISE **32**   Imagine that you are showing a new student the school cafeteria. Use *this, that, these,* and *those,* and a form of *be* to complete each statement. The arrows indicate if the item is near or far.

EXAMPLES   _____*This is*_____ the school cafeteria. →

_____*Those are*_____ the clean dishes. ⟶

1. _____ the trays. →

2. _____ today's special. →

3. _____ the napkins. →

4. _____ the forks, knives, and spoons. ⟶

5. _____ the cashier. →

6. _____ the vending machines. ⟶

7. _____ the eating area. ⟶

8. _____ the teachers' section. ⟶

1. Uses of *Be*

DESCRIPTION:	Chicago **is** big.
IDENTIFICATION / CLASSIFICATION:	This **is** Chicago. It **is** a city.
LOCATION:	Chicago **is** in Illinois.
PLACE OF ORIGIN:	The teacher **is** from Chicago.
AGE:	I **am** 25 (years old).
PHYSICAL OR MENTAL CONDITION:	He **is** hungry. I **am** thirsty. She **is** worried.
TIME:	It **is** 6 p.m.
WEATHER:	It **is** warm today.

2. Subject Pronouns

I   we   he   she   it   you   they

3. Contractions

Subject pronoun + form of *be:* I'm, you're, he's, she's, it's, we're, they're

Subject noun + *is:* the teacher's, Tom's, Mary's

Is or *are* + *not:* isn't, aren't

Wh- word + *is:* what's, when's, where's, why's, how's

4. *This / That / These / Those*

This is an English book.
These are pencils.
That is a pen.
Those are pens.

5. Articles *a / an*

Chicago is **a** big city.
Puerto Rico is **an** island.

6. Statements and Questions with *Be*

AFFIRMATIVE:	She **is** busy.
NEGATIVE:	She **isn't** lazy.
YES/NO QUESTION:	**Is** she busy on Saturday?
SHORT ANSWER:	No, she **isn't.**
WH- QUESTION:	When **is** she busy?
NEGATIVE QUESTION:	Why **isn't** she busy on Saturday?

AFFIRMATIVE:	You **are** late.
NEGATIVE:	You **aren't** on time.
YES/NO QUESTION:	**Are** you OK?
SHORT ANSWER:	Yes, I **am.**
WH- QUESTION:	Why **are** you late?
NEGATIVE QUESTION:	Why **aren't** you on time?

EDITING ADVICE

1. Don't repeat the subject with a pronoun.

   My father ~~he~~ lives in Australia.

2. Use correct word order. Put the subject at the beginning of the statement.
   Cuba is small.
   ~~Is small Cuba.~~

3. Use the correct word order. Put the adjective before the noun.
   small country.
   Cuba is a ~~country small.~~

4. Use the correct word order in a question.
   is he
   Where ~~he is~~ from?

5. Every sentence has a verb. Don't omit *be*.
   is
   My sister ^ a teacher.

6. Every sentence has a subject. For time and weather, the subject is *it*.
   It's
   ~~Is~~ 6 o'clock now.
   It's
   ~~Is~~ very cold today.

7. Don't confuse *your* (possession) with *you're*, the contraction for *you are*.
   You're
   ~~Your~~ a good teacher.

8. Don't confuse *this* and *these*.
   This
   ~~These~~ is my coat.
   These
   ~~This~~ are my shoes.

9. The plural of the subject pronoun *it* is *they*, not *its*.
   They're
   Dogs are friendly animals. ~~Its~~ good pets.

10. Use *the* before *U.S.* and *United States*.
   the
   My sister is in ^ U.S.

11. Use a singular verb after *the U.S.*

   is
   The U.S. ~~are~~ a big country.

12. Do not use a contraction for *am not.*

   I'm not
   ~~I amn't~~ an American.

13. Put the apostrophe in place of the missing letter.

   isn't
   She ~~is'nt~~ here today.

14. Use an apostrophe, not a comma, for a contraction.

   I'm
   ~~I,m~~ a good student.

15. Use the article *a* or *an* before a singular noun.

   a
   New York is ^ big city.

   an
   San Francisco is ^ interesting city.

16. Don't use *a* before plural nouns.

   July and August are ~~a~~ warm months.

17. Don't use the article *a* before an adjective with no noun.

   New York is ~~a~~ big.

18. Use *an* before a vowel sound.

   an
   Puerto Rico is ~~a~~ island.

19. Don't make an adjective plural.

   My daughters are beautiful~~s~~.

20. Don't make a contraction with *is* after *s, z, sh,* or *ch* sounds.

   is
   Los Angeles~~'s~~ ^ a big city.

21. For age, use a number only or a number + *years old.*

   He's 12 ~~years.~~ OR *He's 12 years old.*

22. Don't use a contraction for a short *yes* answer.

   I am
   Are you from Mexico? Yes, ~~I'm.~~

23. Don't separate *how* from the adjective or adverb.

   old is he?
   How ~~is he old?~~

PART 1   Find the mistakes with the underlined words and correct them. Not every sentence has a mistake. If the sentence is correct, write *C*.

EXAMPLES   *He's*
~~He,s~~ my brother.

Chicago's a big city.   *C*

1. New York and Los Angeles are <u>a big cities</u>.

2. The <u>teacher's</u> not here today.

3. She <u>is'nt</u> in the library.

4. I <u>amn't</u> from Pakistan. <u>I'm</u> from India.

5. <u>The students they</u> are very smart.

6. We are <u>intelligents</u> students.

7. <u>We're</u> not hungry. We <u>aren't</u> thirsty.

8. <u>It's</u> warm today.

9. I'm from Ukraine. My <u>wife from</u> Poland.

10. My little brother <u>is 10 years</u>.

11. <u>French's</u> a beautiful language.

12. <u>It's</u> 4:35 now.

13. <u>Your</u> in the U.S. now.

14. <u>These</u> is a good book.

15. <u>These</u> are my pencils.

16. Those dogs are beautiful. <u>Its</u> friendly.

17. I live in <u>U.S.</u>

18. January is <u>cold month</u>.

19. My father is <u>a tall</u>.

20. New York City and Los Angeles are <u>bigs</u>.

21. This is <u>a</u> interesting book.

22. Is he from Peru? Yes, <u>he's</u>.

23. Chicago <u>it's</u> a big city.

PART 2 Find the mistakes with word order and correct them. Not every sentence has a mistake. If the sentence is correct, write *C*.

EXAMPLES   I have a book ⟨new⟩.
          She is 25 years old.   *C*

1. Is very long this book.
2. She has a car very beautiful.
3. Why you are late?
4. How old are you?
5. What nationality your wife is?
6. What color is your new coat?
7. Why the teacher is absent?
8. Is your father a doctor?

PART 3 Fill in the blanks to complete this conversation. Not all blanks need a word. If the blank doesn't need a word, write Ø.

A: Where are you ___*from*___?
              (example)

B: I'm from ___Ø___ Mexico.
           (example)

A: Are you happy in _____ U.S.?
                            (1)

B: Yes. I _____. The U.S. is _____ great country.
           (2)   *(3)*

A: _____ from _____ big city?
        (4)   *(5)*

B: Yes. I'm from Mexico City. It's _____ very big city. This city is
                                    (6)

_____ big and beautiful too. But _____ cold in the winter.
    (7)   *(8)*

A: _____ from Mexico too?
            (9)

B: No, my roommate _____ from Taiwan. I'm happy in the
                        (10)

U.S., but he _____ happy here.
                    (11)

A: Why _____ happy?
              (12)

B: He _____ homesick. His parents _____ in Taiwan.
(13)   (14)

He _____ alone here.
(15)

A: How _____ ?
(16)

B: He's very young. He _____ only 18 years _____ .
(17)   (18)

A: What _____ his name?
(19)

B: His name _____ Lu.
(20)

PART 4 Write a contraction of the words shown. If it's not possible to make a contraction, put an *X* in the blank.

EXAMPLES   she is ___*she's*___

English is ___*X*___

1. we are _____   6. Los Angeles is _____

2. you are not _____   7. Mary is not _____

3. I am not _____   8. he is not _____

4. they are _____   9. what is _____

5. this is _____   10. what are _____

PART 5 Read the conversation between two students, Sofia (S) and Danuta (D). They are talking about their classes and teachers. Fill in the blanks.

D: Hi, Sofia. How's your English class?

S: Hi, Danuta. It___*'s*___ wonderful. I _____ very happy with it.
(example)   (1)

D: _____ 'm in level 3. What level _____ in?
(2)   (3)

S: I' _____ in level 2.
(4)

D: My English teacher _____ Ms. Kathy James. _____ a very
(5)   (6)

good teacher. Who _____ ?
(7)

36 Lesson **1**

S: Mr. Bob Kane is my English teacher. _____ very good, too.
(8)

D: _____ an old man?
(9)

S: No, he _____. He's _____ young man. He _____
(10)   (11)   (12)

about 25 years _____. How _____?
(13)   (14)

D: Ms. James _____ about 50 years old.
(15)

S: How _____?
(16)

D: She's about 5 feet, 6 inches tall.

S: Is she American?

D: Yes, she _____. She's from New York.
(17)

S: _____?
(18)

D: Yes. My class is very big. The students _____ from many
(19)

countries. Ten students _____ from Asia, six students
(20)

_____ from Europe, one student _____ from Africa, and
(21)   (22)

five are _____ Central America. Is your class big?
(23)

S: No, it _____.
(24)

D: Where _____?
(25)

S: The students _____ all from the same country. We _____
(26)   (27)

from Russia.

D: _____ Russian?
(28)

S: No. Mr. Kane isn't Russian. He's from Canada, but he's _____
(29)

American citizen now.

D: _____?
(30)

S: No. That's not Mr. Kane. That _____ my husband. I _____
(31)   (32)

late! See you later.

EXPANSION ACTIVITIES

Classroom Activities

1. Write a few sentences about yourself. Give your height, a physical description, your nationality, your occupation, your age (optional), your gender (man or woman). Put the papers in a box. The teacher will read each paper. Guess which classmate is described.

   EXAMPLE   I'm 5 feet, 8 inches tall.
   I'm Mexican.
   I'm thin.
   I'm 21 years old.

2. Work with a partner. Describe a famous person (an actor, a singer, an athlete, a politician). Report your description to the class. Do not give the person's name. See if your classmates can guess who it is.

   EXAMPLE   He is a former basketball player.
   He's tall.
   He's famous.
   He's an African American.

3. Check the words that describe you. Find a partner and ask each other questions using these words. See how many things you have in common. Tell the class something interesting you learned about your partner.

   a. ____ happy   i. ____ afraid to speak English

   b. ____ from Africa   j. ____ an only child[5]

   c. ____ from Asia   k. ____ from the capital of my country

   d. ____ from Europe

   e. ____ interested in politics   l. ____ an American citizen

   f. ____ a grandparent   m. ____ hungry

   g. ____ under 20 years old   n. ____ married

   h. ____ in love   o. ____ athletic

[5]An *only child* has no sisters or brothers.

4. Fill in the blanks. Then find a partner and read your sentences to your partner. See how many times you match your partner's sentence.

   a. Love is _____

   b. This city is _____

   c. Children are _____

   d. The teacher is _____

   e. Money is _____

   f. The American president is _____

   g. My friends are _____

   h. I am _____

   i. Public transportation in this city is _____

   j. This book is _____

5. Work with a partner from the same country, if possible. Fill in a few items for each category. Report some information to the class.

EXAMPLE Typical of the U.S.

Common last names	Common cars	Popular tourist attractions	Popular sports	Language(s)	Capital city	Other big cities
Johnson Wilson	Ford Chevy Toyota	Disneyland Grand Canyon	baseball basketball football	English	Washington	New York Los Angeles Chicago

Typical of _____ (your country)

Common last names	Common cars	Popular tourist attractions	Popular sports	Language(s)	Capital city	Other big cities

Write
About it

Write a paragraph using Exercise 21 as a model. For every negative statement that you write, add an affirmative statement. You may add other information, too.

EXAMPLE

My name is Mohammad. I'm not from an English speaking country. I'm from Iran. I'm not a student at City College. I'm a student at Roosevelt University. I'm in English class now....

Outside
Activity

Interview a native speaker of English (a neighbor, a coworker, another student or a teacher at this college). Ask him or her the following questions. Report this person's answers to the class.

  a. What city are you from?
  b. Are your parents or grandparents from another country? Where are they from?
  c. Is most of your family in this city?
  d. Are you happy with this city? Why or why not?
  e. What are your favorite places in this city?

Internet
Activity

Using the Internet, find the Web site of a college you are interested in. Or find the Web site of the college or school you are at now. What information is on the home page? What links are on the home page?

Additional Activities at http://elt.heinle.com/gic

LESSON 2

GRAMMAR
The Simple Present Tense

CONTEXT: The U.S. Government
Washington, D.C.
The IRS

The White House, Washington, D.C.

WASHINGTON, D.C.

Before You Read

1. What capital cities do you know?
2. What do you know about Washington, D.C.?

The Lincoln Memorial

The Capitol

The Vietnam War Memorial

Read the following article. Pay special attention to the present-tense verbs.

Washington, D.C., **is** the capital of the United States. "D.C." **means** District of Columbia. The District of Columbia **is** not a state; it **is** a special government district. It **is** very small. It **is** only 61 square miles (158 square kilometers.) More than half a million people **live** in Washington. Washington **doesn't have** factories. Government and tourism **are** the main businesses of Washington. Washington **doesn't have** tall buildings like other big cities.

Some people who work in Washington **don't live** there. They **live** in the nearby states: Virginia and Maryland. Washington **has** a good subway (metro) system. It **connects** Washington to nearby cities in Virginia and Maryland.

The Capitol, the building where Congress **meets, is** on a hill. State senators and representatives **work** in the capital. They **make** the country's laws.

Tourists from all over the United States and many other countries **visit** Washington. They **come** to see the White House and the Capitol building. Many visitors **want** to see the Vietnam War Memorial. This wall of dark stone **lists** all the names of American soldiers who died in the war in Vietnam.

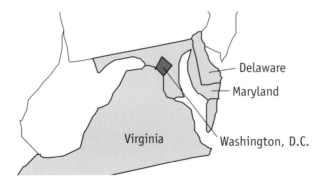

Did You Know?
The first location of the U.S. capital was in New York City.

Besides government buildings, Washington also **has** many important museums and monuments to presidents. The Smithsonian Institution **has** 16 museums and galleries and a zoo. The Smithsonian **includes** the Air and Space Museum. This very popular museum **shows** visitors real spaceships, such as the Apollo 11, which landed on the moon in 1969.

Tourists **don't pay** to see government buildings and museums. However, they **need** tickets to see many places because these places **are** crowded. Government buildings and museums **have** a lot of security. Guards **check** visitors' bags as they **enter** these buildings.

A trip to Washington **is** an enjoyable and educational experience.

2.1 | Simple Present Tense—Forms

A simple present-tense verb has two forms: the base form and the -*s* form.

Examples	Explanation
Subject **Base Form** **Complement** I You We **live** in Washington. They My friends	We use the base form when the subject is *I, you, we, they,* or a plural noun.
Subject **-s Form** **Complement** He She It **lives** in Washington. The president My family	We use the -s form when the subject is *he, she, it,* or a singular noun. *Family* is a singular subject.

Washington **has** many museums.
The metro **goes** to Virginia.
The president **does** a lot of work.
	Three verbs have an irregular -s form.
	   have → has (pronunciation /hæz/)
	   go → goes
	   do → does (pronunciation /dʌz/)

EXERCISE **1** Fill in the blanks with the correct form of the verb.

EXAMPLE Visitors ___like___ the museums.
(like/likes)

1. The president _____ in the White House.
(live/lives)

2. Many people in Washington _____ for the government.
(work/works)

3. Washington _____ many beautiful museums.
(have/has)

4. Millions of tourists _____ Washington every year.
(visit/visits)

5. The metro _____ Washington to nearby cities.
(connect/connects)

6. The Vietnam War Memorial _____ the names of men and
women who died in the war. (list/lists)

7. "D.C." _____ District of Columbia.
(mean/means)

2.2 | Simple Present Tense—Uses

Examples	Uses
The president **lives** in the White House. Washington **has** a good subway (metro) system.	With general truths, to show that something is consistently true
The president **shakes** hands with many people. He **waves** to people.	With customs
We **take** a vacation every summer. We sometimes **go** to Washington.	To show regular activity (a habit) or repeated action
I **come** from Bosnia. He **comes** from Pakistan.	To show place of origin

EXERCISE 2 ABOUT YOU Write the correct form of the verb. Add more words to give facts about you.

EXAMPLE I ___come from Colombia___.
(come)

1. The capital of my country _____.
(have)

2. Most people in my country _____.
(have)

3. In my native city, I especially _____.
(like)

4. Tourists in my country _____.
(visit)

5. My native city _____.
(have)

6. My family _____.
(live)

7. In the U.S., I _____.
(live)

8. The U.S. _____.
(have)

9. I _____ College/School.
(attend)

10. This school _____.
(have)

2.3 | Spelling of the -*s* Form

Rule	Base Form	-*s* Form
Add **s** to most verbs to make the -*s* form.	hope eat	hopes eats
When the base form ends in *ss, sh, ch,* or *x*, add **es** and pronounce an extra syllable.	miss wash catch mix	misses washes catches mixes
When the base form ends in a consonant + *y*, change the *y* to *i* and add **es.**	carry worry	carries worries
When the base form ends in a vowel + *y*, add **s.** Do not change the *y*.	pay enjoy	pays enjoys

EXERCISE **3**   Write the -s form of the following verbs.

EXAMPLES   eat _____ *eats* _____

study _____ *studies* _____

watch _____ *watches* _____

1. try _____

2. play _____

3. have _____

4. go _____

5. worry _____

6. finish _____

7. do _____

8. push _____

9. enjoy _____

10. think _____

11. say _____

12. change _____

13. brush _____

14. obey _____

15. reach _____

16. fix _____

17. work _____

18. raise _____

19. charge _____

20. see _____

2.4 | Pronunciation of the -s Form

Pronunciation	Rule	Examples	
/s/	Pronounce /s/ after voiceless sounds: /p, t, k, f/.	hope—hopes eat—eats	pick—picks laugh—laughs
/z/	Pronounce /z/ after voiced sounds: /b, d, g, v, m, n, ŋ, l, r/ and all vowel sounds.	grab—grabs read—reads hug—hugs live—lives hum—hums run—runs	sing—sings fall—falls hear—hears see—sees borrow—borrows
/əz/	Pronounce /əz/ when the base form ends in *ss, ce, se, sh, ch, ge, x.*	miss—misses dance—dances use—uses wash—washes	watch—watches change—changes fix—fixes

Language Note: The following verbs have a change in the vowel sound. Listen to your teacher pronounce these examples.
do/du/—does/dʌz/
say/sei/—says/sɛz/

EXERCISE 4 Go back to Exercise 3 and pronounce the base form and -s form of each verb.

EXERCISE 5 Fill in the blanks with the -s form of the verb in parentheses ( ). Pay attention to the spelling rules on page 45. Then say each sentence.

EXAMPLE   A teacher _____*tries*_____ to help students learn.
(try)

1. A pilot _____ an airplane.
(fly)

2. A dishwasher _____ dishes.
(wash)

3. A babysitter _____ children.
(watch)

4. A soldier _____ an officer.
(obey)

5. A citizen _____ taxes.
(pay)

6. A mechanic _____ machines.
(fix)

7. A student _____.
(study)

8. A student _____ homework.
(do)

9. A carpenter _____ a hammer.
(use)

10. A teacher _____ students.
(teach)

EXERCISE 6 Choose one of the following professions. Write at least three sentences to tell what someone in this profession does. You may work with a partner.

mechanic	teacher	bus driver
secretary	cook	tour guide
carpenter	banker	salesperson
plumber	writer	lawyer

_____

_____

_____

_____

2.5 | Comparing Affirmative Statements—*Be* and Other Verbs

Examples	Explanation
I **am** a student.	Don't include a form of *be* with a simple present-tense verb.
I **study** English.	
You **are** right.	*Wrong: I'm study English.*
You **know** the answer.	*Wrong: You're know the answer.*
He **is** busy.	*Wrong: He's works hard.*
He **works** hard.	

EXERCISE 7 A student is comparing himself to his friend. Fill in the blanks with the correct form of the underlined verb.

EXAMPLES My friend and I are very different.

I <u>get</u> up at 7 o'clock. He _____*gets*_____ up at 10.

I'<u>m</u> a good student. He _____*'s*_____ a lazy student.

1. I <u>study</u> every day. He _____ only before a test.
2. I always <u>get</u> A's on my tests. He _____ C's.
3. I <u>have</u> a scholarship. He _____ a government loan.
4. I'<u>m</u> a good student. He _____ an average student.
5. He <u>lives</u> in a dormitory. I _____ in an apartment.
6. He'<u>s</u> from Japan. I _____ from the Philippines.
7. He <u>studies</u> with the radio on. I _____ in a quiet room.
8. He <u>watches</u> a lot of TV. I _____ TV only when I have free time.
9. He <u>eats</u> a lot of meat. I _____ a lot of fish.
10. He <u>uses</u> a laptop computer. I _____ a desktop computer.

2.6 | Negative Statements with the Simple Present Tense

Examples	Explanation
The president **lives** in the White House. The vice president **doesn't live** in the White House. Washington **has** many government buildings. It **doesn't have** tall buildings.	Use *doesn't* + the base form with *he, she, it,* or a singular noun. **Compare:** lives → doesn't **live** has → doesn't **have** *Doesn't* is the contraction for *does not*.
Visitors **pay** to enter museums in most cities. They **don't pay** in Washington museums. We **live** in Maryland. We **don't live** in Washington.	Use *don't* + the base form with *I, you, we, they,* or a plural noun. **Compare:** pay → don't **pay** live → don't **live** *Don't* is the contraction for *do not*.

Usage Note: American English and British English use different grammar to form the negative of *have*. Compare:

American: He *doesn't have* a dictionary.

British: He *hasn't* a dictionary. OR He *hasn't got* a dictionary.

EXERCISE 8 Fill in the blanks with the negative form of the underlined verb.

EXAMPLE You <u>need</u> tickets for some museums. You _____*don't need*_____ money for the museums.

1. Washington <u>has</u> tourism. It _____ factories.

2. Tourists <u>need</u> to pass through security in Washington museums.

They _____ to pay to enter a museum.

3. The metro runs all day. It _____ after midnight.

4. You need a car in many cities. You _____ a car in Washington.

5. Washington has a subway system (the metro). Miami _____ _____ a subway system.

6. My friend lives in Virginia. He _____ in Washington.

7. I like American history. I _____ geography.

8. The president lives in Washington. He _____ in New York.

9. The president serves for four years. He _____ for six years.

10. We have a president. We _____ a prime minister.

11. The U.S. Congress makes the laws. The president _____ the laws.

12. Many Washingtonians work in tourism. They _____ for the government.

EXERCISE 9 Tell if this school has or doesn't have the following items.

EXAMPLES ESL courses
This school has ESL courses.

classes for children
It doesn't have classes for children.

1. a library	5. a swimming pool	9. dormitories
2. a cafeteria	6. a gym	10. classes for children
3. copy machines	7. a student newspaper	11. a computer lab
4. a parking lot	8. a theater	12. e-mail for students

EXERCISE 10 Make an affirmative statement or a negative statement with the words given to state facts about the teacher. Use the correct form of the verb.

EXAMPLE speak Arabic
The teacher speaks Arabic.
OR
The teacher doesn't speak Arabic.

1. talk fast	6. pronounce my name correctly
2. speak English well	7. wear glasses
3. speak my language	8. wear jeans to class
4. give a lot of homework	9. teach this class every day
5. give tests	10. watch the students during a test

EXERCISE 11 ABOUT YOU Check (✓) the items that describe you and what you do. Exchange your book with another student. Make statements about the other student.

EXAMPLES ____ I have children.
Marta doesn't have children.

✓ I like cold weather.
Marta likes cold weather.

1. ____ I speak Chinese.
2. ____ I live alone.
3. ____ I live near school.
4. ____ I walk to school.
5. ____ I speak Spanish.

6. ____ I like summer.
7. ____ I like cold weather.
8. ____ I have a laptop.
9. ____ I use the Internet.
10. ____ I have a dog.

2.7 | Comparing Negative Statements with *Be* and Other Verbs

Examples	Explanation
I'm **not** from Mexico. I **don't speak** Spanish.	Don't use *be* to make the negative of a simple present-tense verb.
You **aren't** sick. You **don't need** a doctor.	*Wrong:* I *am* don't speak Spanish. *Wrong:* You *aren't* need a doctor. *Wrong:* He *isn't want* dinner.
He **isn't** hungry. He **doesn't want** dinner.	

EXERCISE 12 ABOUT YOU Check (✓) the items that describe you and what you do. Exchange your book with another student. Make statements about the other student.

EXAMPLES ____ I'm an immigrant.
Margarita isn't an immigrant. She comes from Puerto Rico.

✓ I have a laptop.
Margarita has a laptop.

1. ____ I'm married.
2. ____ I have children/a child.
3. ____ I have a laptop.
4. ____ I'm an American citizen.
5. ____ I like this city.
6. ____ I have a job.

7. ____ I'm a full-time student.
8. ____ I have a pet.[1]
9. ____ I'm an immigrant.
10. ____ I'm happy in the U.S.
11. ____ I like baseball.
12. ____ I understand American TV.

[1] A *pet* is an animal that lives in someone's house. Dogs and cats are common pets.

EXERCISE 13 Choose one of the items from the list below. Write sentences telling what this person does or is. Include negative statements. You may work with a partner. Read some of your sentences to the class.

EXAMPLE   a good teacher

A good teacher explains the lesson.

A good teacher doesn't get angry at students.

A good teacher doesn't walk away after class when students have

questions.

A good teacher is patient.

1. a good friend

2. a good mother or father

3. a good doctor

4. a good adult son or daughter

_____

_____

_____

_____

EXERCISE 14 Fill in the blanks with the correct form of the verb in parentheses ( ).

Sara Harris ____is____ a 30-year-old woman. She _____ in
        Example: (be)   *(1 live)*

Arlington, Virginia. She _____ in Washington because rent is
                              (2 not/live)

cheaper in Arlington. Arlington _____ far from Washington.
                                    (3 be/not)

Sara _____ a car because her apartment _____ near
        (4 not/need)   *(5 be)*

a metro stop. She _____ the metro to go to work every day.
                      (6 use)

Sara works in Washington, but she _____ for the government.
                                      (7 not/work)

She _____ a tour guide. She _____ groups on tours of
        (8 be)   *(9 take)*

the Capitol. Tour groups _____ to pay to enter the Capitol,
                              (10 not/need)

but they do _____ a reservation.
                (11 need)

Sara _____ married. She _____ two
       (12 be/not)   *(13 have)*

roommates. They _____ in government offices. Sara and her
                    (14 work)

roommates _____ hard, so they _____ much time to
              (15 work)   *(16 not/have)*

visit the museums. When Sara's friends _____ from out of town,
                                            (17 visit)

Sara _____ them to museums and other tourist attractions.
         (18 take)

THE IRS

Before You **Read**

1. Do you pay income tax?

2. What other kinds of taxes do you pay?

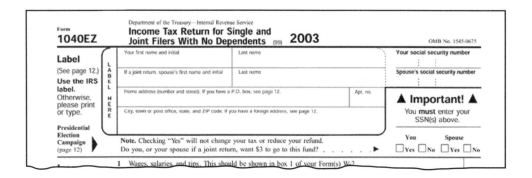

 Read the following conversation between Annie (A) and Bob (B) in Washington, D.C. Pay special attention to questions.

A: **Do** you **live** in Washington?
B: No, I don't. I live in Virginia.
A: **Do** you **work** in Washington?
B: Yes, I do.
A: How **do** you **go** to work?
B: I use the metro.
A: How much **does** it **cost**?
B: That depends on how far you ride. I pay $1.50 per ride.
A: Where **do** you **work**?
B: I work at the IRS.

(continued)

A: What **does** IRS **mean**?

B: It means Internal Revenue Service. This is the government agency that collects taxes. Whenever I tell people that I work at the IRS, they give me funny looks or say funny things.

A: Why?

B: Because everyone hates the IRS. No one likes to pay taxes. But taxes are necessary.

A: How **does** the IRS **use** the money?

B: For the military, education, health care, social security, and many other things.

A: **Does** everyone **pay** the same amount of tax?

B: No. Poor people pay a smaller percentage. Middle income people pay more. The tax law is very complicated[2].

A: When **do** people in the U.S. **pay** tax?

B: They pay little by little. Money comes out of their paychecks. Then they fill out a form and send it to the IRS every year by April 15.

A: My friend gets a refund[3] every year. **Does** everyone **get** a refund?

B: No. Only people who pay too much during the year get a refund. If we pay too little, we send a check to the IRS by April 15.

A: I hope to win the lottery some day. Then I won't need to pay taxes.

B: You're wrong! The IRS takes a percentage from every lottery winning.

A: How **does** the IRS **know** who wins the lottery?

B: The lottery reports the winner's name to the IRS. A famous American, Benjamin Franklin, said, "In this world nothing is certain but death and taxes."

2.8 | *Yes/No* Questions and Short Answers with the Present Tense

Examples				Explanation
Does	**Subject**	**Verb**	**Complement**	To form a question with *he, she, it, everyone, family,* or a singular subject, use:
Does	Barbara	**work**	in Washington?	
Does	she	**live**	in Virginia?	*Does* + subject + base form
Does	everyone	**pay**	taxes?	*Wrong:* Does she *works* in Washington?
Does	your family	**visit**	you?	
Do	**Subject**	**Verb**	**Complement**	To form a question with *I, we, you, they,* or a plural noun, use:
Do	you	**work**	hard?	
Do	they	**pay**	taxes?	*Do* + subject + base form
Do	Americans	**like**	the IRS?	

(continued)

---

[2] *Complicated* means not simple.
[3] A *refund* is money that the government returns to you if you pay too much in taxes.

Examples	Explanation

Do lottery winners pay taxes?
Yes, they do.
Do Americans like taxes?
No, they don't.
Does Barbara use the metro?
Yes, she does.
Does she live in Washington?
No, she doesn't.
	We usually answer a *yes/no* question with a short answer.
	Short answer:
	   Yes, + subject pronoun + *do/does*.
	   No, + subject pronoun + *don't/doesn't*.

Usage Note: American English and British English use different grammar to form a question with *have*. Compare:
   American: Does she *have* a car? Yes, she *does*.
   British: *Has* she a car? OR *Has* she *got* a car? Yes, she *has*.

Compare Statements and Questions

Do/Does	Subject	Verb	Complement	Short Answer
	Barbara	works	in Washington.	
Does	she	work	for the government?	No, she doesn't.
	You	pay	taxes.	
Do	you	pay	a lot?	Yes, I do.

EXERCISE 15   Answer with a short answer.

EXAMPLE   Does Barbara work in Washington, D.C.? _____ *Yes, she does.* _____

1. Does Barbara live in Washington, D.C.? _____

2. Does she work for the government? _____

3. Does the Washington metro go to Virginia? _____

4. Does tax money pay for the military? _____

5. Do poor people pay taxes? _____

6. Do people like to pay taxes? _____

7. Do lottery winners pay taxes? _____

8. Does Annie have a lot of questions for Barbara? _____

EXERCISE 16 Ask your teacher a question with "Do you . . . ?" and the words given. Your teacher will respond with a short answer.

EXAMPLE   drive to school
A: Do you drive to school?
B: Yes, I do. **OR** No, I don't.

1. like your job
2. teach in the summer
3. have another job
4. speak another language
5. learn English from TV
6. know my language

7. like to read students' homework.
8. live far from the school
9. have a fax machine
10. have trouble with English spelling
11. have a scanner
12. like soccer

EXERCISE 17 ABOUT YOU Put a check (✓) next to customs from your native country. Then make an affirmative or negative statement about your native country or culture. Ask another student if this is a custom in his or her native country or culture.

EXAMPLE   __✓__ People take off their shoes before they enter a house.
A: Russians take off their shoes before they enter a house. Do Mexicans take off their shoes before they enter a house?
B: No, we don't.

1. _____ People take off their shoes before they enter a house.
2. _____ People bow when they say hello.
3. _____ People shake hands when they say hello.
4. _____ People bring a gift when they visit a friend's house.
5. _____ People eat with chopsticks.
6. _____ On the bus, younger people stand up to let an older person person sit down.
7. _____ High school students wear a uniform.
8. _____ People visit friends without calling first.
9. _____ Men open doors for women.
10. _____ Men give flowers to women for their birthdays.
11. _____ People celebrate children's day.
12. _____ Women cover their faces with a veil.

A tourist in Washington, D.C., has a lot of questions. Fill in the blanks to make questions.

EXAMPLE Most big cities have tall buildings. ___*Does Washington have*___ tall buildings?
No, it doesn't.

1. The metro trains run all day. _____ 24 hours a day?
No, they don't. They only run from early morning to midnight. On weekends they run later.

2. In my city, all passengers pay the same fare on the metro.

_____ the same fare in the metro in Washington?
No, they don't. Passengers pay according to the distance they ride.

3. I need a ticket to enter museums back home. _____

_____ ticket to enter museums in Washington?
Yes, you do, but the museums are free.

4. The Washington Monument is very tall. _____ an elevator?
Yes, it has an elevator.

5. The president works in Washington. _____ on Capitol Hill?
No, he doesn't. He works in the White House.

6. _____ the laws?
No, he doesn't. The president doesn't make the laws. Congress makes the laws.

EXERCISE **19** Two students are comparing teachers. Fill in the blanks to complete this conversation.

A: Do you ___*like*___ your English class?
(example: like)

B: Yes, I _____ . I _____ a very good teacher.
(1)   (2 have)
Her name is Ms. Lopez.

A: _____ Spanish?
(3)

B: No, she doesn't. She comes from the Philippines. She _____
English and Tagalog.   (4 speak)

A: My teacher is very good too. But he _____ fast, and sometimes
(5 talk)

I _____ him. He _____ a lot of homework.
(6 not / understand)   (7 give)

_____ a lot of homework?
(8)

B: Yes, she does. And she _____ a test once a week.
(9 give)

A: My teacher _____ jeans to class. He's very informal.
(10 wear)

_____ jeans to class?
_(11)_

B: No, she doesn't. She always wears a dress.

A: My teacher always _____ to us about American culture.
(12 talk)

_____ your teacher _____ to you about American culture?
_(13)_ _(14)_

B: Yes, she _____.
_(15)_

2.9 | Comparing *Yes/No* Questions—*Be* and Other Verbs

Examples		Explanation
Are you lost?	No, I**'m** not.	Don't use *be* to make a question with a simple present-tense verb.
Do you **need** help?	No, I **don't**.	
Am I right?	Yes, you **are**.	*Wrong: Are* you need help?
Do I **have** the answer?	Yes, you **do**.	*Wrong: Am* I have the answer?
Is he from Haiti?	Yes, he **is**.	*Wrong: Is* he speak French?
Does he speak French?	Yes, he **does**.	

EXERCISE 20 Read each statement. Write a *yes/no* question about the words in parentheses ( ). Then write a short answer.

EXAMPLES Workers pay tax. (lottery winners) (yes)

Do lottery winners pay tax? Yes, they do.

Washington, D.C., is on the east coast. (New York) (yes)

Is New York on the east coast? Yes, it is.

1. Sara works from Monday to Friday. (on the weekend) (no)

_____

2. You are interested in American culture. (the American government) (yes)

_____

3. The president lives in the White House. (the vice president) (no)

_____

_____

4. The museums are free. (the metro) (no)

_____

5. Washington has a space museum. (a zoo) (yes)

_____

6. Taxes are necessary. (popular) (no)

_____

7. Security is high in government offices. (in airports) (yes)

_____

8. People hate the IRS. (you) (yes)

_____

9. The metro runs all day. (after midnight) (no)

_____

10. The metro in Washington is clean. (quiet) (yes)

_____

Washington, D.C. Subway Map

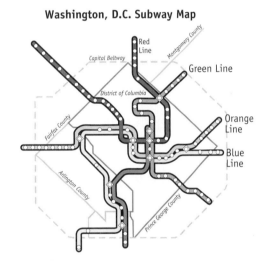

2.10 | *Or* Questions

Examples	Explanation
Do you study English **or** French? I study English. Is Washington, D.C., on the east coast **or** the west coast? It's on the east coast.	An *or* question gives a choice of answers.
Pronunciation Note: The first part of an *or* question has rising intonation; the second part has falling intonation. Listen to your teacher pronounce the examples above.	

ABOUT YOU Circle the words that are true for you, and make a statement about yourself. Then ask an *or* question. Another student will answer.

EXAMPLE I drink (coffee)/ *tea* in the morning. *I drink coffee in the morning* .

A: Do you drink coffee or tea in the morning?
B: I drink coffee, too.

1. I speak *English / my native language* at home.

   _____

2. I prefer *classical music / popular music.*

   _____

3. I'm *a resident of the U.S. / a visitor.*

   _____

4. I'm *married / single.*

   _____

5. I live in *a house / an apartment / a dormitory.*

   _____

6. I write with my *right hand / left hand.*

   _____

7. I'm from *a big city / a small town.*

   _____

8. I prefer *morning classes / evening classes.*

   _____

9. I prefer to *eat out / eat at home.*

   _____

10. English is *easy / hard* for me.

    _____

11. I live *with someone / alone.*

    _____

2.11 | *Wh*- Questions with the Simple Present Tense

Examples					Explanation
Wh- Word	*Does*	Subject	Verb	Complement	To form a question with *he, she, it, everyone, family,* or a singular subject, use:
Where	**does**	Barbara	**work?**		*Wh-* word + *does* + subject + base form
When	**does**	she	**use**	the metro?	Use the base form after *do* or *does*.
How	**does**	the IRS	**use**	your money?	*Wrong:* Where does Barbara *works?*
Wh- Word	*Do*	Subject	Verb	Complement	To form a question with *I, you, we, they,* or a plural subject, use:
When	**do**	we	**pay**	taxes?	*Wh-* word + *do* + subject + base form
Where	**do**	they	**work?**		
Why	**do**	I	**get**	a refund?	
Wh- Word	*Do/ Does*	Subject	Verb	Preposition	In informal written and spoken English, we usually put the preposition at the end of a *wh-* question.
Where	do	you	come	**from?**	
Who	does	she	live	**with?**	
What floor	do	you	live	**on?**	
Preposition	*Wh- Word*	*Do/Does*	Subject	Verb	In formal written and spoken English, we put the preposition before the question word.
With	whom	does	she	live?	
On	what floor	do	you	live?	

Language Note:
We use *whom,* not *who,* after a preposition. We often use *who* when the preposition is at the end of the sentence. Compare:

> **Formal: With whom** do you study?
> **Informal: Who** do you study **with**?

EXERCISE 22 ABOUT YOU Answer the questions.

EXAMPLE Where do you live?
I live near the school.

1. Who do you live with?

2. What do you bring to class?

3. What does the teacher bring to class?

4. What do you do after class?

5. How do you come to school?

6. Where do you live?

7. What do you like to do on weekends?

8. Why does the teacher give homework?

2.12 | Comparing Statements and Questions in the Simple Present Tense

Affirmative Statements and Questions

Wh- Word	Do/Does	Subject	Verb	Complement	Short Answer
		My sister	works	in Washington.	
	Does	she	work	for the IRS?	No, she doesn't.
Where	does	she	work?		
		You	pay	tax.	
	Do	you	pay	income tax?	Yes, I do.
Why	do	you	pay	tax?	

Negative Statements and Questions

Wh- Word	Don't/Doesn't	Subject	Verb	Complement
		People	don't like	taxes.
Why	don't	they	like	taxes?
		Sara	doesn't get	a tax refund.
Why	doesn't	she	get	a tax refund?

EXERCISE 23   ABOUT YOU Ask and answer questions with the words given. First ask another student a *yes/no* question. Then use the words in parentheses ( ) to ask a *wh-* question, if possible.

EXAMPLES   live near school (where)

A: Do you live near school?
B: Yes, I do.
A: Where do you live?
B: I live on Green and Main.

have cable TV (why)

A: Do you have cable TV?
B: No, I don't.
A: Why don't you have cable?
B: Because it's too expensive.

1. speak Spanish (what language)

2. have American friends (how many)

3. live near the school (where)

4. plan to go back to your country (when) (why)

5. live alone (with whom OR who . . . with)

6. practice English outside of class (with whom OR who . . . with)

7. bring your dictionary to class (why)

8. have a cell phone (why)

First ask the teacher a *yes/no* question. After you get the answer, use the words in parentheses ( ) to ask a *wh-* question, if possible. Your teacher will answer.

EXAMPLE   teach summer school (why)

A: Do you teach summer school?
B: No, I don't.
A: Why don't you teach summer school?
B: Because I like to travel in the summer.

1. have a laptop computer (what kind of computer)

2. speak another language (what language)

3. teach summer school (why)

4. correct the homework in school (where)

5. drive to school (how . . . get to[4] school)

6. like to teach English (why)

7. come from this city (what city . . . from)

EXERCISE **25**   Ask and answer questions about another teacher with the words given. First ask another student a *yes/no* question. Then use the words in parentheses ( ) to ask a *wh-* question, if possible.

EXAMPLE   speak your language (what languages)

A: Does your teacher speak your language?
B: No, he doesn't.
A: What languages does he speak?
B: He speaks English and French.

1. give a lot of homework (why)

2. write on the chalkboard (when)

3. come to class late (what time)

4. pronounce your name correctly (how)

5. use a textbook (what textbook)

6. wear jeans to class (what)

[4]*Get to* means arrive at.

2.13 | Questions About Meaning, Spelling, and Cost

Wh- Word	Do/Does	Subject	Verb	Complement	Explanation
What	does	"D.C."	mean?		*Mean, spell, say,* and *cost* are verbs and should be in the verb position of a question.
How	do	you	spell	"government"?	
How	do	you	say	"government" in your language?	
How much	does	a metro ticket	cost?		

EXERCISE 26 Fill in the blanks in the conversation below with the missing words.

A: What _____'s_____ your name?
(example)

B: My name is Martha Gomez.

A: How _____ spell "Gomez"?
(1)

B: G-O-M-E-Z. It's a Spanish name.

A: Are you _____ Spain?
(2)

B: No, I'm _____.
(3)

A: What country _____ you come _____?
(4)   (5)

B: I come from Guatemala.

A: What language _____ they _____ in Guatemala?
(6)   (7)

B: They speak Spanish in Guatemala.

A: _____ your family here?
(8)

B: No. My family is still in Guatemala. I call them once a week.
A: Isn't that expensive?

B: No, it _____. I use a phone card.
(9)

A: How much _____ cost?
(10)

B: It _____ five dollars. We can talk for 35 minutes. I like
(11)

to say hello to my family every week.

A: How _____ "hello" in Spanish?
(12)

B: We say "hola." Please excuse me now. I'm late for my class. *Hasta luego.*

A: What _____ "hasta luego" _____?
    (13)   (14)

B: It means "see you later" in Spanish.

2.14 | Comparing *Wh-* Questions—*Be* and Other Verbs

Examples	Explanation
Who **is** she? Where **does** she **live**? How **are** you? How **do** you **feel**? Where **am** I? What **do** I **need**?	Don't forget to use *do* or *does* in a question with a simple present-tense verb. *Wrong: Where she lives?* *Wrong: How you feel?* Don't use *be* to form a simple present-tense question. *Wrong: What am I need?*

EXERCISE 27 Read this conversation between two new students, Ricardo (R) and Alexander (A). Fill in the blanks with the missing words.

R: Hi. My name _____'s_____ Ricardo.
                    (example)

What _____?
                            (1)

A: Alexander.

R: Nice to meet you, Alexander. Where _____?
                                                    (2)

A: I _____ from Ukraine.
            (3)

R: What languages _____?
                                    (4)

A: I speak Ukrainian and Russian.

R: _____ a new student?
                    (5)

A: Yes, I am. What about you? Where _____ from?
                                                (6)

R: I _____ from Peru.
                    (7)

A: Where _____?

(8)

R: It's in South America. We speak Spanish in Peru. I want to learn English and then go back to my country.

A: Why _____ to go back to Peru?

(9)

R: Because my father has an export business there, and I want to work with him.

A: What _____?

(10)

R: "Export" means to sell your products in another country.

A: Why _____ to know English?

(11)

R: I need to know English because we have many American customers.

A: How many languages _____?

(12)

R: My father speaks four languages: English, French, German, and Spanish.

A: Tell me about your English class. _____ your

(13)
English teacher?

R: Oh, yes. I like her very much.

A: Who _____ your English teacher?

(14)

R: Barbara Nowak.

A: _____?

(15)

R: N-O-W-A-K. It's a Polish name.

A: How many students _____?

(16)

R: It has about 35 students. The classroom is very big.

A: What floor _____?

(17)

R: It's on the second floor.

A: When _____ your class _____?

(18)   (19)

R: It begins at 6 o'clock. I'm late. See you later.

A: _____ "see you later" in Spanish?

(20)

R: We say "hasta luego."

1. The simple present tense has two forms: the base form and the -s form:

Base Form	-s Form
I	Everyone
You	He
We eat.	She eats.
They	It
(Plural noun)	(Singular noun)

2. Simple present-tense patterns with the -s form:

AFFIRMATIVE:	The president **lives** in Washington, D.C.
NEGATIVE:	He **doesn't live** in New York.
YES/NO QUESTION:	**Does** he **live** in the White House?
SHORT ANSWER:	Yes, he **does.**
WH- QUESTION:	Where **does** the vice president **live?**
NEGATIVE QUESTION:	Why **doesn't** the vice president **live** in the White House?

3. Simple present-tense patterns with the base form:

AFFIRMATIVE:	We **study** English in class.
NEGATIVE:	We **don't study** American history in class.
YES/NO QUESTION:	**Do** we **study** grammar?
SHORT ANSWER:	Yes, we **do.**
WH- QUESTION:	Why **do** we **study** grammar?
NEGATIVE QUESTION:	Why **don't** we **study** history?

4. Present-tense patterns with the verb *be:*

AFFIRMATIVE:	The teacher **is** absent.
NEGATIVE:	She **isn't** here today.
YES/NO QUESTION:	**Is** she sick?
SHORT ANSWER:	No, she **isn't.**
WH- QUESTION:	Where **is** she?
NEGATIVE QUESTION:	Why **isn't** she here?

5. We use the simple present tense with:

General truths and facts	Washington, D.C., **has** over half a million people. Americans **speak** English.
Customs	Japanese people **take** off their shoes when they enter a house. Americans **don't visit** friends without an invitation.
Regular activities (*More on this use in Lesson 3*)	He **visits** his parents every summer. I **play** soccer once a week.

1. Don't forget to use the *-s* form when the subject is *he, she, it,* or a singular noun.

          s
   He need ^ more money.

          has
   This school ~~have~~ a big library.

2. Use the base form after *does* and *doesn't.*

             have
   My father doesn't ~~has~~ a car.

   Does your mother speaks English well?

3. If you are living in the U.S., use the American form, not the British form, with *have.*

       doesn't have
   He ~~hasn't~~ a car.

       Do you have
   ~~Have you~~ a car?

4. Don't forget *do/does* in a question.

        do
   Where ^ your parents live?

5. Use correct word order in a question.

            your brother live
   Where does ~~live your brother~~?

             does your father have
   What kind of car ~~has your father~~?

         don't you
   Why ~~you don't~~ like pizza?

6. Don't use *be* with another verb to form the simple present tense.

      I
   ~~I'm~~ have three brothers.
   She's lives in New York.

      I don't
   ~~I'm not~~ have a car.

7. Don't use *be* in a simple present-tense question that uses another verb.

      Does
   ~~Is~~ your college have a computer lab?

      Do
   ~~Are~~ you speak French?

8. Use correct spelling for the -s form.

      studies
    She ~~studys~~ in the library.

      watches
    He ~~watchs~~ TV every evening.

9. Use the correct negative form.

      doesn't
    He ~~not~~ know the answer.

      don't
    They ~~no~~ speak English.

10. Don't use an -*ing* form for simple present tense.

      write
    I ~~writing~~ a letter to my family once a week.

11. *Family* is a singular word. Use the -s form.

             s
    My family live ^ in Germany.

12. Use the same auxiliary verb in a short answer as in a *yes/no* question.

            am
    Are you hungry? Yes, I ~~do~~.

                do
    Do you like baseball? Yes, I ~~am~~.

13. Use the correct word order with questions about meaning, spelling, and cost.

      does "wonderful" mean
    What ~~means "wonderful"~~?

              do bananas cost
    How much ~~cost bananas~~ this week?

      do you
    How ^ spell "opportunity"?

      do you
    How ^ say "opportunity" in your language?

PART 1 Find the mistakes with the underlined words and correct them. Not every sentence has a mistake. If the sentence is correct, write *C*.

EXAMPLES   ~~I'm not speak~~ English well.   *I don't*

What <u>does</u> the teacher <u>want</u>?   *C*

1. My mother <u>washes</u> my clothes every Sunday.

2. I <u>haven't</u> a dictionary.

3. <u>Where you</u> live?

4. He <u>no need</u> help from you.

5. My sister <u>talks</u> a lot.

6. You <u>aren't need</u> a dictionary for the test.

7. My brother <u>goes</u> to a state university.

8. <u>Are</u> you want to buy a new computer?

9. <u>Does</u> your apartment <u>have</u> a dishwasher? Yes, it <u>is</u>.

10. What kind of computers <u>has this school</u>?

11. <u>How spell</u> "computer"?

12. What <u>does the teacher want</u>?

13. Why <u>you don't</u> want to practice English at home?

14. How many children <u>do</u> your sister <u>have</u>?

15. How much <u>costs a stamp</u>?

16. The teacher <u>doesn't speak</u> my language.

17. My mother <u>worries</u> a lot about me.

18. Miami <u>don't have</u> cold winters.

19. I'm <u>not like</u> to use public transportation.

20. <u>How say</u> "potato" in your language?

21. My friend <u>going</u> to Puerto Rico every winter.

22. My family <u>has</u> a big house.

23. How many states <u>does the U.S. have</u>?

24. What <u>means</u> "adjective"?

PART 2   Write the *-s* form of the following verbs. Use correct spelling.

EXAMPLE   take _____*takes*_____

1. go _____

2. carry _____

3. mix _____

4. drink _____

5. play _____

6. study _____

7. catch _____

8. say _____

PART 3   Fill in the first blank with the affirmative form of the verb in parentheses ( ). Then write the negative form of this verb.

EXAMPLES   A monkey _____*lives*_____ in a warm climate.
            (live)

It _*doesn't live*_ in a cold climate.

Brazil _____*is*_____ a big country.
        (be)

Haiti _____*isn't*_____ a big country.

1. The English language _____ the Roman alphabet.
   (use)

   The Chinese language _____ the Roman alphabet.

2. We _____ English in class.
   (speak)

   We _____ our native languages in class.

3. March _____ 31 days.
   (have)

   February _____ 31 days.

4. Mexico and Canada _____ in North America.
   (be)

   Colombia and Ecuador _____ in North America.

5. You _____ the "k" in "bank."
   (pronounce)

   You _____ the "k" in "knife."

6. The teacher _____ the English language.
   (teach)

   He/She _____ American history.

7. A green light _____ "go."
   (mean)

   A yellow light _____ "go."

8. I _____ from another country.
   (come)

   I _____ from the U.S.

9. English _____ hard for me.
   (be)

   My language _____ hard for me.

PART 4 Write a *yes/no* question about the words in parentheses ( ).
Then write a short answer.

EXAMPLES   January has 31 days. (February) (no)
       Does February have 31 days? No, it doesn't.

         China is in Asia. (Korea) (yes)
       Is Korea in Asia? Yes, it is.

1. The U.S. has 50 states. (Mexico) (no)

   _____

2. The post office sells stamps. (the bank) (no)

   _____

3. San Francisco is in California. (Los Angeles) (yes)

   _____

4. The metro runs all day. (all night) (no)

   _____

5. January and March have 31 days. (April and June) (no)

   _____

6. The president lives in the White House. (the vice president) (no)

_____

7. Americans speak English. (Canadians) (yes)

_____

8. We come to class on time. (the teacher) (yes)

_____

9. The museums have good security. (the White House) (yes)

_____

PART 5 Read each statement. Then write a _wh-_ question about the words in parentheses ( ). You don't need to answer the question.

EXAMPLES February has 28 days. (March)
How many days does March have?

Mexico is in North America. (Venezuela)
Where is Venezuela?

1. Mexicans speak Spanish. (Canadians)

_____

2. The U.S. has 50 states. (Mexico)

_____

3. The president lives in the White House. (the vice president)

_____

4. Thanksgiving is in November. (Christmas)

_____

5. You spell "occasion" O-C-C-A-S-I-O-N: ("tomorrow")

_____

6. "Occupation" means job or profession. ("occasion")

_____

7. The president doesn't make the laws. (why)

_____

8. Marek comes from Poland. (you)

_____

PART 6

Read this interview. Fill in the blanks with the missing word.

A: How old _____*are you*_____?
                    (example)

B: I'm 30 years old.

A: _____ married?
                    (1)

B: No I'm single.

A: _____ with your parents?
                    (2)

B: No, I don't live with my parents.

A: Why _____ with your parents?
                    (3)

B: I don't live with my parents because they live in another city.

A: Where _____?
                    (4)

B: They live in Chicago.

A: _____ you _____ Washington?
            (5)   *(6)*

B: Yes, I like it very much.

A: Why _____ Washington?
                    (7)

B: I like it because it has so many interesting museums and galleries. But I don't have time to visit these places very often. I work every day. When my parents visit, we go to galleries and museums.

A: When _____?
                    (8)

B: They visit me in the spring. They love Washington.

A: Why _____ Washington?
                    (9)

B: They love it because it's a beautiful, interesting city. And they love it because I'm here.

A: What kind of job _____?
                    (10)

B: I have a job with the government. I work in the Department of Commerce.

A: What _____?
                    (11)

B: Commerce means "business."

A: How _____?
                    (12)

B: C-O-M-M-E-R-C-E.

A: _____ your job?

(13)

B: Yes, I like my job very much.

A: _____?

(14)

B: I live a few blocks from the White House.

A: _____ have a car?

(15)

B: No, I don't. I don't need a car.

A: How _____ to work?

(16)

B: I go to work by metro. If I'm late, I take a taxi.

A: How much _____?

(17)

B: A taxi ride from my house to work costs about $12.

A: _____ clean?

(18)

B: Oh, yes. The metro is very clean.

A: _____ all night?

(19)

B: No, the trains don't run all night. They run until midnight.

A: In my city, we don't say "metro." We use a different word.

B: How _____ "metro" in your city?

(20)

A: We say "subway."

EXPANSION ACTIVITIES

Classroom Activities

1. Check (✓) all the items below that are true of you. Find a partner and compare your list to your partner's list. Write three sentences telling about differences between you and your partner. (You may read your list to the class.)

   a. _____ I have a cell phone.   g. _____ I play a musical instrument.

   b. _____ I own a home.   h. _____ I sing well.

   c. _____ I live in an apartment.   i. _____ I'm a good driver.

   d. _____ I exercise regularly.   j. _____ I like pizza.

   e. _____ I'm a vegetarian.   k. _____ I use an electronic calendar.

   f. _____ I live with my parents.   l. _____ I write with my left hand.

2. **Game:** One student thinks of the name of a famous person and writes this person's initials on the chalkboard. Other students ask questions to try to guess the name of this person.

SAMPLE QUESTIONS

Is he an athlete?   Is he tall?
Where does he come from?   How old is he?

3. **Game:** One student comes to the front of the room. He or she thinks of an animal and writes the name of this animal on a piece of paper. The other students try to guess which animal it is by asking questions. The person who guesses the animal is the next to come to the front of the room.

EXAMPLE
lion
Does this animal fly? No, it doesn't.
Does it live in water? No, it doesn't.
What does it eat? It eats meat.
Does this animal live in Africa? Yes, it does.

4. In a small group, discuss differences between classes and teachers in this school and another school you know.

EXAMPLES
In my college back home, students stand up when they speak. This class has some older people. In my native country, only young people study at college.

Write About it

Write about a tourist attraction in your country (or in another country you know something about).

Outside Activity

Interview an American about his or her favorite tourist place in the U.S. Why does he or she like this place? What does this place have?

Internet Activities

1. Using the Internet, find information about one of the following places: Disneyland, the White House, the Holocaust Museum, Ellis Island, Epcot Center, the Alamo, or any other American tourist attraction that interests you. Then answer these questions:

What is it?   What does it cost to enter?
Where is it?   What does it have?

2. Using the Internet, find information about a museum or place of special interest in this city. Then answer these questions:

What is it?   What does it cost to enter?
Where is it?   What does it have?

Additional Activities at http://elt.heinle.com/gic

GRAMMAR

Frequency Words with the Simple Present Tense
Prepositions of Time

CONTEXT: American Holidays

Three Special Days
The Fourth of July

THREE SPECIAL DAYS

Before You **Read**

1. What is your favorite holiday? When is it?

2. Do you celebrate Mother's Day? When?

3. Do you send cards for special occasions?

 Read the following article. Pay special attention to the frequency words.

Did You Know?

Valentine's Day began in ancient Rome to honor Juno, the Roman goddess of women and marriage.

Valentine's Day is a day of love. It is **always** on February 14. On this day, people **often** give flowers or candy to their spouses or sweethearts. Candy manufacturers make candy or candy boxes in the shape of a heart. People **sometimes** send cards, called valentines, to close friends and relatives. Red is the color associated with Valentine's Day. A valentine **usually** has a red heart and a message of love. It **often** has a picture of Cupid, a symbol of romantic love. Florists sell a lot of red roses on Valentine's Day. Young children **usually** have a party at school and exchange cards.

Another special day is Saint Patrick's Day. It is **always** on March 17. It is really an Irish holiday, but many Americans like St. Patrick's Day even if they are not Irish. We **sometimes** say that on St. Patrick's Day everybody is Irish. In New York City, there is **always** a parade on St. Patrick's Day. Green is the color associated with St. Patrick's Day. People **often** wear green clothes on this day. One symbol of St. Patrick's Day is the shamrock.

Businesses are **never** closed for Valentine's Day or St. Patrick's Day. People **never** take a day off from work for these days. Schools and government offices are **always** open (except if these days fall on a Sunday).

Another special day is Mother's Day. It is **always** in May, but it isn't **always** on the same date. It is **always** on the second Sunday in May. People **usually** buy presents for their mothers and grandmothers or send special cards. Families **often** have dinner in a restaurant. Florists sell a lot of flowers on Mother's Day.

People enjoy these holidays. Greeting card companies also enjoy these holidays. They **always** sell a lot of cards and make a lot of money at these times.

3.1 | Frequency Words with the Simple Present Tense

Frequency Word	Frequency	Examples
Always	100%	Mother's Day is **always** in May.
Usually	↑	I **usually** take my mother out to dinner.
Often		People **often** wear green on St. Patrick's Day.
Sometimes		I **sometimes** watch the parade.
Rarely/Seldom	↓	We **rarely** give flowers to children.
Never	0%	Businesses are **never** closed for Valentine's Day.

EXERCISE **1** Choose the correct word to fill in the blanks.

EXAMPLE People _____*often*_____ give flowers or candy on Valentine's
(never, seldom, often)

Day.

1. Valentine's Day is _____ on February 14.
(always, sometimes, never)

2. People _____ send valentine cards to their
(rarely, often, never)

sweethearts.

3. A valentine card _____ has a red heart and a
(never, rarely, usually)

message of love.

4. Young children _____ have a Valentine's Day party
(usually, always, never)

at school.

5. Saint Patrick's Day is _____ on March 17.
(always, sometimes, never)

St. Patrick's Day Parade

6. A St. Patrick's Day card _____ has a red heart.
   (always, usually, never)

7. In New York City, there is _____ a parade on Saint
   (always, seldom, never)

   Patrick's Day.

8. Card companies _____ do a lot of business before
   (never, always, seldom)

   holidays.

9. Businesses are _____ closed for St. Patrick's Day
   (always, usually, never)

   and Valentine's Day.

10. Mother's Day is _____ in May.
    (always, usually, never)

11. Mother's Day is _____ on a Saturday in the U.S.
    (always, never, sometimes)

EXERCISE **2**   Fill in the blank with an appropriate frequency word about this
class or this school.

EXAMPLE   We _sometimes_ use a dictionary in class.

1. The teacher _____ wears a suit to class.

2. The school is _____ closed on Labor Day.

3. The students _____ ask questions in class.

4. The windows of the classrooms are _____ open.

5. The students _____ talk to each other during a test.

6. The door of the classroom is _____ open.

7. We _____ write a composition in class.

8. The teacher _____ writes on the
   blackboard (chalkboard).

9. The students _____ write on the
   blackboard (chalkboard).

10. The students _____ stand up
    when the teacher enters the room.

11. The teacher is _____ late to class.

12. We _____ read stories in class.

3.2 | Position of Frequency Words and Expressions

Examples	Explanation
Businesses *are* **never** closed for St. Patrick's Day. Mother's Day *is* **always** in May.	The frequency word comes after the verb *be*.
I **usually** *buy* a card for my mother. I **sometimes** *wear* green on St. Patrick's Day.	The frequency word comes before other verbs.
Sometimes I take my mother to a restaurant. **Usually** the weather is nice in May. **Often** we give gifts.	*Sometimes, usually,* and *often* can come at the beginning of the sentence, too.

EXERCISE **3**   ABOUT YOU Add a frequency word to each sentence to make a **true** statement about yourself.

EXAMPLE   I eat fish.
I usually eat fish on Fridays.

1. I cook the meals in my house.

2. I stay home on Sundays.

3. I buy the Sunday newspaper.

4. I read the newspaper in English.

5. I use public transportation.

6. I'm tired in class.

7. I use my dictionary to check my spelling.

8. I buy greeting cards.

EXERCISE 4   Add a verb (phrase) to make a **true** statement about people from your country or cultural group.

EXAMPLE   people / often

Russian people often go to the forest on the weekends to pick

mushrooms.

1. people / often

   _____

2. people / seldom

   _____

3. women / usually

   _____

4. women / rarely

   _____

5. men / usually

   _____

6. men / rarely

   _____

EXERCISE 5   ABOUT YOU Add a verb phrase to make a **true** statement about yourself.

EXAMPLE   I / never

I never go to bed after 11 o'clock.

OR

I'm never in a good mood in the morning.

1. I / never

   _____

2. I / always / in the morning

   _____

3. I / usually / on Sunday

   _____

4. I / often / on the weekend

   _____

5. I / sometimes / in class

   _____

EXERCISE 6   Use the words below to make sentences.

EXAMPLE   mechanics / sometimes

Mechanics sometimes charge too much money.

1. American doctors / rarely

   _____

2. American teachers / sometimes

   _____

3. students at this school / often

   _____

4. this classroom / never

   _____

5. American hospitals / always

   _____

6. people in this country / often

   _____

THE FOURTH OF JULY

Before You Read

1. Do you like to see fireworks?

2. Do you celebrate any American holidays? What's your favorite American holiday?

Read the following student composition. Pay special attention to prepositions of time.

My favorite holiday in the U.S. is American Independence Day. We celebrate it **on** July 4. In fact, we often call this holiday "The Fourth of July."

In the morning, my family and I prepare hamburgers for a barbecue. Our guests arrive **in** the afternoon, and we cook hamburgers and hotdogs on the grill in the backyard. We usually start to eat **at** about three o'clock. We have a lot of barbecues **in** the summer, but my favorite is **on** the Fourth of July.

We usually stay in our yard **from** about two o'clock **to** six o'clock Then **in** the evening, we usually go to the park. Most of our town goes there too, so we visit with each other while we wait for the fireworks. Finally, **at** night when it's completely dark, the fireworks show begins.

This is an exciting time for all of us. We celebrate our nation's independence and we have a lot of fun.

3.3 | Prepositions of Time

Preposition	Examples	Explanation
in	We prepare for the barbecue **in the morning.** We eat **in the afternoon.** We go to the park **in the evening.**	Use *in* with morning, afternoon, and evening.
in	Americans elect a president every four years: **in 2004, 2008, 2012,** etc.	Use *in* with years.
in	We often have a barbecue **in the summer.** It's too cold to have a barbecue **in the winter.**	Use *in* with seasons: summer, fall, winter, spring.
in	We celebrate Independence Day **in July.** We celebrate Mother's Day **in May.**	Use *in* with months.
on	We celebrate Independence Day **on July 4.** This year the holiday is **on Tuesday.**	Use *on* with dates and days.
at	We start to eat **at** three o'clock. We start the grill **at noon.** We go to bed **at midnight.**	Use *at* with a specific time of day.
at	The firework show starts **at night.**	Use *at* with night.
from . . . to	We stay in the backyard **from** two **to** six o'clock.	Use *from . . . to* with a beginning and an ending time. We can also say *from . . . till* or *until.*

EXERCISE 7 ABOUT YOU Answer these questions. Use the correct preposition.

1. What time do you get up in the morning?
2. What time do you go to bed at night?
3. What time does your English class begin?
4. What days does your English class meet?
5. What time do you get to school?
6. When do students have vacation?
7. When do you do your homework?
8. What hours do you go to school?
9. When is your birthday?

3.4 | Questions with *Ever*

We use *ever* in a question when we want an answer that has a frequency word.

Do/Does	Subject	Ever	Verb	Complement	Short Answer
Do	you	**ever**	cook	outside?	Yes, we **sometimes** do.
Does	your brother	**ever**	work	on a holiday?	Yes, he **often** does.

Be	Subject	Ever	Complement	Short Answer
Are	the stores	**ever**	open on a holiday?	Yes, they **sometimes** are.
Is	the park	**ever**	crowded on the Fourth of July?	Yes, it **always** is.

Language Notes:
1. In a short answer, the frequency word comes between the subject and the verb.
2. If the frequency word is *never*, don't use a negative verb.

   Is the school **ever** open on the Fourth of July?

   No, it **never** is.

   Do you **ever** buy fireworks?

   No, I **never** do.

EXERCISE **8** ABOUT YOU Add *ever* to ask these questions. Another student will answer.

EXAMPLES Do you eat in a restaurant?

A: Do you ever eat in a restaurant?
B: Yes, I often do. OR Yes, often.

Are you bored in class?

A: Are you ever bored in class?
B: No, I never am. OR No, never.

1. Do you use public transportation?
2. Do you drink coffee at night?
3. Do you drink tea in the morning?
4. Do you speak English at home?
5. Do you watch TV at night?
6. Do you rent DVDs?
7. Are you late to class?
8. Do you drive and use your cell phone at the same time?
9. Are you homesick?
10. Are you lazy on Saturdays?
11. Does it snow in March?
12. Do you ask for directions on the street?

EXERCISE **9** Add *ever* to these questions to ask about Americans. Another student will answer.

EXAMPLES Do Americans eat fast food?

A: Do Americans ever eat fast food?
B: Yes, they sometimes do.

Are Americans friendly to you?

A: Are Americans ever friendly to you?
B: Yes, they usually are.

1. Do Americans eat with chopsticks?
2. Do Americans carry radios?
3. Do Americans say, "Have a nice day"?
4. Do Americans kiss when they meet?
5. Do Americans pronounce your name incorrectly?
6. Are Americans impolite to you?
7. Do Americans shake hands when they meet?
8. Do Americans ask you what country you're from?
9. Are Americans curious about your native country?

EXERCISE 10 ABOUT YOU Fill in the blanks with a frequency word to make a statement about yourself. Then ask a question with *ever*. Another student will answer.

EXAMPLE   I ____never____ jog in the morning.

A: Do you ever jog in the morning?
B: No, I never do.

1. I _____ ride a bike in the summer.

2. I _____ visit relatives on Sunday.

3. I _____ go to sleep before 9 p.m.

(Women: Do **A**. Men: Do **B**.)

4. **A.** I _____ wear high heels.

   B. I _____ wear a suit and tie.

5. I _____ do exercises.

6. I _____ eat meat.

7. I _____ drink colas.

8. I _____ buy the Sunday newspaper.

9. I _____ put sugar in my coffee.

10. I _____ take a nap in the afternoon.

11. I _____ eat in a restaurant.

12. I _____ use a fax machine.

13. I _____ bake bread.

14. I _____ use cologne or perfume.

15. I _____ take a bubble bath.

16. I _____ check my e-mail in the morning.

17. I _____ borrow money from a friend.

18. I _____ leave a light on when I sleep.

19. I _____ drink coffee at night.

20. I _____ listen to the radio when I'm driving.

3.5 | Questions with *How Often* and Answers with Frequency Expressions

We ask a question with *how often* when we want to know the frequency of an activity.

Examples	Explanation

How often do you eat hamburgers?
   Once in a while.
How often do you visit your mother?
   Once a week.
How often do you go to the park?
   Every week.
	Expressions that show frequency are:
	 • every day (week, month, year)
	 • every other day (week, month, year)
	 • from time to time
	 • once in a while

I learn more about life in America **every day.** **Every day** I learn more about life in America. **From time to time,** I eat hamburgers. I eat hamburgers **from time to time.**	Frequency expressions can come at the beginning or the end of the sentence.

EXERCISE **11**   ABOUT YOU Ask a question with "How often do you . . . ?" and the words given. Another student will answer.

EXAMPLE   get a haircut

A: How often do you get a haircut?
B: I get a haircut every other month.

1. come to class
2. shop for groceries
3. wash your clothes
4. use your cell phone
5. go out to dinner
6. use public transportation
7. renew your driver's license
8. buy the newspaper
9. go to the movies
10. check your e-mail

EXERCISE 12 Linda has a list to remind her of the things she has to do on a regular basis. Write questions and answers about her activities.

- drive daughter to ballet lessons—Tu, Th
- pick up son at baseball practice—Mon, Wed
- shop for groceries—Sat
- take the dog for a haircut—3rd day of every month
- go to the beauty salon—5th day of every month
- visit Mom—Fri
- go to the gym—Mon, Wed, Fri morning
- prepare the kids' lunches—Mon to Fri
- change oil in car—Jan, April, July, Oct

EXAMPLE *How often does she drive her daughter to ballet lessons?*

She drives her daughter to ballet lessons twice a week.

1. _____
_____

2. _____
_____

3. _____
_____

4. _____
_____

5. _____
_____

6. _____
_____

7. _____
_____

8. _____
_____

EXERCISE 13 ABOUT YOU Write a few sentences about a member of your family or another person you know. Use frequency words.

EXAMPLE   *My sister never helps with the housework.*

_____ *She sometimes leaves dirty dishes in the sink.* _____

_____ *She always gets good grades.* _____

_____

_____

EXERCISE 14 Use the words in parentheses ( ) to complete this conversation. Put the words in the correct order. Use the correct form of the verb.

A: Let's go to a movie tonight.

B: I can't. My mother ___*always makes*___ dinner for me on Fridays.
              (example: make/always)

If I don't visit her, she _____.
                              (1 complain/usually)

And if I don't call her, she worries.

A: _____ her?
         (2 how/often/you/call)

B: _____.
         (3 I/every day/call her)

A: Why do you call her so often?

B: She's old now, and she_____ lonely.
                                  (4 often/be)

A: Well, invite your mother to go to the movies.

B: Thanks, but she has a favorite TV show on Friday nights.

She _____ it.
         (5 watch/always)

A: _____ go out?
         (6 ever/she)

B: She _____. She prefers to stay home.
              (7 rarely/do)

She likes to cook, knit, and watch TV.

A: Is she a good cook?

B: Not really. She _____ the
                           (8 usually/cook)

same thing every week: chicken on Friday, fish on Saturday, meatloaf

on Sunday. . . . Her routine _____.
                                   (9 change/never)

Only Mother's Day is different.

A: What _____ on Mother's Day?
　　　　　(10 you/do/usually)

B: My sister and I _____ her flowers
　　　　　　　　(11 usually/buy)

and take her to a restaurant.

A: Does she like that?

B: Not really. She _____ ,
　　　　　　　　　　(12 usually/say)

"Don't waste your money. Flowers _____ in a day
　　　　　　　　　　　　　　　(13 die/always)

or two. And my cooking is better than restaurant food."

A: _____ hard to please?
　　　　(14 be/she/always)

B: Yes, she is.

A: _____ satisfied?
　　　　(15 be/she/ever)

B: Not usually. She _____ ,
　　　　　　　　　　　(16 always/say)

"I don't want Mother's Day once a year. I want it every day."

EXERCISE 15 *Combination Exercise.* Read a student's composition about the Fourth of July. Find the mistakes with the underlined words and correct them. Add a form of the verb *be* where necessary. If the underlined words are correct, write *C.*

　　　　　　　　　　　　　　　　　　　　　　　　　C
　　　　My favorite holiday in the U.S. is the Fourth of July. My
　　　　　　　always puts
family puts always an American flag in front of the house.

My friends and relatives always get together for a BBQ.

We usually cook hamburgers and hotdogs on the grill.

Sometimes we cook fried chicken and steaks. The men in

the family usually cooking. (They rarely cook the rest of

the year!) We usually have the BBQ at my house, but

sometimes we're have the BBQ in a park. We always has

a potluck; everyone brings a different dish. My mother

always bake a delicious apple pie.

Our city always has a parade <u>at</u> the Fourth of July <u>from</u> noon <u>at</u> one o'clock. <u>In the</u> night, we usually go to see the fireworks at the main park. The park <u>always is</u> crowded. The weather usually nice, but <u>it's</u> sometimes rains and the fireworks show is canceled. When that <u>happen</u>, we are very disappointed. Luckily, that <u>seldom happens</u>.

Most businesses and schools <u>is</u> closed on the Fourth of July. The library, banks, and offices <u>are always</u> closed. <u>I'm</u> never work on this holiday, but my brother is a police officer and he sometimes <u>work</u> on the Fourth of July. Some businesses, such as supermarkets, <u>stays</u> open for half the day. People often <u>forgets</u> to buy something and need to get some last minute items.

I always look forward to this holiday because I <u>see</u> all my family and we <u>has</u> a lot of fun together. Also my birthday is <u>on</u> July and I get a lot of presents.

SUMMARY OF LESSON 3

1. Frequency Words:

Most Frequent	always	100%
↑	usually	↑
	often	
	sometimes	
↓	rarely/seldom	↓
Least Frequent	never	0%

2. The Position of Frequency Words:

AFTER THE VERB *BE*: He is **always** late.

BEFORE A MAIN VERB: I **usually** walk to work.

3. The Position of Frequency Expressions:
   Every day I watch TV.
   I watch TV **every day.**

4. Frequency Questions and Answers:
   Do you **ever** wear a suit? I seldom do.
   Are you **ever** bored in class? Yes, sometimes.
   How often do you go to the library? About once a month.

5. Review prepositions of time on page 84. Review the simple present tense in Lessons 1 and 2.

EDITING ADVICE

1. Put the frequency word in the correct place.

   am never
   I ~~never am~~ bored in class.

   I always
   ~~Always I~~ drink coffee in the morning.

2. Don't separate the subject and the verb with a frequency phrase.

   once in a while
   She ~~once in a while~~ visits her grandmother ^.

   Every other day we
   ~~We every other day~~ write a composition.

3. Don't use a negative verb with *never*.

   do
   Do you ever take the bus to school? No, I never ~~don't~~.
   We never ~~don't~~ eat in class.

4. Use *ever* in questions. Answer the question with a frequency word.

   sometimes
   Do you ever listen to the radio in the morning? Yes, I ~~ever~~ do.

LESSON 3 TEST/REVIEW

PART 1 Find the mistakes with the underlined words and correct them (including mistakes with word order). Not every sentence has a mistake. If the underlined words are correct, write *C*.

do
EXAMPLES Do you ever drink coffee? No, I never ~~don't~~.
I <u>never eat</u> spaghetti. *C*

1. <u>Always I give</u> my mother a present for Mother's Day.

2. <u>I rarely go</u> downtown.

3. <u>They never are</u> on time.

4. <u>It snows seldom</u> in April.

5. <u>Do you ever</u> take the bus? <u>Yes, I never do.</u>

6. <u>Are you ever</u> late to class? Yes, <u>always I am.</u>

7. <u>Do you ever use</u> chopsticks? Yes, <u>I ever do.</u>

8. <u>What often</u> do you go to the library? I go to the library <u>twice a month.</u>

9. <u>I once in a while</u> eat in a restaurant.

10. <u>Every other day</u> she cooks chicken.

PART 2 This is a conversation between two students. Fill in the blanks to complete the conversation.

A: Who _____<u>is</u>_____ your English teacher?
   (example)

B: His name _____ David.
   _(1)_

A: _____ David?
   _(2)_

B: Yes. I like him very much.

A: _____ he wear a suit to class?
   _(3)_

B: No, he _____. He always _____
   _(4)_   _(5)_

   jeans and running shoes.

A: _____?
   _(6)_

B: He _____ about 60 years old.
   _(7)_

A: _____ your language?
   _(8)_

B: No, he doesn't speak Spanish, but he _____ Polish
   _(9)_

   and Russian. And English, of course.

A: _____ does your class meet?
   _(10)_

B: It meets three days a week: Monday, Wednesday, and Friday.

A: My class _____ two days a week: Tuesday and
(11)

Thursday.

B: Tell me about your English teacher.

A: Her name _____ Dr. Misko. She never
(12)

_____ jeans to class. She _____
(13)   (14)

wears a dress or suit. She _____ my language.
(15)

She only _____ English.
(16)

B: Do you like her?

A: Yes, but she _____ a lot of homework and tests.
(17)

B: _____ does she give a test?
(18)

A: Once a week. She gives a test every Friday. I _____
(19)

like tests.

B: My teacher sometimes teaches us American songs.

_____ your teacher _____
(20)   (21)

_____ you American songs?
(22)

A: No, she never _____.
(23)

B: What book _____?
(24)

A: My class uses *Grammar in Context*.

B: What _____?
(25)

A: "Context" means the words that help you understand a new word or
idea.

B: How _____?
(26)

A: C-O-N-T-E-X-T.

PART 3 Fill in the blanks with the correct preposition.

EXAMPLE Many people go to church ___*on*___ Sundays.

1. We have classes _____ the evening.

2. Valentine's Day is _____ February.

3. Valentine's Day is _____ February 14.

4. A news program begins _____ 6 o'clock.

5. I watch TV _____ night.

6. We have vacation _____ the summer.

7. Many Americans work _____ 9 _____ 5 o'clock.

8. I drink coffee _____ the morning.

9. I study _____ the afternoon.

PART 4 Read this student's composition about his teacher. Find the mistakes with the underlined words, and correct them. Add the verb *be* where necessary. If the underlined words are correct, write *C*.

My English teacher ᴬis᷿ Barbara Nowak. She ~~teach~~ *teaches* grammar and composition at City College. <u>She very</u> nice, but <u>she's</u> very strict. She <u>give</u> a lot of homework, and we <u>take</u> a lot of tests. If I pass the test, <u>I very</u> happy. <u>English's</u> hard for me.

<u>Every day</u>, at the beginning of the class, she <u>takes</u> attendance and we <u>hand</u> in our homework. Then <u>she's explains</u> the grammar. We <u>do</u> exercises in the book. The book <u>have</u> a lot of exercises. Most exercises <u>is</u> easy, but some are hard. Sometimes we <u>says</u> the answers out loud, but sometimes we <u>write</u> the answers. Sometimes the teacher <u>asks</u> a student to write the answers on the chalkboard.

The students <u>like</u> Barbara because she <u>make</u> the class interesting. She <u>brings often</u> songs to class, and we <u>learn</u> the words. Sometimes we <u>watch</u> a movie in class. <u>Always I</u> enjoy her lessons.

After class I <u>sometimes going</u> to her office if I want more help. <u>She very</u> kind and always <u>try</u> to help me.

Barbara <u>dresses</u> very informally. <u>Sometimes she wears</u> a skirt, but <u>she wears usually</u> jeans. <u>She about</u> 35 years old, but <u>she's looks</u> like a teenager. (In my country, <u>never a teacher wear</u> jeans.)

<u>I very</u> happy with my teacher. She <u>understand</u> the problems of a foreigner because <u>she's</u> also a foreigner. <u>She's comes</u> from Poland, but she <u>speaks</u> English very well. She <u>know</u> it's hard to learn another language.

Classroom Activities

1. Find a partner. Interview your partner about one of his or her teachers, friends, or relatives. Ask about this person's usual activities.

    EXAMPLE
    A: What's your math teacher's name?
    B: Her name is Kathy Carlson.
    A: Does she give a lot of homework?
    B: No, she doesn't.
    A: What does she usually wear to class?
    B: She usually wears a skirt and blouse.
    A: Does she ever wear jeans to class?
    B: No, she never does.

2. In a small group or with the entire class, use frequency words to talk about the activities of a famous person (the president, a singer, an actor, etc.).

    EXAMPLE   The president of the U.S. often meets with leaders of other countries.

3. Find a partner. Talk about a special holiday that you and your family celebrate. Ask your partner questions about the date of the holiday, food, clothing, preparations, activities, and so on.

    EXAMPLE
    A: We celebrate the Lunar New Year.
    B: Do you wear special clothes?
    A: Yes, we do.
    B: What kind of clothes do you wear?

4. Look at the list of Linda's activities on page 89. Write a list to remind yourself of things you do on a regular basis. Find a partner. Compare your list to your partner's list.

5. Describe your favorite holiday to your classmates.

6. In the left column is a list of popular customs in the U.S. Do people in your native country or cultural group have similar customs? If so, put a check (✓) in Column A. If not, put a check (✓) in Column B. Discuss your answers in a group.

American Customs	A Similar custom in my native country or cultural group	B Completely different custom in my native country or cultural group
1. Americans often say, "Have a nice day."		
2. When someone sneezes, Americans usually say, "God bless you."		
3. Americans often ask, "How are you?" People usually reply, "I'm fine, thanks. How are you?"		
4. Americans rarely visit their friends without calling first.		
5. Americans are often in a hurry. They rarely have free time.		
6. Americans often eat popcorn in a movie theater.		
7. Americans often eat in fast-food restaurants.		
8. Americans often say, "OK."		
9. Americans often wear shorts and sandals in the summer.		
10. Americans often listen to a personal stereo.		
11. When eating, Americans usually hold a fork in the right hand and a knife in the left hand.		
12. Banks in the U.S. often have a time/temperature sign.		
13. American restaurants usually have salt and pepper shakers on the table.		
14. When a radio or TV breaks down, Americans often buy a new one. They rarely try to repair it.		
15. Americans often send greeting cards to close friends and relatives for birthdays, anniversaries, holidays, and illnesses.		
16. The Sunday newspaper often has store coupons.		
17. There is a special day for sweethearts, like Valentine's Day.		

Write About it

1. Write about one of your teachers. Describe your teacher and tell about his or her classroom behavior and activities.

2. Write about a holiday that you celebrate. Explain how you celebrate this holiday. Or write about how you celebrate your birthday or another special day.

Outside Activities

1. Ask an American-born person to do Exercise 4. See how your answers compare to this person's answers. Report this person's answers to the class.

2. Go to a drugstore, supermarket, or card store. Is there a special holiday at this time (for example, Father's Day, Thanksgiving, Christmas, Chanukah)? Read the messages in a few cards. Make a card for someone you know. Write your own message.

Internet Activities

1. Find a greeting card site on the Internet. Send an electronic greeting card to someone you know.

2. Using the Internet, find the answers to these questions:
   a. When is Father's Day in the U.S.?
   b. What is the origin of Mother's Day?
   c. When is Thanksgiving?
   d. What is the history of the Fourth of July?

 Additional Activities at **http://elt.heinle.com/gic**

LESSON

4

GRAMMAR

Singular and Plural
Articles and Quantity Words
There + Be + Noun

CONTEXT: Americans and Where They Live

Americans and Where They Live
Finding an Apartment
Calling About an Apartment

4.1 | Singular and Plural—An Overview

Examples	Explanation
Some kids live with one **parent.** Some kids live with two **parents.** Everyone pays **taxes.**	Singular means one. Plural means more than one. Plural nouns usually end in -s or -es.
Some young **men** and **women** live with their parents. Some **children** live with their grandparents.	Some plural forms are irregular. They don't end in -s. **Examples:** man → men woman → women child → children

AMERICANS AND WHERE THEY LIVE[1]

Before You Read

1. Do you know anyone who lives alone?

2. Does your family own a house or rent an apartment?

Read the following information. Pay special attention to plural nouns.

There are about 292 million **people** in the U.S.

- The average family has 3.17 **people.**
- 5.5% of **children** live in **households** run by one or both **grandparents.**
- 69% of **children** live with two **parents.**
- 15% of **males** 25–34 live at home with one or both **parents.**
- 8% of **females** 25–34 live at home with one or both **parents.**
- 26% of **Americans** live alone. (Compare this figure to 1940—8%.)
- 31% of **households** have a dog.
- 27% of **households** have a cat.

Homes

- 67% of American **families** own their **homes.**
- 25% of **homeowners** are over 65 **years** old.
- The price of **homes** depends on the city where you live. Some **cities** have very expensive **homes:** San Francisco, Boston, San Diego, Honolulu, and New York.
- The average American moves a lot. In a five-year period, 46% of **Americans** change their address. **Renters** move more than **owners.** Young **people** move more than older people.

[1] Statistics are from the 2000 census.

Average home prices in the most expensive American cities (2002)	
San Francisco	$541,000
Boston	$398,000
San Diego	$362,000
Honolulu	$330,000
New York City	$304,000

EXERCISE 1 Tell if the statement is true (*T*) or false (*F*).

EXAMPLE Homes in Boston are very expensive. **T**

1. Most children live with their grandparents.

2. Houses in New York City are more expensive than houses in San Francisco.

3. Most people rent an apartment.

4. Americans stay in the same house for most of their lives.

5. Cats are more popular than dogs in American homes.

6. Families in the U.S. are small (under five people).

7. Most children live with both parents.

8. The price of homes depends on where you live.

4.2 | Regular Noun Plurals

Word Ending	Example Words	Plural Addition	Plural form
Vowel	bee banana pie	+ s	bees bananas pies
Consonant	bed pin month	+ s	beds pins months
ss, sh, ch, x	class dish church box	+ es	classes dishes churches boxes
Vowel + y	boy day monkey	+ s	boys days monkeys
Consonant + y	lady story party	y + ies	ladies stories parties
Vowel + o	patio stereo radio	+ s	patios stereos radios
Consonant + o	mosquito tomato potato	+ es	mosquitoes tomatoes potatoes
Exceptions: photos, pianos, solos, altos, sopranos, autos, avocados.			
f or fe	leaf calf knife	f̶ + ves fe̶ + ves	leaves calves knives
Exceptions: beliefs, chiefs, roofs, chefs			

EXERCISE 2 Write the plural form of each noun.

EXAMPLES leaf _____*leaves*_____

toy _____*toys*_____

1. dish _____

2. country _____

3. half _____

4. book _____

5. boy _____

6. girl _____

7. bench _____

8. box _____

9. shark _____

10. stereo _____

11. knife _____

12. story _____

13. sofa _____

14. key _____

15. movie _____

16. squirrel _____

17. mosquito _____

18. lion _____

19. fly _____

20. cow _____

21. table _____

22. roach _____

23. fox _____

24. house _____

25. turkey _____

26. chicken _____

27. wolf _____

28. dog _____

29. bath _____

30. pony _____

31. duck _____

32. moth _____

4.3 | Pronunciation of Plural Nouns

The plural ending has three pronunciations: /s/, /z/, and /əz/

Pronunciation	Rule	Examples	
/s/	Pronounce /s/ after voiceless sounds: /p, t, k, f, θ/	lip—lips cat—cats rock—rocks cuff—cuffs month—months	
/z/	Pronounce /z/ after voiced sounds: /b, d, g, v, m, n, ŋ, l, r/ and all vowels	cab—cabs lid—lids bag—bags stove—stoves sum—sums	can—cans thing—things bill—bills car—cars bee—bees
/əz/	Pronounce /əz/ when the base form ends in *s, ss, ce, se, sh, ch, ge, x*	bus—buses class—classes place—places cause—causes dish—dishes beach—beaches garage—garages tax—taxes	

EXERCISE 3 Go back to Exercise 2 and pronounce the plural form of each word.

4.4 | Irregular Noun Plurals

Singular	Plural	Explanation
man woman mouse tooth foot goose	men women mice teeth feet geese	Some nouns have a vowel change in the plural form. **Singular:** Do you see that old **woman?** **Plural:** Do you see those young **women?**
sheep fish deer	sheep fish deer	Some plural forms are the same as the singular form. **Singular:** I have one **fish** in my tank. **Plural:** She has ten **fish** in her tank.
child person mouse	children people (OR persons) mice	For some plurals we change to a different form. **Singular:** She has one **child.** **Plural:** They have two **children.**
	pajamas clothes pants/slacks (eye)glasses scissors	Some words have no singular form. **Example:** My **pants** are new. Do you like them?
dozen (12) hundred thousand million		Exact numbers use the singular form. **Examples:** The U.S. has over 290 **million** people. I need to buy **a dozen** eggs.
	dozens hundreds thousands millions	The plural form of a number is *not* an exact number. **Example:** **Thousands** of people live alone.

Language Notes:
1. You hear the difference between *woman* (singular) and *women* (plural) in the first syllable.
2. The plural of *person* can also be *persons*, but *people* is more common.

EXERCISE 4   The following nouns have an irregular plural form. Write the plural.

EXAMPLE   man ____men____

1. foot _____
2. woman _____
3. policeman _____
4. child _____

5. fish _____
6. mouse _____
7. sheep _____
8. tooth _____

EXERCISE 5   Fill in the blanks with the correct plural form of the noun in parentheses.

EXAMPLE   Some ____people____ like to live alone.
    (person)

1. Most _____ in the U.S. own a house.
        (family)

2. The U.S. has over 290 million _____.
                                    (person)

3. Americans move many _____.
                            (time)

4. Most single _____ are _____.
                (parent)   (woman)

5. Some _____ earn more money than their _____.
          (woman)   (husband)

6. _____ are very expensive in some _____.
      (Home)   (city)

7. Divorce is very high in some _____.
                                    (country)

8. Some _____live with only one parent.
              (child)

9. How many square _____ does your house or apartment have?
                        (foot)

10. Some _____ live with _____.
              (child)   (grandparent)

11. The average family has 3.17 _____.
                                    (person)

12. Some apartments have a problem with _____.
                                            (mouse)

FINDING AN APARTMENT

Before You Read

1. Do you live in a house, an apartment, or a dorm?[2] Do you live alone?
2. Do you like the place where you live? Why or why not?

Read the following article. Pay special attention to *there + be* followed by singular and plural nouns.

There are several ways to find an apartment. One way is to look in the newspaper. **There is** an "Apartments for Rent" section in the back of the newspaper. **There are** many ads for apartments. **There are** also ads for houses for rent and houses for sale. Many newspapers also put their listings online.

Another way to find an apartment is by looking at the buildings in the neighborhood where you want to live. **There are** often "For Rent" signs on the front of the buildings. **There is** usually a phone number on the sign. You can call and ask for information about the apartment that you are interested in. You can ask:

- How much is the rent?
- Is heat included?
- What floor is the apartment on?
- **Is there** an elevator?
- How many bedrooms **are there** in the apartment?
- How many closets **are there** in the apartment?
- Is the apartment available[3] now?

If an apartment interests you, you can make an appointment to see it. When you go to see the apartment, you should ask some more questions, such as the following:

- **Is there** a lease?[4] How long is the lease?

[2] *Dorm* is short for *dormitory*, a building where students live.
[3] *Available* means ready to use now.
[4] A *lease* is a contract between the owner (landlord or landlady) and the renter (tenant). It tells how much the rent is, how long the tenant can stay in the apartment, and other rules.

APARTMENTS FOR RENT

5 rooms, 2 baths, fenced yard, pets allowed. References required. Call 555-112-3345 after 6:00 p.m.

4 rooms, 1 bath, quiet dead end street. 2 car driveway. Call 555-122-3445 for appointment.

5 rooms, 1 bath, new kitchen and ~~ting. Dish wash-~~

- **Is there** a janitor or manager?
- **Is there** a parking space for each tenant? Is it free, or do I have to pay extra?
- **Are there** smoke detectors? (In many places, the law says that the landlord must put a smoke detector in each apartment and in the halls.)
- **Is there** a laundry room in the building? Where is it?

The landlord may ask you a few questions, such as:

- How many people **are there** in your family?
- Do you have any pets?

You should check over the apartment carefully before you sign the lease. If **there are** some problems, you should talk to the landlord to see if he will take care of them before you move in.

4.5 | Using *There + Is/Are*

We use *there + is* or *there + are* to introduce a subject into the conversation when we show location or time.

	Examples				
Singular	*There*	*is*	*a/an/one*	singular subject	location/time
	There	is	a	janitor	in my building.
	There	is	an	open house	at 1:00.
	There	is	one	dryer	in the basement.
	There	is	a	rent increase	this year.
	Note: *There's* is the contraction for *there is*.				
Negative Singular	*There*	*isn't*	*a*	singular subject	location/time
	There	isn't	a	back door	in my apartment.
	There's	*no*		singular subject	location/time
	There's	no		balcony	in my apartment.
	There's	no		heat	this month.
Plural	*There*	*are*	plural word	plural subject	location/time
	There	are	several	windows	in the bedroom.
	There	are	many	children	in the building.
	There	are	some	cats	in the building.
	There	are	two	closets	in the hall.
	There	are	—	curtains	on the windows.
	Note: We don't write a contraction for *there are*.				
Negative Plural	*There*	*aren't*	plural word	plural subject	location/time
	There	aren't	any	shades	on the windows.
	There	aren't	any	new tenants	this month.
	There	*are*	*no*	plural subject	location/time
	There	are	no	cabinets	in the kitchen.

Language Notes:

1. When two nouns follow *there,* use a singular verb (*is*) if the first noun is singular. Use a plural verb (*are*) if the first noun is plural.

   There is a closet in the bedroom and two closets in the hall.

   There are two closets in the hall and one closet in the bedroom.

   There is a washer and dryer in the basement.

2. *There* never introduces a specific or unique noun. Don't use a noun with the definite article (*the*) after *there*.

   Wrong: *There's* the Eiffel Tower in Paris.

   Right: The Eiffel Tower is in Paris.

EXERCISE 6 ABOUT YOU Use the words given to make a statement about the place where you live (house or apartment). If you live in a dorm, use Exercise 7 instead.

EXAMPLES   carpet / in the living room
There's a carpet in the living room.

trees / in front of the building
There are no trees in front of the building.

1. porch

2. blinds / on the windows

3. door / in every room

4. window / in every room

5. lease

6. closet / in the living room

7. number / on the door of the apartment

8. overhead light / in every room

9. microwave oven / in the kitchen

10. back door

11. fireplace

12. smoke detector

EXERCISE 7 ABOUT YOU Make a statement about your dorm and dorm room with the words given. (If you live in an apartment or house, skip this exercise.)

EXAMPLES   window / in the room
There's a window in the room.

curtains / on the window
There are no curtains on the window.
There are shades.

1. closet / in the room

2. two beds / in the room

3. private bath / for every room

4. men and women / in the dorm

5. cafeteria / in the dorm

6. snack machines / in the dorm

7. noisy students / in the dorm

8. numbers / on the doors of the rooms

9. elevator(s) / in the dorm

10. laundry room / in the dorm

4.6 | Questions and Short Answers Using *There*

Compare statements (S) and questions (Q) with *there*. Observe short answers (A).

	Examples	Explanation

Singular Statement
 	
Yes/No **Question**
	S: **There is** a laundry room in the building.
	
	Q: **Is there** an elevator in the building?
	A: Yes, there is.
	
	S: **There's** a closet in the bedroom.
	Q: **Is there** a closet in the hall?
	A: No, there isn't.
		Question word order:
		
		Is + there + a/an + singular noun . . . ?
		
		Short answers:
		  Yes, there is. (no contraction)
		  No, there isn't. OR No, there's not.

Plural Statement *Yes/No* **Question**	S: **There are** some children in the building. Q: **Are there** (any) children on your floor? A: Yes, there are. S: **There are** trees in back of the building. Q: **Are there** (any) trees in front of the building? A: No, there aren't.	**Question word order:** *Are + there + (any) +* plural noun . . . ? We often use *any* to introduce a plural noun in a *yes/no* question. **Short answers:** No, there aren't.
Plural Statement **Information Question**	S: **There are** ten apartments in my building. Q: **How many** apartments **are there** in your building? A: Thirty.	**Question word order:** *How many +* plural noun *+ are there* . . . ?

EXERCISE **8**   ABOUT YOU Ask and answer questions with *there* and the words given to find out about another student's apartment and building. (If you live in a dorm, use Exercise 9 instead.)

EXAMPLES   a microwave oven / in your apartment

A: Is there a microwave oven in your apartment?
B: No, there isn't.

closets / in the bedroom

A: Are there any closets in the bedroom?
B: Yes. There's one closet in the bedroom.

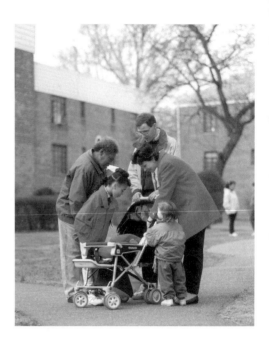

1. children / in your building
2. a dishwasher / in the kitchen
3. a yard / in front of your building
4. trees / in front of your building
5. a basement / in the building
6. a laundry room / in the basement
7. a janitor / in the building
8. noisy neighbors / in the building
9. nosy[5] neighbors / in the building
10. an elevator / in the building
11. parking spaces / for the tenants
12. a lot of closets / in the apartment
13. how many apartments / in your building
14. how many parking spaces / in front of your building

EXERCISE 9 ABOUT YOU Ask and answer questions with *there* and the words given to find out about another student's dorm. (If you live in an apartment or house, skip this exercise.)

EXAMPLE a bicycle room / in your dorm

A: Is there a bicycle room in your dorm?
B: No, there isn't.

1. married students
2. private rooms
3. a bicycle room
4. a computer room
5. an elevator
6. a bulletin board

7. graduate students
8. a quiet place to study
9. an air conditioner / in your room
10. a parking lot / for your dorm
11. how many rooms / in your dorm
12. how many floors / in your dorm

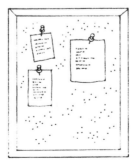

---

[5] A *nosy* person is a person who wants to know everyone's business.

Use the words given to ask the teacher a question about his or her office. Your teacher will answer.

EXAMPLES pencil sharpener

A: Is there a pencil sharpener in your office?
B: No, there isn't.

books

A: Are there any books in your office?
B: Yes. There are a lot of books in my office.

1. phone
2. file cabinet
3. photos of your family
4. radio
5. copy machine
6. windows

7. calendar
8. bookshelves
9. plants
10. voice mail
11. fax machine
12. computer

EXERCISE 11 A student is calling about an apartment for rent. Fill in the blanks with *there is*, *there are*, *is there*, *are there*, and other related words to complete this phone conversation between the student (S) and the landlord (L).

S: I'm calling about an apartment for rent on Grover Street.

L: We have two apartments available. ___*There's*___ a four-room
        (example)

apartment on the first floor and a three-room apartment on the fourth floor. Which one are you interested in?

S: I prefer the smaller apartment. _____ an elevator in the building?
                                            (1)

L: Yes, there is. How many people _____ in your family?
                                          (2)

S: It's just for me. I live alone. I'm a student. I need a quiet apartment. Is this a quiet building?

L: Oh, yes. _____ no kids in the building.
                            (3)

This is a very quiet building.

S: That's good. I have a car. _____ parking spaces?
                                          (4)

L: Yes. _____ 20 spaces in the back of the building.
                  (5)

S: How _____ apartments _____ in the building?
              (6)   (7)

L: _____ 30 apartments.
                        (8)

S: Twenty parking spaces for 30 apartments? Then _____

_____ enough spaces for all the tenants.
(9)

L: Don't worry. Not everyone has a car. Parking is on a first-come,

first-served basis.[6] And _____ plenty
(10)

of[7] spaces on the street.

S: _____ a laundry room in the building?
(11)

L: Yes. There are washers and dryers in the basement.
S: How much is the rent?
L: It's $850 a month.
S: I hear a dog. Is that your dog?

L: Yes, but don't worry. I don't live in the building. _____
(12)

no dogs in the building.
S: When can I see the apartment?
L: How about tomorrow at six o'clock?
S: That'll be fine. Thanks.

4.7 | *There* vs. *They* and Other Pronouns

Examples		Explanation
There's a *janitor* in the building.	**He's** in the basement.	To introduce a new noun, we use *there* + *is/are*. When we use this noun again as the subject of another sentence, we use *he, she, it,* or *they*.
There's a little *girl* in the next apartment.	**She's** cute.	
There's an empty *apartment* on the first floor.	**It's** available now.	
There are two washing *machines*.	**They're** in the basement.	

Pronunciation Note: We pronounce *there* and *they're* exactly the same. Listen to your teacher pronounce the sentences from the box above.

Spelling Note: Don't confuse *there* and *they're*.
   There are dogs in the next apartment.
   They're very friendly.

---

[6] A *first-come, first-served* basis means that people who arrive first will get something first (parking spaces, theater tickets, classes at registration).
[7] *Plenty of* means "a lot of."

EXERCISE 12   Fill in the blanks with *there's*, *there are*, *it's*, or *they're*.

EXAMPLE   _There's_ a small apartment for rent in my building.

           _It's_ on the fourth floor.

1. _____ two apartments for rent. _____ not on the same floor.

2. _____ a laundry room in the building. _____ in the basement.

3. The parking spaces are in the back of the building. _____ _____ for the tenants with cars.

4. The parking spaces don't cost extra. _____ free for the tenants.

5. The apartment is small. _____ on the fourth floor.

6. The building has 30 apartments. _____ a big building.

7. The student wants to see the apartment. _____ on Grover Street.

8. The building is quiet because _____ no kids in the building.

9. How much is the rent? _____ $850 a month.

10. Is the rent high? No, _____ not high.

11. _____ no dogs in the building.

12. _____ a quiet building.

EXERCISE 13   Ask a question about this school using *there* and the words given. Another student will answer. If the answer is "yes," ask a question with *where*.

EXAMPLE   lockers

A: Are there any lockers at this school?
B: Yes, there are.
A: Where are they?
B: They're near the gym.

1. a library
2. vending machines
3. public telephones
4. a computer room
5. a cafeteria
6. a gym
7. a swimming pool

8. tennis courts
9. dormitories
10. a parking lot
11. a bookstore
12. copy machines
13. a student lounge
14. a fax machine

Before You Read

1. Does your neighborhood have more apartment buildings or houses?

2. Do you prefer to live alone, with a roommate, or with your family? Why?

Read the following phone conversation between a student (S) and the manager (M) of a building. Pay special attention to the definite article (*the*), the indefinite articles (*a, an*), and indefinite quantity words (*some, any*).

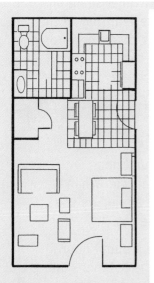

S: Hello? I want to speak with **the landlord.**

M: I'm **the manager** of **the building.** Can I help you?

S: I need to find **a** new **apartment.**

M: Where do you live now?

S: I live in **a** big **apartment** on Wright Street. I have **a roommate,** but he's graduating, and I need **a** smaller **apartment.** Are there **any** small **apartments** for rent in your building?

M: There's one.

S: What floor is it on?

M: It's on **the** third **floor.**

S: Does it have **a bedroom?**

M: No. It's **a** studio **apartment.** It has **a living room** and **a kitchen.**

S: Is **the living room** big?

M: So-so.

S: Does **the kitchen** have **a stove** and **a refrigerator?**

M: Yes. **The refrigerator** is old, but it works well. **The stove** is pretty new.

S: Can I see **the apartment?**

M: I have a question for you first. Do you have **a dog?** We don't permit **dogs.** **Some dogs** make a lot of noise.

S: I don't have **a dog.**

M: I'm happy to hear that.

S: But I have **a snake.**

M: **A snake?**

S: **Snakes** are quiet.

M: Yes, but . . .

S: Don't worry. I keep **the snake** in a glass box.

M: I hope **the box** is always closed.

S: It is. I only open it to feed **the snake.** I feed it **mice.**

M: Oh.

S: When can I see **the apartment?**

M: I have to speak to **the landlord.** I'm not sure if you can have **snakes** and **mice** in **the apartment.**

4.8 | Articles with Definite and Indefinite Nouns

Singular

Indefinite	Definite	Explanation
I live in **a** big building. There's **a** janitor in the building.	**The** building is near the college. **The** janitor lives on the first floor.	We introduce a singular noun with the indefinite articles (*a* or *an*). When we refer to this noun again, we use the definite article *the*.
	May I speak to **the** landlord? He lives on **the** third floor. **The** basement is dirty.	We use *the* before a singular noun if this noun is the only one or if the speaker and listener share an experience and are referring to the same one. (In this case, they are talking about the same building.)

Plural

Indefinite	Definite	Explanation
My building has **(some)** washing machines. Are there **(any)** dryers?	**The** washing machines are in the basement. Where are **the** dryers?	We introduce a plural noun with *some*, *any*, or no article. When we refer to this noun again, we use the definite article *the*.
	The tenants are angry. **The** washing machines don't work.	We use *the* before a plural noun if the speaker and the listener share the same experience. (In this case, they are talking about the same building.)

EXERCISE 14 Fill in the blanks in the conversations between two students. Use *the, a, an, some,* or *any.*

CONVERSATION 1

A: Is there ____a____ cafeteria at this school?
      (example)

B: Yes, there is.

A: Where's _____ cafeteria?
                (1)

B: It's on _____ first floor.
              (2)

A: Are there _____ snack machines in _____ cafeteria?
                  (3)   *(4)*

B: Yes, there are.

A: I want to buy _____ soft drink.
                      (5)

B: _____ soft drink machine is out of order today.
      (6)

A: Is there _____ bookstore for this college?
(1)

B: Yes, there is.

A: Where's _____ bookstore?
(2)

B: It's on Green Street.

A: I need to buy _____ dictionary.
(3)

B: Today's _____ holiday. _____ bookstore is closed today.
(4)   (5)

EXERCISE 15 Fill in the blanks in the conversation about apartment problems. Use *the, a, an, some,* or *any.*

A: I have ____a____ problem in my apartment.
(example)

B: What's _____ problem?
(1)

A: _____ landlord doesn't provide enough heat. I have
(2)

to wear _____ sweater or _____ coat all the
(3)   (4)

time in the apartment.

B: Why don't you talk to _____ building manager?
(5)

Maybe _____ heating system is broken. If he doesn't
(6)

solve _____ problem, you can send _____
(7)   (8)

letter to _____ Department of Housing.
(9)

A: That's _____ good idea. There's one more problem.
(10)

I have _____ neighbor who has _____ small dog.
(11)   (12)

_____ dog barks all the time when _____ neighbor isn't
(13)   (14)

home. We share _____ wall, and I can hear _____ dog
(15)   (16)

barking through _____ wall.
(17)

B: Talk to _____ neighbor. Tell him there are dog services. For
                    (18)

_____ price, someone can go to his house every day and play
   (19)

with _____ dog and take it out for a walk.
          (20)

A: I don't think he wants to pay _____ price for this service.
                                              (21)

B: Then talk to _____ landlord. Tell him about _____ problem.
                        (22)   (23)

4.9 | Making Generalizations

A generalization says that something is true of all members of a group.

Singular	Plural	Explanation
A snake is quiet. **A dog** makes noise.	**Snakes** are quiet. **Dogs** make noise.	To make a generalization about the **subject**, use the indefinite article (*a* or *an*) with a singular subject or no article with a **plural** subject.
	I don't like **snakes.** Snakes eat **mice.**	To make a generalization about the **object**, use the plural form with no article.

EXERCISE 16   The following sentences are generalizations. Change the subject from singular to plural. Make other necessary changes.

EXAMPLE: A single parent has a difficult life.
Single parents have a difficult life.

1. A house in San Diego is expensive.

   _____

2. A homeowner pays property tax.

   _____

3. A dog is part of the family.

   _____

4. A renter doesn't have freedom to make changes.

   _____

5. An owner has freedom to make changes.

   _____

EXERCISE 17 ABOUT YOU Use the noun in parentheses ( ) to give general information about your native country or hometown. Use the plural form with no article.

EXAMPLE (woman)
Generally, women don't work outside the home in my native country.

1. (person)   5. (house)
2. old (person)   6. poor (person)
3. (woman)   7. (car)
4. (man)   8. (doctor)

EXERCISE 18 Add a plural subject to these sentences to make a generalization.

EXAMPLE _____ Small children _____ need a lot of sleep.

1. _____ make a lot of money.
2. _____ have a hard life.
3. _____ talk on the phone a lot.
4. _____ are in good physical condition.
5. _____ believe in Santa Claus.
6. _____ worry about children.

EXERCISE 19 ABOUT YOU Use the plural form of each noun to tell if you like or don't like the following living conditions.

EXAMPLE tall building
I like tall buildings.

1. white wall   7. high ceiling
2. curtain on the window   8. bright light
3. picture on the wall   9. two-story house
4. plant   10. digital clock
5. friendly neighbor   11. carpet
6. blind on the window   12. hardwood floor

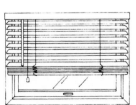

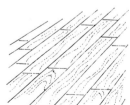

EXERCISE 20 ABOUT YOU Ask *Do you like* + the plural form of the noun. Another student will answer.

EXAMPLES child

    A: Do you like children?
    B: Yes, I do.

dog

    A: Do you like dogs?
    B: No, I don't.

1. cat
2. dog
3. American doctor
4. American car
5. American movie
6. fashion magazine

7. comic book
8. computer
9. computer game
10. strict teacher
11. American supermarket
12. American textbook

EXERCISE 21 Combination Exercise. This is a conversation between two students. Fill in the blanks with *the, a, an, some, any,* or *X* for no article.

A: Is there _____*a*_____ copy machine in our library?
           (example)

B: Yes. There are several copy machines in _____ library.
                                       (1)

A: Are _____ copy machines free?
          (2)

B: No. You need to use _____ nickel[8] for
                         (3)

_____ copy machines. Why do you need
    (4)

_____ copy machine?
    (5)

A: I want to copy my classmate's textbook.

B: The whole thing? Why?

A: _____ textbooks in the U.S. are too expensive.
    (6)

B: There's _____ rule about copying an entire book.
          (7)

A: What's _____ rule?
         (8)

B: You can't copy _____ books without permission
                     (9)

from the publisher.

---

[8] A *nickel* is a five-cent coin.

A: In my country, we copy _____ books all the time.
   (10)

B: But it's illegal. People who copy _____ books, and
   (11)

CDs, and movies are called "pirates."

SUMMARY OF LESSON 4

1. **Singular and Plural**
   boy—boys
   box—boxes
   story—stories
   (Exceptions: men, women, people, children, feet, teeth)

2. *There + be*
   There's an empty apartment in my building.
   There are two washing machines in the basement.
   Are there any parking spaces?

3. **Articles**

   - To make a generalization:
     | SINGULAR | **A dog** has good hearing. |
     | PLURAL | **Dogs** have good hearing. |
     | | I like **dogs.** |

   - To introduce a new noun into the conversation:
     | SINGULAR | I have **a dog.** |
     | PLURAL | I have **(some) turtles.** |
     | | I don't have **(any) birds.** |

   - To talk about a previously mentioned noun:
     | SINGULAR | I have a dog. **The dog** barks when the letter carrier arrives. |
     | PLURAL | I have some turtles. I keep **the turtles** in the bathroom. |

   - To talk about specific items or people from our experience:
     | SINGULAR | **The janitor** cleans the basement once a week. |
     | PLURAL | **The tenants** have to take out their own garbage. |

   - To talk about the only one:
     The president lives in Washington, D.C.
     The Statue of Liberty is in New York.

1. *People* is a plural noun. Use a plural verb form.

   People in my country ~~is~~ *are* very poor.

2. Don't use *the* with a generalization.

   ~~The~~ *D*dogs are friendly animals.

3. Don't confuse *there* with *they're*.

   I have two brothers. ~~There~~ *They're* in Florida.

4. Use *there + is/are* to introduce a new subject.

   In my class ^*there are* five students from Haiti.

5. Don't confuse *it's* and *there's*.

   ~~It's~~ *There's* a closet in my bedroom.

6. Don't confuse *have* and *there*.

   ~~Have~~ *There's* a closet in my bedroom.

7. Don't use *the* + a unique noun after *there*.

   ~~There's~~ *T*the Golden Gate Bridge ^*is* in California.

8. Don't use *the* with the first mention of a noun when you and the listener do not share a common experience with this noun.

   I have ~~the~~ *a* new watch.

9. Don't use an apostrophe for a plural ending.

   She has three ~~brother's~~ *brothers*.

PART 1 A woman is showing her new apartment to her friend. Find the mistakes with the underlined words in this conversation and correct them. If the sentence is correct, write *C*.

A: Let me show you around my new apartment.

B: <u>It's</u> a big apartment.   *C*

A: It's big enough for my family. ~~They're~~ *There* are four bedrooms and two bathrooms. <u>Has each bedroom a large closet.</u> Let me show you my
(1)
kitchen too.

B: Oh. <u>It's</u> a new dishwasher in your kitchen.
(2)

A: <u>It's</u> wonderful. You know how I hate to wash dishes.
(3)

B: <u>Is there</u> a microwave oven?
(4)

A: No, <u>there isn't.</u>
(5)

B: <u>Are any</u> washers and dryers for clothes?
(6)

A: Oh, yes. <u>They're</u> in the basement. In the laundry room <u>are</u> five
*(7)**(8)*
washers and five dryers. I never have to wait.

B: <u>There are</u> a lot of people in your building?
(9)

A: <u>In my building 30 apartments.</u>
(10)

B: <u>Is a janitor</u> in your building?
(11)

A: Yes. <u>There's</u> a very good janitor. He keeps the building very clean.
(12)

B: I suppose this apartment costs a lot.

A: Well, yes. The rent is high. But I share the apartment with my
cousins. *(13)*

PART 2 Write the plural form for each noun.

box ____boxes____   month _____   child _____

card _____   match _____   desk _____

foot _____   shelf _____   key _____

potato _____   radio _____   story _____

woman _____   mouse _____   bus _____

PART 3 Fill in the blanks with *there, is, are, it,* or *they* or a combination of more than one of these words.

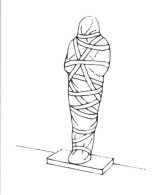

A: ____Are there____ any museums in Chicago?
   (example)

B: Yes, _____ a lot of museums in Chicago.
        (1)

A: _____ a history museum in Chicago?
        (2)

B: Yes, _____ is.
        (3)

A: Where _____ the history museum?
            (4)

B: _____ near downtown.
        (5)

A: _____ any mummies in this museum?
        (6)

B: Yes, there are. _____ from Egypt.
                    (7)

A: _____ a dinosaur in this museum?
        (8)

B: Yes, there is. _____ on the first floor.
                   (9)

A: How many floors _____ in this museum?
                        (10)

B: _____ two floors and a basement.
        (11)

A: _____ a parking lot near this museum?
        (12)

B: Yes, _____, but _____ not very big.
             (13)   (14)

126   Lesson 4

PART 4 Fill in the blanks with *the*, *a*, *an*, *some*, *any*, or *X* for no article.

A: Do you like your apartment?

B: No, I don't.

A: Why not?

B: There are many reasons. First, I don't like ___*the*___ janitor.
    (example)
   He's impolite.

A: Anything else?

B: I want to get _____ dog.
                    (1)

A: So?

B: It's not permitted. _____ landlord says that _____ dogs
                        (2)   (3)
   make a lot of noise.

A: Can you get _____ cat?
                (4)

B: Yes, but I don't like _____ cats.
                          (5)

A: Is your building quiet?

B: No. There are _____ children in _____ building. When
                  (6)   (7)
   I try to study, I can hear _____ children in the next apartment.
                               (8)
   They watch TV all the time.

A: You need to find _____ new apartment.
                     (9)

B: I think you're right.

Classroom Activities

1. Make a list of things you have, things you don't have but would like to have, and things you don't need. Choose from the list below and add any other items you can think of. Then find a partner and compare lists.

a computer	a house	a credit card
a DVD player	a diamond ring	a speaker phone
a digital camera	a CD player	a cell phone
an encyclopedia	an electric can opener	a big-screen TV
a pager	a microwave oven	a letter opener
an electric toothbrush	a waterbed	a blow dryer
a scale	an electronic calendar	an orange juice squeezer

I have:	I don't have, but I would like to have:	I don't need:

Discuss your chart with a partner. Tell why you need or don't need some things. Tell why you want some things that you don't have.

2. People often use the newspaper to look for an apartment. The Sunday newspaper has the most ads. Bring in a copy of the Sunday newspaper. Look at the section of the newspaper that has apartments for rent. Ask the teacher to help you understand the abbreviations.

3. What other sections are there in the Sunday newspaper? Work with a partner and make a list of everything you can find in the Sunday paper.

EXAMPLE   There's a TV schedule for this week's programs.
There are a lot of ads and coupons.
There's a crossword puzzle.

4. Look at the information about two apartments for rent below. What are some of the advantages and disadvantages of each one? Discuss your answers with a partner or with the entire class.

Apartment 1	Apartment 2
a view of a park	on a busy street
rent = $950	rent = $750
fifth floor (an elevator in the building)	third floor walk-up
a new kitchen with a dishwasher	old appliances in the kitchen
pets not allowed	pets allowed
hardwood floors	a carpet in the living room
the janitor lives in the building	the owner lives in the building on the first floor
management controls the heat	the tenant controls the heat
no air conditioners	air conditioners in the bedroom and living room
faces north only	faces east, south, and west
a one-year lease	no lease
a large building—50 apartments	a small building—6 apartments
washers and dryers on each floor	a laundry room in the basement
parking spaces on first-come, first-served basis	a parking space for each tenant

5. Do you have a picture of your house, apartment, or apartment building? Bring it to class and tell about it.

6. Find a partner and pretend that one of you is looking for an apartment and the other person is the landlady, landlord, or manager. Ask and answer questions about the apartment, the building, parking, laundry, and rent. Write your conversation. Then read it to the class.

7. In a small group or with the entire class, discuss the following:
   a. How do people rent apartments in your hometown? Is rent high? Is heat usually included in the rent? Does the landlord usually live in the building?
   b. What are some differences between a typical apartment in this city and a typical apartment in your hometown?

8. Use the plural form of the word in parentheses ( ) to make a generalization. Remember, don't use an article with the plural form to make a generalization. You may work with a partner.

EXAMPLES   (child)

Children like to watch cartoons.

American (highway)

American highways are in good condition.

1. (American)

2. American (child)

3. big (city) in the U.S.

4. (teacher) at this college

5. (student) at this college

6. American (doctor)

7. old (person) in the U.S.

8. American (woman)

Write About it

1. Write a description of a room or place that you like very much. (Review prepositions in Lesson 1.)

EXAMPLE   My favorite place is my living room. There are many pictures on the walls. There's a picture of my grand-parents above the sofa. There are a lot of pictures of my children on the wall next to the sofa.

There's a TV in the corner. Under the TV there is a DVD player. There's a box of movies next to the DVD player . . . .

2. Write a comparison of your apartment in this city and your apartment or house in your hometown.

EXAMPLE   There are many differences between my apartment here and my apartment in Kiev, Ukraine. In my Kiev apartment, there is a door in every room. In my apartment here, only the bedrooms and bathrooms have doors. In my Kiev apartment, there is a small window inside each large window. In the winter, I can open this small window to get some fresh air. My apartment here doesn't have this small window. I have to open the whole window to get air. Sometimes the room becomes too cold. . . .

Internet Activity

Use the Internet to look for apartments for rent and houses for sale in this city (or nearby suburbs). What parts of this city or the suburbs have the highest rents and housing prices?

Additional Activities at http://elt.heinle.com/gic

GRAMMAR

Possession

Object Pronouns

Questions About the Subject

CONTEXT: Families and Names

Names

William Madison's Name

Who Helps Your Parents?

131

Before You Read

1. What is your complete name? What do your friends call you?

2. Do you like your name?

Read the following article. Pay special attention to possessive forms.

Americans usually have three names: a first name, a middle name, and a last name (or surname). For example: Marilyn Sue Ellis or Edward David Orleans. Some people use an initial when they sign **their** names: Marilyn S. Ellis, Edward D. Orleans. Not everyone has a middle name.

American women often change **their** last names when they get married. For example, if Marilyn Ellis marries Edward Orleans, **her** name becomes Marilyn Orleans. Not all women follow this custom. Sometimes a woman keeps **her** maiden name[1] and adds **her husband's** name, with or without a hyphen (-): For example, Marilyn Ellis-Orleans or Marilyn Ellis Orleans. Sometimes a woman does not use **her husband's** name at all. In this case, if the couple has children, they have to decide if **their** children will use **their father's** name, **their mother's** name, or both. A man does not usually change **his** name when he gets married.

Some people have **their mother's** last name as a middle name: John Fitzgerald Kennedy, Franklin Delano Roosevelt.[2]

Did You Know?

The five most common last names in the U.S. are Smith, Johnson, Williams, Jones, and Brown.

[1] A *maiden name* is a woman's family name before she gets married.
[2] These are the names of two American presidents.

5.1 | Possessive Form of Nouns

We use the possessive form to show ownership or relationship.		
Noun	**Ending**	**Examples**
Singular Noun father mother dog	Add apostrophe + *s*	I use my **father's** last name. I don't use my **mother's** last name. My **dog's** name is PeeWee.
Plural Noun Ending in -s parents boys	Add apostrophe only	My **parents'** names are Ethel and Herman. My **sons'** names are Ted and Mike.
Irregular Plural Noun children women	Add apostrophe + *s*	What are your **children's** names? Marilyn and Sandra are **women's** names.
Names That End in -s Mr. Harris Charles	Add apostrophe only OR Add apostrophe + *s*	Do you know **Charles'** wife? OR Do you know **Charles's** wife?
Inanimate Objects the classroom the school	Use "*the* _____ *of* _____." Do not use apostrophe + *s*.	**The door of the classroom** is closed. Washington College is **the name of my school.**

EXERCISE **1** Fill in the blanks with the possessive form of a noun to make a true statement.

EXAMPLE I use my _____ *father's* _____ last name.

1. I use my _____ last name.

2. I don't use my _____ last name.

3. An American married woman often uses her _____ last name.

4. A married woman in my native culture uses her _____ last name.

5. A single American woman usually uses her _____ last name.

6. An American man rarely uses his _____ last name.

7. John Kennedy had his _____ maiden name as a middle name.

EXERCISE 2 Some of the following sentences can show possession with 's or '. Rewrite these sentences. Write "no change" for the others.

EXAMPLES The teacher knows the names of the students.

The teacher knows the students' names.

The door of the classroom is usually closed.

No change.

1. The teacher always corrects the homework of the students.

2. The name of the textbook is *Grammar in Context*.

3. The job of the teacher is to explain the grammar.

4. What are the names of your parents?

5. The color of this book is blue.

6. Do you use the last name of your father?

7. What is the name of your dog?

8. The names of the children are Jason and Jessica.

5.2 | Possessive Adjectives

Possessive adjectives show ownership or relationship.

Examples	Explanation
Compare subject pronouns and possessive adjectives	Subject Pronouns / Possessive Adjectives
I like **my** name.	I — my
You're a new student. What's **your** name?	you — your
He likes **his** name.	he — his
She doesn't like **her** name.	she — her
Is this your dog? Is *it* friendly? What's **its** name?	it — its
We use **our** nicknames.	we — our
They are my friends. **Their** last name is Jackson.	they — their
Be careful not to confuse *his* **and** *her*. **My sister** loves **her** husband. **My uncle** lives with **his** daughter.	*Wrong:* My sister loves *his* husband. *Wrong:* My uncle lives with *her* daughter.
My sister's name is Marilyn. **Her son's** name is David.	We can use a possessive adjective (*my, her*) and a possessive noun (*sister's, son's*) together.
My **sister's husband's** name is Edward.	We can use two possessive nouns together (*sister's husband's*).

EXERCISE 3 Fill in the blanks with the possessive adjective that relates to the subject.

EXAMPLE   I like _____*my*_____ teacher.

1. He loves _____ mother.

2. She loves _____ father.

3. A dog loves _____ master.

4. Many American women change _____ names when they get married.

5. Sometimes a woman keeps _____ maiden name and adds _____ husband's name.

6. American men don't usually change _____ names when they get married.

7. Do you use _____ father's last name?

8. I bring _____ book to class.

9. We use _____ books in class.

10. The teacher brings _____ book to class.

11. Some students do _____ homework in the library.

5.3 | Questions with *Whose*

Whose + noun asks about possession or ownership.

Questions	Answers
Whose + noun + aux. verb + subject + verb	
Whose name do you use?	I use **my father's** name.
Whose composition do you like?	I like **Lisa's** composition.
Whose + noun + *be* verb + subject	
Whose book is that?	It's **Bob's** book.
Whose glasses are those?	They're **my** glasses.

EXERCISE 4 Write a question with *whose* and the words given. Answer with the words in parentheses ( ).

EXAMPLES wife / that (Robert)

Whose wife is that? That's Robert's wife.

children / these (Robert)

Whose children are these? These are Robert's children.

1. office / this (the dean)

   _____

2. offices / those (the teachers)

   _____

3. dictionary / that (the teacher)

   _____

4. books / those (the students)

   _____

5. car / that (my parents)

   _____

6. house / this (my cousin)

   _____

7. papers / those (Mr. Ross)

   _____

8. CDs / these (the programmer)

   _____

5.4 | Possessive Pronouns

We use possessive pronouns to avoid repetition of a noun.	
Examples	**Explanation**
You don't know my name. I know **yours.** (*yours = your name*) Your name is easy for Americans. **Mine** is hard. (*mine = my name*) My parents are in the U.S. **Theirs** are in Russia. (*theirs = their parents*)	When we omit the noun, we use the possessive pronoun. **Compare:** Possessive Adjectives Possessive Pronouns my mine your yours his his her hers our ours their theirs
Robert's wife speaks English. **Peter's** doesn't. (*Peter's = Peter's wife*)	After a possessive noun, we can omit the noun.

EXERCISE 5   In each pair of sentences below, replace the underlined words with a possessive pronoun.

EXAMPLE   Your book is new. <u>My book</u> is old.
Your book is new. <u>Mine</u> is old.

1. His name is Charles. <u>Her name</u> is Paula.

2. My teacher comes from Houston. <u>Paula's teacher</u> comes from El Paso.

3. I like my English teacher. Does your brother like <u>his English teacher</u>?

4. I have my dictionary today. Do you have <u>your dictionary</u>?

5. Please let me use your book. I don't have <u>my book</u> today.

6. My parents' apartment is big. <u>Our apartment</u> is small.

7. My car is old. <u>Your car</u> is new.

EXERCISE 6 Circle the correct word in parentheses ( ) to complete this conversation.

A: Do you live with ((your,) yours) parents?
(example)

B: No, I don't. Do you live with (your, yours)?
(1)

A: No. I live with (my, mine) sister. (Our, Ours) parents are back
(2)   *(3)*

home. They live with (my, mine) brother.
(4)

B: (Your, Yours) brother is single, then?
(5)

A: No, he's married. He lives with his wife and (our, ours) parents.
(6)

B: If he's married, why does he live with (your, yours) parents?
(7)

A: In (our, ours) country, it's an honor to live with parents.
(8)

B: Not in (my, mine). Grown children don't usually want to live with
(9)

(their, theirs) parents, and parents don't usually want to live with
(10)

(their, theirs) grown children.
(11)

A: Where do (your, yours) parents live?
(12)

B: They live in another state.

A: Isn't that hard for you?

B: Not really. I have (my, mine) own life, and they have (their, theirs).
(13)   *(14)*

5.5 | The Subject and the Object

Examples	Explanation
S V 0 Bob likes Mary. We like movies.	The **subject** (S) comes before the verb (V). The **object** (0) comes after the verb. The object is a person or a thing.
S V 0 S V 0 Bob likes Mary because **she** helps **him**. S V 0 S V 0 I like movies because **they** entertain **me**.	We can use pronouns for the **subject** and the **object.**

Before You Read

1. What are common American names?

2. What is a very common first name in your country or native culture? What is a very common last name? Is your name common in your country or native culture?

Read the following conversation. Pay special attention to object pronouns.

A: I have many questions about American names. Can you answer **them** for me?

B: Of course.

A: Tell **me** about your name.

B: My name is William, but my friends call **me** Bill.

A: Why do they call **you** Bill?

B: Bill is a common nickname for William.

A: Is William your first name?

B: Yes.

A: What's your full name?

B: William Michael Madison.

A: Do you ever use your middle name?

B: I only use **it** for very formal occasions. I sign my name William M. Madison, Jr. (junior).

A: What does "junior" mean?

B: It means that I have the same name as my father. His name is William Madison, Sr. (senior).

A: What's your wife's name?

B: Anna Marie Simms-Madison. I call **her** Annie.

A: Why does she have two last names?

B: Simms is her father's last name, and Madison is mine. She uses both names with a hyphen (-) between **them.**

A: Do you have any children?

B: Yes. We have a son and a daughter. Our son's name is Richard, but we call **him** Dick. Our daughter's name is Elizabeth, but everybody calls **her** Lizzy.

A: What do your children call **you**?

B: They call **us** Mommy and Daddy, of course.

5.6 | Object Pronouns

Subject		Object	Examples		
			Subject	**Verb**	**Object**
I	→	me	You	love	me.
you	→	you	I	love	you.
he	→	him	She	loves	him.
she	→	her	He	loves	her.
it	→	it	We	love	it.
we	→	us	They	love	us.
they	→	them	We	love	them.

They love us.

He loves her.

We can use an object pronoun after the verb or after a preposition.		
Object Noun	**Object Pronoun**	**Explanation**
I have a **middle name.**	I use **it** when I sign my name.	We can use an object pronoun to substitute for an object noun.
He loves **his wife.**	The kids love **her** too.	
You know **my son.**	Friends call **him** Dick.	
We have **two children.**	We love **them.**	We use *them* for plural people and things.
I need **my books.**	I use **them** in class.	
I have **two last names.**	I use both **of** **them.**	An object pronoun can follow a preposition (*of, about, to, from, in,* etc.).
My sister has **a son.**	She always talks **about** him.	

EXERCISE 7 Fill in the blanks. Substitute an object pronoun for the underlined words.

EXAMPLE I look like my father, but my brother doesn't look like ___*him*___.

1. My brother's name is William, but we call _____ Bill.
2. I understand the teacher, and the teacher understands _____.
3. I use my dictionary when I write, but I don't use _____ when I speak.
4. I like this city. Do you like _____ too?
5. I talk to Americans, but I don't always understand _____.
6. We listen to the teacher, and we talk to _____.
7. When we make a mistake, the teacher corrects _____.
8. The president has advisers. They help _____ make decisions.
9. You understand me, and I understand _____.
10. My friends sometimes visit me, and I sometimes visit _____.

EXERCISE 8 This is a conversation between two students, one from China (A), one from the U.S. (B). Fill in the blanks with an appropriate object pronoun.

A: Americans are very informal about names. The teacher calls

___*us*___ by our first names.
(example)

B: What does the teacher call _____ in your country?
(1)

A: In my country, when a teacher talks to a woman, he calls

_____ "Miss" or "Madam." When he talks to a man, he calls
(2)

_____ "Sir."
(3)

B: I like it when the teacher calls _____ by my first name.
(4)

A: I don't. There's another strange thing: In my country, we never use a

first name for our teachers. We call _____ "Professor" or
(5)

"Teacher." Our teacher here gets mad when we call _____
(6)

"Teacher." She doesn't like _____. She says it's impolite. But in
(7)

my country, "Teacher" is a term of great respect.

B: Only small children in the U.S. call their teacher "Teacher." If you

know your teacher's name, use _____.
(8)

A: Do you mean I should call _____ Dawn?
_(9)_

B: If that's what she likes.

A: I'm sorry. I can't do _____. She's about 50 years old, and
_(10)_
I'm only 20.

B: Then call _____ Ms. Paskow.
_(11)_

A: She doesn't like to use her last name. She says everyone

mispronounces _____. Sometimes I call _____ Ms. Dawn, but
_(12)_   _(13)_
she says no one does that here.

B: We have an expression, "When in Rome, do as the Romans do."[3]

A: It's hard for _____ to change my customs after a lifetime of
_(14)_
following _____.
_(15)_

EXERCISE 9 Fill in the blanks with *I*, *I'm*, *my*, *mine*, or *me*.

EXAMPLES _____*I'm*_____ a foreign student. _____*I*_____ come from Japan.

_____*My*_____ roommate's parents live in the U.S., but _____*mine*_____ live in

Japan. _____*My*_____ parents write to _____*me*_____ twice a month.

1. _____ roommate's name is Kelly. _____ is Yuki.

2. _____ roommate helps _____ with my English.

3. _____ study at the University of Wisconsin.

4. _____ major is engineering.

5. _____ have a roommate.

6. _____ 20 years old.

7. _____ parents don't live in
the U.S.

[3] This expression means that you should follow the customs of the country you are in.

EXERCISE 10 Fill in the blanks with *he*, *he's*, *his*, or *him*.

EXAMPLE   I have a good friend. _____His_____ name is Paul. _____He's_____ Puerto Rican.
_____He_____ lives in New York. I like _____him_____.

1. _____ married.

2. _____ works in an office.

3. _____ an accountant.

4. _____ son helps _____ in _____ business.

5. _____ 37 years old. _____ wife is 35.

6. My wife and _____ wife are friends.

7. My wife is a doctor. _____ is a computer programmer.

EXERCISE 11 Fill in the blanks with *she*, *she's*, *her*, or *hers*.

EXAMPLE   I have a friend. _____Her_____ name's Diane. _____She's_____ American.
_____She_____ lives in Boston. My native language is Korean. _____Hers_____
is English.

1. _____ an interesting person.

2. I like _____ very much.

3. _____ married.

4. _____ has two children.

5. My children go to Dewey School. _____ go to King School.

6. _____ a nurse. _____ likes _____ job.

7. _____ husband is a teacher.

EXERCISE 12 Fill in the blanks with *they*, *they're*, *their*, *theirs*, or *them*.

EXAMPLE   Diane and Richard are my friends. _____They_____ live in Boston. _____Their_____
house is beautiful. _____They're_____ happy. I see _____them_____ on the weekends.

1. _____ Americans.

2. _____ both work.

3. _____ have two children.

4. _____ children go to public school.

5. My house is small. _____ is big.

6. _____ interested in art.

7. I talk to _____ once a week.

EXERCISE **13**   Fill in the blanks about a cat. Use *it*, *it's*, or *its*.

EXAMPLE   _____*It's*_____ an independent animal. _____*It*_____ always lands on
_____*its*_____ feet.

1. _____ likes to eat fish.

2. _____ a small animal.

3. _____ fur is soft.

4. _____ catches mice.

5. _____ claws are sharp.

6. _____ a clean animal.

7. Do you see that cat? Yes, I see _____.

EXERCISE **14**   Fill in the blanks with *we*, *we're*, *our*, *ours*, or *us*.

EXAMPLE   _____*We*_____ study English. _____*We're*_____ foreign students.
_____*Our*_____ teacher is American. He helps _____*us*_____.

1. _____ come from different countries.

2. _____ in class now.

3. _____ classroom is comfortable.

4. The teacher asks _____ a lot of questions.

5. The teacher's textbook has the answers. _____ don't have the answers.

6. _____ interested in English.

EXERCISE **15**   Fill in the blanks with *you*, *you're*, *your*, or *yours*.

EXAMPLE   _____*You're*_____ a good teacher. Students like _____*you*_____. My other teacher's
name is hard to pronounce. _____*Yours*_____ is easy to pronounce.

1. _____ explain the grammar well.

2. We all understand _____.

3. Our pronunciation is sometimes hard to understand. _____ is clear.

4. _____ a kind teacher.

5. _____ class is very interesting.

6. _____ have a lot of experience with foreign students.

1. At what age should adult children leave home if they're not married?

2. Should adult children take care of their parents?

 Read the following conversation. Pay special attention to questions.

A: Where does your dad live?

B: He lives back in our country.

A: Is he in good health?

B: His health is so-so.

A: Who takes care of him?

B: My brother and his wife do.

A: Do they go to his house every day?

B: No. They live with him.

A: Why do they live with him?

B: It's the custom in my country. What about in America? Do you live with your parents?

A: Don't be ridiculous. I'm 25. I live with my roommate.

B: Where do your parents live?

A: My parents are divorced. My mother lives just a couple of miles from me. My dad lives in another state.

B: How often do you see your parents?

A: I see my dad a couple of times a year. I see my mom about once or twice a month.

B: Is that all? **Who helps them? Who shops for them? Who cooks for them?**

A: They're in their 60s and in great health. They can do everything. No one takes care of them. **What's wrong with that?**

B: What about when they get older?

A: I never think about it. **Who knows about the future?** I have my life to live, and they have theirs.

5.7 | Questions About the Subject or About the Complement

Compare these statements and related questions about the complement:

Subject	Verb	Complement	Wh- Word	Does/ Do	Subject	Verb	
Dad	lives	in Korea.	Where	does	Dad	live?	We use *do* and *does* to ask a question about the complement of the sentence.
Dad	lives	with someone.	Who(m)	does	he	live with?	
I	visit	once a month.	When	do	you	visit?	

Compare these statements and related questions about the subject:

Subject	Verb	Who/ What	Verb -s Form		
Someone	helps my father.	Who	helps	your father?	When we ask a question about the subject, we don't use *do* or *does*. We can use the *-s* form in the question.
Nobody	knows.	Who	knows	about the future?	
Something is wrong.		What	is	wrong with that?	

EXERCISE 16 ABOUT YOU Talk about some jobs in your house. Ask another student, "Who _____s in your house?" The other student will answer.

EXAMPLES

take out the garbage
- A: Who takes out the garbage in your house?
- B: My brother does.

vacuum the carpet
- A: Who vacuums the carpet in your house?
- B: Nobody does. We don't have carpets.

1. dust the furniture
2. shop for groceries
3. pay the bills
4. wash the dishes
5. make your bed

6. vacuum the carpet
7. wash the clothes
8. cook the meals
9. sweep the floor

EXERCISE 17 Fill in the blanks to complete this conversation.

A: ___*Do you like*___ going to school in the U.S.?
   (example)

B: Yes, I like it very much. But I miss my parents.

A: Where ___*do they live*___?
   (example)

B: They live in Peru.

A: How old ___are they___?
   (example)

B: They're in their 60s.

A: Who _____ of them?
   (1)

B: No one takes care of them. They're in great health.

A: _____ alone?
   (2)

B: No, they don't. They live with my oldest sister.

A: _____?
   (3)

B: No, she isn't single. She's married. She's a nurse and her husband is a doctor.

A: How many _____?
   (4)

B: They have three kids. The girl is seven, and the boys are six and two.

A: Who _____ the kids when your sister and her
   (5)

   husband go to work?

B: The older two are in school. My parents take care of the youngest boy.

A: How often _____ your parents?
   (6)

B: I talk to them about once a week.
A: Is it expensive to call your country?
B: Not really. I buy a phone card.

A: How much _____?
   (7)

B: It costs $5.00 We can talk for 30 minutes.
A: Do you plan to see them soon?

B: Who _____? Maybe yes, maybe no. I hope so.
   (8)

5.8 | *Who, Whom, Who's, Whose*

Examples	Explanation
Compare: Who needs the teacher's help? We do. Who(m)* do you love? I love my parents. Who's that man? He's my dad. Whose book is this? It's mine.	*Who* = Subject *Who(m)* = Object *Who's* = *Who is* *Whose* = Possession (ownership)
*Note:** Many native speakers use *who* in place of *whom*.	

EXERCISE 18 Fill in the blanks with *who*, *whom*, *who's*, or *whose*.

EXAMPLE ___Who___ likes ice cream? I like ice cream.

1. _____ last name do you use? I use my father's last name.

2. _____ composition is this? It doesn't have a name on it. It's mine.

3. _____ is your best friend? My best friend is Nina.

4. _____ has my dictionary? I do. Do you need it now?

5. _____ do you call when you have a problem? I call my parents.

6. _____ needs more practice with pronouns? We all do!

EXERCISE 19 *Combination exercise.* Circle the correct word to complete this conversation between two students.

EXAMPLE A: (Who, (Who's,) Whose, Whom) your English teacher?
(example)

B: (My, Mine, Me) teacher's name is Charles Flynn.
(1)

A: (My, Mine, Me) is Marianne Peters. She's Mr. Flynn's wife.
(2)

B: Oh, really? His last name is different from (she, her, hers).
(3)

A: Yes. She uses (her, hers, his, he's) father's last name, not her
(4)

(husband's, husbands', husbands, husband).
(5)

B: Do they have children?

A: Yes.

B: (Whose, Who's, Who, Whom) name do the children use?
(6)

A: (They, They're, Their, Theirs) children use both last names.
(7)

B: How do you know so much about (you, you're, your, yours) teacher
(8)

and (she, she's, her, hers) children?
(9)

A: We talk about (we, us, our, ours) names in class. We also talk about
(10)

American customs. She explains her customs, and we explain
(our, ours, us).
(11)

B: Mr. Flynn doesn't talk about (her, his, he's, hers) family in class.
(12)

A: Do you call (her, his, him, he) "mister"?
(13)

B: Of course. (He, He's, His) the teacher. We show respect.
(14)

A: But we call Marianne by (her, hers, she) first name. (She, She's, Her)
(15) (16)

prefers that.

B: I prefer to call (our, us, ours) teachers by (they, they're, their, theirs)
(17) (18)

last names. That's the way we do it in my country.

A: And in (me, my, mine) too. But (we, we're, us) in the U.S. now.
(19) (20)

There's an expression: When in Rome, do as the Romans do.

SUMMARY OF LESSON 5

1. Pronouns and Possessive Forms

Subject Pronoun	Object Pronoun	Possessive Adjective	Possessive Pronoun
I	me	my	mine
you	you	your	yours
he	him	his	his
she	her	her	hers
it	it	its	—
we	us	our	ours
they	them	their	theirs
who	whom	whose	whose

Subject	**I** come from Cuba	**They** come from Korea.	**Who** comes from Poland?
Object	The teacher helps **me.**	The teacher helps **them.**	**Who(m)** does the teacher help?
Possessive Adjective	**My** name is Rosa.	**Their** names are Kim and Park.	**Whose** name do you use?
Possessive Pronoun	Your book is new. **Mine** is used.	Your book is new. **Theirs** is used.	This is your book. **Whose** is that?

2. Possessive Forms of Nouns
Jack's car is old.
His **parents'** car is new.
The **children's** toys are on the floor.
What's the name of **our textbook?**

1. Don't confuse *you're* (you are) and *your* (possessive form).

   You're
   ~~Your~~ a good person.

   your
   Where's ~~you're~~ book?

2. Don't confuse *he's* (he is) and *his* (possessive form).

   His
   ~~He's~~ name is Paul.

   He's
   ~~His~~ a good student.

3. Don't confuse *it's* (it is) and *its* (possessive form).

   It's
   ~~Its~~ a beautiful day today.

   its
   A monkey uses ~~it's~~ tail to climb trees.

4. Don't confuse *his* (masculine) and *her* (feminine).

   his
   My brother loves ~~her~~ daughter.

   her
   My sister loves ~~his~~ son.

5. Don't confuse *my* and *mine*.

   my
   I don't have ~~mine~~ book today.

6. Don't confuse *they're* and *their*.

   Their
   I have two American friends. ~~They're~~ names are Bob and Sue.

7. Use the correct pronoun (subject or object).

   her
   I have a daughter. I love ~~she~~ very much.

   I
   My father and ~~me~~ like to go fishing.

8. Don't use *the* with a possessive form.

   M
   ~~The~~ my friend is very tall.

   I need ~~the~~ your dictionary.

9. Don't use *do* or *does* in a *who* question about the subject.

   has
   Who ~~does have~~ a Spanish dictionary?

10. Don't separate *whose* from the noun.

    book
    Whose ∧ is this ~~book~~?

11. Don't confuse *whose* and *who's*.

    Whose
    ~~Who's~~ coat is that?

12. Use the correct word order for possession.

    My neighbor's dog
    ~~Dog my neighbor~~ makes a lot of noise.

13. Put the apostrophe in the right place.

    parents'
    My ~~parent's~~ car is new.

14. Don't use the possessive form for nonliving things.

    name of the book
    Grammar in Context is the ~~book's name~~.

LESSON 5 TEST/REVIEW

PART 1 Find the mistakes with the underlined words and correct them. Not every sentence has a mistake. If the sentence is correct, write *C*.

Whose
EXAMPLES ~~Who's~~ book is that?

Who's your best friend? *C*

1. Where does you're brother live?

2. Paul is in my English class, but his not in my math class.

3. Its important to know a second language.

4. Whose name do you use, your father's or your mother's?

5. Who wants to leave early today? We all do.

6. Maria's son goes to a bilingual school. Her son's teacher comes from Cuba.

7. I visit my girlfriend once a week. <u>His</u> son likes to play with <u>mine</u>.

8. <u>The door of the classroom</u> is open.

9. Do you know <u>the first name the teacher</u>?

10. I have two married brothers. <u>My brother's wives</u> are wonderful women.

11. <u>Your</u> always late to class.

12. <u>My the brother's</u> car is new.

13. <u>Whose is this umbrella</u>?

14. She likes her mother-in-law because <u>mother her husband</u> always helps her.

15. Do they visit <u>theirs</u> parents often?

16. A dog wags (moves) <u>its</u> tail when <u>it's</u> happy.

17. Susan and Linda are <u>women's</u> names.

18. <u>Who does have</u> a red pen?

19. <u>My friend and me</u> eat dinner together once a week.

20. <u>Whose pen</u> is this?

PART **2**   Choose the correct word to complete these sentences.

EXAMPLE   Most American women change _____*c*_____ names when they get married, but not all do.

      a. her   **b.** hers   **c.** their   **d.** theirs

1. I have two _____.
   a. sisters   **b.** sister's   **c.** sisters'   **d.** sister

2. _____ names are Marilyn and Charlotte.
   a. Their   **b.** Theirs   **c.** They're   **d.** They   **e.** Hers

3. _____ both married.
   a. Their   **b.** They're   **c.** They   **d.** Them   **e.** There

4. Marilyn uses _____.
   a. the last name her husband
   b. the last name of his husband
   c. her husband's last name
   d. his husband's last name

5. Charlotte uses _____ father's last name.
   a. we   **b.** our   **c.** ours   **d.** us

6. I have one brother. _____ married.
   a. He's   **b.** His   **c.** He   **d.** Him

7. _____ wife is very nice.
   a. Him   **b.** Her   **c.** His   **d.** He's

8. _____ first name is Sandra.
   a. My   **b.** Mine   **c.** I'm   **d.** Me

9. My friends call _____ "Sandy."
   a. me   **b.** my   **c.** mine

10. My sister often uses her middle name, but I rarely use _____.
    a. my   **b.** mine   **c.** me   **d.** I'm

11. You have a dog, but I don't know _____ name.
    a. it   **b.** it's   **c.** its

12. _____ your teacher?
    a. Whom   **b.** Who   **c.** Whose   **d.** Who's

13. Her _____ names are Ricky and Eddie.
    a. childs'   **b.** children's   **c.** childrens   **d.** childrens'

14. _____ has the newspaper?
    a. Whom   **b.** Whose   **c.** Who   **d.** Who's

15. Who _____ more time with the test?
    a. need   **b.** does need   **c.** needs   **d.** does needs

16. The teacher's name is on _____.
    a. the door of her office
    b. her office's door
    c. the door her office
    d. her the office's door

17. _____
    a. Who's is that office?
    b. Whose is that office?
    c. Who's office is that?
    d. Whose office is that?

Two women are talking about names. Fill in the blanks with possessive forms, subject pronouns, or object pronouns. Some blanks need an apostrophe or an apostrophe + s.

A: What's your last name?

B: It's Woods.

A: Woods sounds like an American name. But _____*you're*_____ Polish, aren't
you? *(example)*

B: Yes, but Americans have trouble pronouncing _____ name, so I
(1)
use the name "Woods."

A: What's _____ real last name?
(2)

B: Wodzianicki.

A: My name is hard for Americans too, but _____ like my
(3)
name, and I don't want to change _____. I'm proud of it.
(4)

B: What's _____ last name?
(5)

A: Lopez Hernandez.

B: Why do _____ have two last names?
(6)

A: I come from Mexico. Mexicans have two last names. Mexicans use
both parents _____ names.
(7)

B: What happens when a woman get married? Does she use _____
(8)
parents' _____ names and _____ husband _____
(9) *(10)* *(11)*
name too?

A: No. When a woman gets married, she usually drops _____
(12)
mother _____ name. She adds "of" (in Spanish, "de") and
(13)
_____ husband _____ name. My sister is married.
(14) *(15)*
_____ name is Maria Lopez de Castillo. Lopez is _____
(16) *(17)*
father _____ name and Castillo is her husband _____
(18) *(19)*
name. _____ kids _____ last name is Castillo Lopez.
(20) *(21)*

B: That's confusing. Everybody in the family has a different last name.

A: It's not confusing for us. You understand your customs, and we understand _____.
(22)

B: Do your sister _____ kids have American first names?
(23)

A: My sister gave _____ Spanish names, but _____ friends
(24)   (25)

gave them American names. Her daughter _____ name is Rosa,
(26)

but _____ friends call her Rose. _____ son _____
(27)   (28)   (29)

name is Eduardo, but _____ friends call _____
(30)   (31)

Eddie. Ricardo is the youngest one. _____ still a baby, but
(32)

when he goes to school, _____ friends will probably call
(33)

_____ Rick.
(34)

EXPANSION ACTIVITIES

Classroom Activities

1. Find a partner. Compare yourself to your partner. Compare physical characteristics, clothes, family, home, job, car, and so on. Report some interesting facts to the class.

   EXAMPLE   My hair is straight. Mark's is curly.
   His eyes are blue. Mine are brown.
   My family lives in this city. Mark's family lives in Romania.

2. One student will ask these *who* questions. Raise your hand if this is a fact about you. The first student will answer the question after he or she sees raised hands.

   EXAMPLE   Who has kids?
   Ben, Maria, and Lidia have kids.
   Who has a cell phone?
   No one has a cell phone.

   1. Who has kids?

   2. Who likes cartoons?

   3. Who plays soccer?

   4. Who has a laptop computer?

5. Who is a sports fan?

6. Who likes to swim?

7. Who is a vegetarian?

8. Who wants a grammar test?

9. Who has American friends?

10. Who has a pet?

11. Who lives in a house?

12. Who is over 6 feet tall?

13. Who has a motorcycle?

14. Who has an e-mail address?

15. Who gets a lot of junk mail?

16. Who exercises every day?

17. Who watches TV in the morning?

18. Who has a middle name?

19. Who wants to become an American citizen?

20. Who plays a musical instrument?

3. Think of something unusual that you do or are. Write a sentence telling what you do or are. Then ask a question to find out who else does or is this.

EXAMPLES   I have a pet snake. Who else has a pet snake?
I play volleyball. Who else plays volleyball?
I am a Buddhist. Who else is a Buddhist?

(Variation: On a piece of paper, write something unusual that you do or are. Give the papers to the teacher. The teacher reads a statement. Other students—and the teacher—try to guess who wrote it. Example: Someone has a pet snake. Who has a pet snake?)

4. Discuss naming customs in your native culture. Do people have a middle name? Do fathers and sons ever have the same name? Tell about your name. Does it mean something?

Joke

A woman is outside her house. A dog is near her. A man walks by and is interested in the dog. He wants to pet the dog. He asks the woman, "Does your dog bite?" The woman answers no. The man pets the dog, and the dog bites him. He says, "You told me that your dog doesn't bite." The woman answers, "This is not my dog. Mine is in the house."

Outside Activity

Ask an American to tell you about his or her name. Tell the class something interesting you learned from this American.

Internet Activity

Find a phone directory on the Internet. Look up your last name in a major American city, such as New York City, or in the city where you live. How many people in this city have your last name?

Additional Activities at http://elt.heinle.com/gic

LESSON

6

GRAMMAR
The Present Continuous Tense[1]

CONTEXT: Observations About American Life
Observations in the Park
Observations in the School Cafeteria

[1]The present continuous tense is sometimes called the present progressive tense.

Read

1. Do you ever write in a journal?

2. Do you ever compare the behavior of Americans to the behavior of people from your native culture?

Read the following entry from Dan's journal. Pay special attention to the present continuous tense.

September 9

    I'm taking an ESL course this semester. Our teacher wants us to write in a journal every day. **I'm beginning** my journal now. I'm in the park now. It's a beautiful day. The sun **is shining. I'm sitting** on a park bench and **observing** the behavior of people around me.

    It's warm and most of the people **are wearing** shorts, but **I'm wearing** long pants. Even old people **are wearing** shorts. This surprises me. Some people **are jogging.** They **are** all **carrying** a personal stereo and **wearing** headphones. They **are** all **jogging** alone. A lot of people **are going** by on rollerskates. Some young kids **are using** a skateboard. It seems that these are popular activities here.

    A group of young men **is playing** soccer. I don't think they're Americans. I think Americans don't like soccer. I hear them speaking Spanish. Americans prefer baseball. In another part of the park, small children **are playing** baseball. Their parents **are watching** them. This is called Little League. Little League is very popular here.

    One man **is riding** a bike and **talking** on a cell phone at the same time. Some people **are having** a picnic. They **are barbecuing** hamburgers.

    There is a group of teenagers nearby. They **are talking** very loudly. They have a big boombox and **are listening** to hip-hop music. They**'re making** a lot of noise.

    I'm learning a lot about the American lifestyle.

6.1 | The Present Continuous Tense

To form the present continuous tense, use a form of *be* (*is, am, are*) + verb *-ing*. We use the present continuous tense to describe an action in progress at this moment.

Examples	Explanation
Subject *Be* **Verb + -ing Complement** I **am taking** an ESL class. The sun **is shining.** A man **is jogging.** He **is wearing** shorts. You **are reading** Dan's journal. Kids **are listening** to music. They **are talking** very loudly. We **are learning** about American life.	I → am He/She/It → is Singular Subject → is + verb *-ing* We/You/They → are Plural Subject → are
I'm taking an ESL class this semester. **They're** listening to music. **We're** observing the American lifestyle. **Dan's** writing in his journal.	We can make a contraction with the subject pronoun and a form of *be*. Most nouns can also form a contraction with *is*.[2]

Dan **isn't** writing a composition. He's writing in his journal.
 The teenagers **aren't** paying attention to other people.
	To form the negative, put *not* after the verb *am/is/are*.
	 Negative contractions:
	     is not = isn't
	     are not = aren't
	 There is no contraction for *am not*.

A man **is riding** his bike **and talking** on his cell phone.	When the subject is doing two or more things, we don't repeat the verb *be* after *and*.

EXERCISE **1**   Fill in the blanks with the missing part of each sentence.

EXAMPLE   I'_____*m*_____ writing in my journal.

1. Most people are wear _____ shorts.

2. Some young men _____ playing soccer.

3. Some children are play _____ baseball.

4. Teenagers _____ listening to music.

5. I' _____ looking at people in the park.

6. The sun _____ shining.

7. A man is riding his bike and talk _____ on his cell phone.

8. I'm learn _____ about life in the U.S.

[2]See Lesson 1, page 8 for exceptions.

6.2 | Spelling of the *-ing* Form

Rule	Verbs	*-ing* Form
Add *-ing* to most verbs. (Note: Do not drop the *y* of the base form.)	eat go study	eat**ing** go**ing** study**ing**
For a one-syllable verb that ends in a consonant + vowel + consonant (CVC), double the final consonant and add *-ing*.	p l a n ↓ ↓ ↓ C V C s t o p ↓ ↓ ↓ C V C s i t ↓ ↓ ↓ C V C	plan**ning** stop**ping** sit**ting**
Do not double a final *w, x,* or *y*.	show mix stay	show**ing** mix**ing** stay**ing**
For a two-syllable verb that ends in CVC, double the final consonant only if the last syllable is stressed.	refér admít begín	refer**ring** admit**ting** begin**ning**
When the last syllable of a two-syllable verb is not stressed, do not double the final consonant.	lísten ópen óffer	listen**ing** open**ing** offer**ing**
If the verb ends in a consonant + *e*, drop the *e* before adding *-ing*.	live take write	liv**ing** tak**ing** writ**ing**

EXERCISE 2   Write the *-ing* form of the verb. (Two-syllable verbs that end in CVC have accent marks to show which syllable is stressed.)

EXAMPLES   play _____ *playing* _____

make _____ *making* _____

1. plan _____
2. ópen _____
3. sit _____
4. begín _____
5. hurry _____
6. háppen _____

7. stay _____
8. grow _____
9. marry _____
10. grab _____
11. write _____
12. fix _____

13. wipe _____   17. wait _____

14. carry _____   18. serve _____

15. drink _____   19. vísit _____

16. drive _____   20. prefér _____

EXERCISE **3**   Fill in the blanks with the present continuous tense of the verb in parentheses ( ). Use correct spelling.

EXAMPLE   Dan _____*is observing*_____ people in the park.
  (observe)

1. He _____ about his observations.
   (write)

2. Some men _____ soccer.
   (play)

3. A man _____ a bike.
   (ride)

4. Some people _____.
   (jog)

5. The sun _____.
   (shine)

6. He _____ on a park bench.
   (sit)

7. Some people _____ by on rollerskates and skate-
   boards.   (go)

8. Some people _____ a personal stereo.
   (carry)

6.3 | The Present Continuous Tense—Uses

Examples	Explanation
I **am writing** in my journal now. I **am observing** the American lifestyle. Children **are playing** baseball. Teenagers **are listening** to music.	To show that an action is in progress now, at this moment.
I**'m learning** about the American lifestyle. I**'m taking** an ESL course this semester.	To show a long-term action that is in progress. It may not be happening at this exact moment.
Most people **are wearing** shorts. I**'m sitting** on a park bench.	To describe a state or condition, using the following verbs: *sit, stand, wear, sleep*.

EXERCISE **4** ABOUT YOU Make a **true** affirmative statement or negative statement about your activities now with the words given.

EXAMPLES wear a watch
I'm not wearing a watch (now).

drink coffee
I'm drinking coffee (now).

1. sit in the back of the room
2. speak my native language
3. pay attention
4. ask questions
5. learn the present continuous tense

6. look out the window
7. look at the chalkboard
8. write a composition
9. use my textbook
10. wear jeans

EXERCISE **5** ABOUT YOU Make a true affirmative statement or negative statement about yourself with the words given. Talk about a long-term action.

EXAMPLES look for a job
I'm looking for a job.

live in a hotel
I'm not living in a hotel.

1. look for a new apartment
2. learn a lot of English
3. gain weight
4. lose weight
5. spend a lot of money
6. save my money
7. write a term paper[3]
8. try to understand American customs
9. meet Americans
10. learn how to drive
11. live in a dorm
12. plan to return to my hometown

---

[3]A *term paper* is a paper that students write for class. The student researches a topic. It often takes a student a full semester (or term) to produce this paper.

6.4 | Questions with the Present Continuous Tense

Affirmative Statements and Questions

Wh- Word	Be	Subject	Be	Verb + -ing	Complement	Short Answer
		Dan	is	writing.		
	Is	he		writing	a composition?	No, he isn't.
What	is	he		writing?		A page in his journal.
		The kids	are	playing.		
	Are	they		playing	soccer?	No, they aren't.
What	are	they		playing?		Baseball.

Negative Statements and Questions

Wh- Word	Be + n't	Subject	Be + n't	Verb + -ing	Complement
		The kids	aren't	playing	soccer.
Why	aren't	they		playing	soccer?
		Dan	isn't	using	his computer.
Why	isn't	he		using	his computer?

Language Note:
When the question is "What . . . doing?" we usually answer with a different verb.
  What is Dan **doing?** He's **writing** in his journal.
  What are those kids **doing?** They're **playing** baseball.

EXERCISE **6** Use the words given to ask a question about what this class is doing now. Another student will answer.

EXAMPLE we / use the textbook now
  A: Are we using the textbook now?
  B: Yes, we are.

1. the teacher / wear a sweater
2. the teacher / write on the chalkboard
3. the teacher / erase the chalkboard
4. the teacher / sit at the desk
5. the teacher / take attendance
6. the teacher / explain the grammar
7. the teacher / help the students
8. we / practice the present continuous tense

9. we / practice the past tense
10. we / review Lesson 5
11. we / make mistakes
12. what / the teacher / wear
13. where / the teacher / stand or sit
14. what exercise / we / do
15. what / you / think about

EXERCISE 7 ABOUT YOU Ask a question about a long-term action with the words given. Another student will answer.

EXAMPLE you / study math this semester

A: Are you studying math this semester?
B: Yes, I am.

1. you / plan to buy a car
2. you / study biology this semester
3. you / take other courses this semester
4. you / look for a new apartment
5. you / look for a job
6. your English / improve
7. your vocabulary / grow
8. the teacher / help you
9. the students / make progress
10. you / learn about other students' countries

EXERCISE 8 ABOUT YOU Fill in the blanks with *I'm* or *I'm not* + the *-ing* form of the verb in parentheses ( ) to tell if you are doing these things now or at this general point in time. Then ask another student if he or she is doing this activity now. The other student will answer.

EXAMPLES (plan) _____*I'm planning*_____ to buy a computer.

A: Are you planning to buy a computer?
B: Yes, I am.

(learn) _____*I'm not learning*_____ to drive a car.

A: Are you learning to drive a car?
B: No, I'm not.

1. (wear) _____ jeans.
2. (hold) _____ a pencil.
3. (chew) _____ gum.
4. (think) _____ about the weekend.
5. (live) _____ in a dorm.
6. (plan) _____ to take a vacation.
7. (look) _____ for a job.
8. (plan) _____ to buy a computer.
9. (take) _____ a computer class this semester.
10. (get) _____ tired.
11. (gain) _____ weight.

12. (learn) _____ about the history of the U.S.

13. (learn) _____ how to drive.

EXERCISE **9** ABOUT YOU Read each sentence. Then ask a *wh-* question about the words in parentheses ( ). Another student will answer.

EXAMPLE We're doing an exercise. (What exercise)

A: What exercise are we doing?
B: We're doing Exercise 9.

1. We're practicing a tense. (What tense)

2. We're using a textbook. (What kind of book)

3. You're listening to the teacher. (Why)

4. The teacher's helping the students. (Why)

5. I'm answering a question. (Which question)

6. We're practicing questions. (What kind of questions)

7. Your English is improving. (Why)

8. Your life is changing. (How)

9. You're taking courses. (How many courses)

EXERCISE **10** A woman is calling her husband from a cell phone in her car. Fill in the blanks to complete the conversation.

A: Hello?
B: Hi. It's Betty.

A: Oh, hi, Betty. This connection is so noisy. Where ___*are you calling*___ from?
                                                          (example)

B: I _____ from the car. I _____
        (1)   *(2)*
the cell phone.

A: _____ home now?
                        (3)

B: No, I'm not. I'm driving to the airport.

A: Why _____ to the airport?
                        (4)

B: I'm going to pick up a client.
A: I can't hear you. There's so much noise.

B: Airplanes _____ overhead. They're very low.
                    (5)

A: I can't hear you. Talk louder please.

B: I _____ as loud as I can. I _____
        (6)   (7)

to the airport to pick up a client. I'm late. Her plane _____
                                                                   (8)

now, and I'm stuck[4] in traffic. I'm getting nervous. Cars aren't moving.

A: Why _____ moving?
            (9)

B: There's an accident on the highway.

A: I worry about you. _____?
                                    (10)

B: Of course, I'm wearing my seat belt.
A: That's good.

B: What _____ now?
                            (11)

A: I _____ the computer. I _____
            (12)   (13)

for information about cars on the Internet.

B: What _____ doing?
                            (14)

A: The kids? I can't hear you.
B: Yes, the kids.

A: Meg _____ TV. Pam _____ her
                (15)   (16)

homework.

B: Why _____ Meg doing her homework?
                (17)

A: She doesn't have any homework today.

B: _____ dinner for the kids?
              (18)

A: No, I'm not making dinner. I _____ for you to come
                                              (19)

home and make dinner.
B: Please don't wait for me. Oh. Traffic is finally moving. Talk to you
        later.

---

[4] When you are stuck in traffic, you can't move because other cars aren't moving.

Before You Read

1. When you observe the students at this school, do you see any strange behaviors?

2. Is your behavior in this school different from your behavior when you are with your family or people from your native culture?

 Read the following entry from Dan's journal. Pay special attention to verbs—simple present and present continuous.

March 8

I'm **sitting** in the school cafeteria now. I'm **writing** in my journal. I **want** to know about American customs, so I'm **observing** the behavior of other students. I **see** many strange behaviors and customs around me.

I'm **looking** at a young couple at the next table. The young man and woman **are touching, holding** hands, and even **kissing.** It looks strange because people never **kiss** in public in our country. At another table, a young man and woman **are sitting** with a baby. The man **is feeding** the baby. Men never **feed** the baby in our country. Why **isn't** the woman **feeding** the baby? Students in our country are usually single, not married with children.

Two women **are putting** on makeup. I **think** this is bad public behavior. These women **are wearing** shorts. In our country, women never **wear** shorts.

A group of students **is listening** to the radio. The music is very loud. Their music **is bothering** other people, but they **don't care.** I'm **sitting** far from them, but I **hear** their music.

A young man **is resting** his feet on another chair. His friend **is eating** a hamburger with his hands. Why **isn't** he **using** a fork and knife?

These kinds of behaviors **look** bad to me. I'm **trying** to understand them, but I'm **having** a hard time. I still **think** many of these actions are rude.[5]

---

[5]*Rude* means impolite.

6.5 | Contrast of Present Continuous and Simple Present

Form

Simple Present	Present Continuous
Dan sometimes **wears** a suit. He **doesn't** usually **wear** shorts. **Does** he ever **wear** a hat? Yes, he **does.** When **does** he **wear** a hat? Who **wears** a hat?	He **is wearing** jeans now. He **isn't wearing** a belt. **Is** he **wearing** a T-shirt? No, he **isn't.** What **is** he **wearing?** Who **is wearing** a T-shirt?

Uses

Examples	Explanation
a. Dan **writes** in his journal once a week in the college cafeteria. b. People **eat** hamburgers with their hands. c. The college cafeteria **has** inexpensive food.	We use the *simple present tense* to talk about: a. a habitual activity b. a custom c. a general truth or fact
a. Dan **is writing** in his journal now. b. He **is learning** more and more about life in the U.S.	We use the *present continuous tense* for: a. an action that is in progress at this moment b. a longer action that is in progress at this general time
Compare: Dan's family **lives** in another country. Dan **is living** in a dorm this semester.	When we use *live* in the simple present, we mean that this is a person's home. In the present continuous, it shows a temporary, short-term residence.
Compare: What **does** she **do** for a living? She's a nurse. What **is** she **doing?** She's waiting for the bus. 	*What does she do?* asks about a profession or job. *What is she doing?* asks about her present activity.

EXERCISE 11 Two students meet in the cafeteria and discuss American customs and the customs of their native countries. Fill in the blanks with the correct form of the verb in parentheses ( ). Practice the simple present and the present continuous.

A: Hi. What ___*are you doing*___ here?
                               (example: you/do)

B: I _____ lunch. I always _____
               (1 eat)   *(2 eat)*

lunch at this time. But I _____ behaviors and
                                (3 also/observe)

customs in this country.

A: What do you mean?

B: Well, look at that man over there. He _____ an
(4 wear)

earring. It looks so strange. Only women _____
(5 wear)

earrings in my country.

A: It *is* strange. And look at that woman. She _____
(6 wear)

three earrings in one ear.

B: And she _____ running shoes with a dress. In my
(7 wear)

country, people only _____ running shoes for sports
(8 use)

activities.

A: Look at that student over there. He _____ a colored
(9 use)

pen to mark his textbook. In my country, we never _____
(10 write)

in our textbooks because they _____ to the college,
(11 belong)

not to the students.

B: Many college activities are different here. For example, my English

teacher usually _____ at the desk in class. In my
(12 sit)

country, the teacher always _____ in class. And the
(13 stand)

students always _____ when the teacher
(14 stand up)

_____ the room.
(15 enter)

A: And college students always _____ English or
(16 study)

another foreign language. Here, nobody knows another language.

My American roommate _____ five courses this
(17 take)

semester, but no foreign language.

B: By the way, how many classes _____ this semester?
(18 you/take)

The Present Continuous Tense

A: Four. In my country, I usually _____ eight courses a
  (19 take)
  semester, but my adviser here says I can only take four.

B: I have to go now. My girlfriend _____ for me at the
  (20 wait)
  library.

6.6 | Nonaction Verbs

Some verbs are nonaction verbs. Nonaction verbs describe a state or condition, not an action.

Examples	Explanation
He **hears** the music now. The music is bothering Dan, but the other students **don't care.** Dan **needs** a quiet place to write. He **doesn't understand** the behavior of some students. He **thinks** these behaviors are rude.	We do not usually use the present continuous tense with nonaction verbs. We use the *simple present tense,* even if we are talking about now.

Nonaction Verbs

like	know	see	cost
love	believe	smell	own
hate	think (that)	hear	have (for possession)
want	care (about)	taste	
need	understand	feel	
prefer	remember	seem	

Compare action and nonaction verbs.

Action (uses the present continuous tense)	Nonaction (uses the simple present tense)
The music **is bothering** Dan.	He **prefers** soft music.
Dan **is learning** about American customs.	He **cares** about good behavior.
He **is looking** at two people kissing.	This behavior **looks** strange to him.
He **is writing** about the students.	He **wants** to understand their customs.
He **is using** a laptop.	He **has** a PC in his dorm room.
The students **are listening** to the music.	Dan **hears** the music.
Dan **is looking** at students in the cafeteria.	He **sees** some strange behaviors.

Language Notes:
Hear and *see* are nonaction verbs. *Listen* and *look* are action verbs.
Hear and *see* are involuntary. *Listen* and *look* are voluntary.

EXERCISE 12 Fill in the blanks with the simple present or the present continuous tense of the verb in parentheses ( ).

EXAMPLES   I ___understand___ the explanation now.
                (understand)

I ___am writing___ now.
      (write)

1. I _____ English this semester.
          (study)

2. We _____ the textbook now.
          (use)

3. We _____ a lot of practice with verb tenses.
          (need)

4. We _____ action and nonaction verbs.
          (compare)

5. I _____ every grammar rule.
       (not/remember)

6. I _____ the chalkboard.
          (see)

7. I _____ at the clock now. I _____
     (not/look)   (look)

at my book.

8. I _____ my dictionary now.
        (not/need)

9. We _____ a composition now.
         (not/write)

10. We _____ the students in the next room.
           (not/hear)

11. We _____ about nonaction verbs.
            (learn)

12. We _____ a lot of grammar.
            (know)

6.7 | *Think, Have,* and the Sense Perception Verbs

Think, have, and the sense perception verbs can be action or nonaction verbs.

Examples	Explanation
Action: He **is thinking** about his mother's cooking. **Nonaction:** He **thinks** it is wrong to kiss in public.	When we think <u>about</u> something, *think* is an action verb. When we *think* <u>that</u> something is true, *think* is a nonaction verb. We are giving an opinion about something.
Action: He **is having** lunch in the cafeteria. **Action:** He **is having** new experiences in the U.S. **Nonaction:** He **has** free time now. **Nonaction:** He **has** new American friends. **Nonaction:** His best friend **has** the flu now.	When *have* means to experience something or to eat or drink something, it is an action verb. When *have* shows possession, relationship, or illness, it is a nonaction verb.
Action: He **is looking** at a woman wearing shorts. **Nonaction:** This behavior **looks** bad to him. **Action:** He is **smelling** the coffee. **Nonaction:** The coffee **smells** delicious.	The sense perception verbs (*look, taste, feel, smell, sound, seem*) can be action or nonaction verbs. When the sense perception verbs describe a state, they are nonaction verbs. When they describe an action, they are action verbs.

EXERCISE 🔟 Fill in the blanks with the simple present or the present continuous tense of the verb in parentheses ( ).

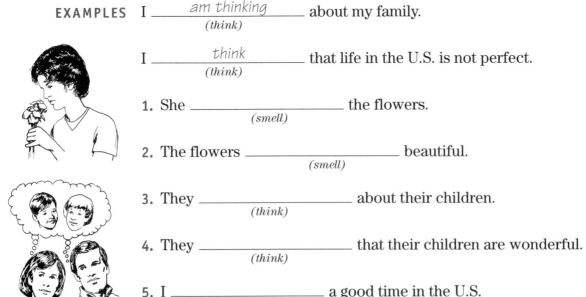

EXAMPLES   I ___am thinking___ about my family.
              (think)

       I ___think___ that life in the U.S. is not perfect.
              (think)

1. She _____ the flowers.
        (smell)

2. The flowers _____ beautiful.
              (smell)

3. They _____ about their children.
        (think)

4. They _____ that their children are wonderful.
        (think)

5. I _____ a good time in the U.S.
      (have)

6. I _____ a lot of new friends.
(have)

7. I _____ a lot of free time.
(not/have)

8. My friend _____ a cold now and she can't go out
(have)

today, so I _____ lunch alone now.
(have)

9. He _____ at a car now.
(look)

10. The car _____ new.
(look)

EXERCISE **14** Fill in the blanks with the simple present or the present continuous of the verb in parentheses ( ). Use the simple present for regular activity and with nonaction verbs.

EXAMPLES Dan _____*wants*_____ to understand American behavior.
(want)

He _____*is looking*_____ at some Americans in the cafeteria now.
(look)

1. Dan _____ in his journal now.
(write)

2. He _____ in the school cafeteria now.
(sit)

3. He _____ a couple with a baby.
(see)

4. He often _____ to the cafeteria between classes.
(go)

5. He _____ in his journal once a week.
(write)

6. He _____ that his family _____
(think) (want)

to know about American customs.

7. He _____ at a young man and woman. They
(look)

_____ hands.
(hold)

8. This behavior _____ bad in his country.
(look)

9. He _____ about American customs now.
   (think)

10. Some women _____ shorts now.
    (wear)

11. Women in Dan's country never _____ shorts.
    (wear)

12. American customs _____ strange to him.
    (seem)

EXERCISE 15 Read each sentence. Write the negative form of the underlined word, using the word(s) in parentheses ( ).

EXAMPLES Dan <u>is looking</u> at Americans. (people from his country)
He isn't looking at people from his country.

He <u>knows</u> about customs from his country. (American customs)
He doesn't know about American customs.

1. The father <u>is feeding</u> the baby. (the mother)

   _____

2. Dan's <u>sitting</u> in the cafeteria. (in class)

   _____

3. He <u>understands</u> customs from his country. (American customs)

   _____

4. American men and women sometimes <u>kiss</u> in public. (men and women in his country)

   _____

5. Americans <u>use</u> their hands to eat a hamburger. (to eat spaghetti)

   _____

6. A man <u>is wearing</u> an earring in one ear. (in both ears)

   _____

7. Americans <u>seem</u> strange to him. (to me)

   _____

8. American men <u>like</u> to take care of babies. (Dan)

   _____

9. American women often <u>wear</u> shorts in the summer. (women in Dan's country never)

   _____

EXERCISE 16 Read each sentence. Then write a *yes/no* question about the words in parentheses ( ). Write a short answer.

EXAMPLES American women sometimes wear earrings. (American men/ever)
Do American men ever wear an earring? Yes, they do.

The women are wearing shorts. (the men)
Are the men wearing shorts? No, they aren't.

1. Dan is writing. (his homework)

_____

2. He's watching people. (American people)

_____

3. He understands his own customs. (American customs)

_____

4. American men wear shorts in the summer. (American women)

_____

5. The man is eating. (a hot dog)

_____

EXERCISE 17 Read each statement. Then write a *wh-* question about the words in parentheses ( ). An answer is not necessary.

EXAMPLES A young man is resting his feet on a chair. (why)
Why is he resting his feet on a chair?

Dan lives in the U.S. (where/his family)
Where does his family live?

1. Dan is writing a letter. (to whom) OR (who . . . to)

_____

2. Dan wants to know about American customs. (why)

_____

3. Two women are putting on makeup. (where)

_____

4. American men and women touch and hold hands in public. (why)

_____

5. Dan writes to his family. (how often)

_____

6. The man isn't using a fork. (why/not)

_____

7. Women don't wear shorts in some countries. (why)

_____

8. Americans often wear blue jeans. (why)

_____

9. "Custom" means tradition or habit. (what/"behavior")

_____

EXERCISE 18 *Combination exercise.* This is a phone conversation between Dan (D) and his mother (M). Fill in the blanks with the correct form of the words in parentheses ( ) to complete the conversation.

D: Hello?

M: Hi. This is Mom.

D: Hi, Mom. How _____*are you doing*_____?
   (example: you/do)

M: We _____ fine. And you?
   (1 be)

   How _____ college in the U.S.?
   (2 you/like)

D: Great. I _____ it a lot. I _____
   (3 like)   *(4 have)*

   a lot of fun.

M: Fun? _____?
   (5 why/you/not/study)

D: I *am* studying. But I _____ new people from all over
   (6 meet)

   the world. I _____ about getting an earring.
   (7 think)

M: What? Earrings are for women.

D: But, Mom, all the guys _____ it these days.
   (8 do)

M: I _____. You _____ an earring in your
   (9 not/care)   *(10 not/need)*

   ear. You just _____ to study. _____
   (11 need)   *(12 you/get)*

   good grades?

D: You _____ I'm a good student. Of course,
(13 know)

I _____ good grades.
(14 get)

M: _____ your guitar these days?
(15 you/practice)

D: Yes, I am. But I _____ as much time as before.
(16 not/have)

I _____ five classes this semester.
(17 take)

M: Only five? Students here _____ eight classes.
(18 usually/take)

D: The system is different here. Freshmen only take four or five classes.

M: What _____?
(19 freshman/mean)

D: A freshman is a student in the first year of college.

M: How's the food? _____ enough to eat?
(20 you/get)

D: Yes, I am. In fact, I _____ weight. But I
(21 gain)

_____ the food here.
(22 not/like)

M: What _____ about the food?
(23 not/like)

D: It's too greasy. And it _____ like food back home.
(24 not/taste)

I really _____ your food.
(25 miss)

M: I _____ your favorite dish now.
(26 make)

D: Really? I _____ hungry just thinking about it.
(27 get)

M: You and Dad _____ that my food is the best.
(28 always/think)

D: Where's Dad?

M: He _____ in the garden now. He's planting a new tree.
(29 work)

D: Thanks for sending me the sweater. I _____ it now.
(30 wear)

M: _____ enough warm clothes?
        (31 you/have)

D: For now, I do. But it _____ to get cold these days.
                              (32 start)

   And the days _____ shorter. Fall is beautiful here.
                     (33 get)

   The trees _____ color. I _____
                 (34 change)   *(35 look)*

   out my window now and I _____ a beautiful maple
                                 (36 see)

   tree with red leaves. But I _____ the climate back
                                   (37 prefer)

   home. It's warm all year. Here it's really cold in December and January.

M: I _____ a new sweater for you now. Your sister Ruby
       (38 make)

   _____ you a scarf.
       (39 make)

D: Thanks, Mom. Where's Ruby? _____ to talk to me now?
                                   (40 she/want)

M: I _____ so. She _____ a video
       (41 not/think)   *(42 watch)*

   with her friends.

D: _____ good grades this semester?
          (43 she/get)

M: She _____ too much time with her friends these days.
          (44 spend)

D: Well, she's 16. Friends are really important when you're 16.
M: I'm worried about her.
D: Don't worry so much, Mom.

M: Of course I worry. I'm a mother. Dad _____ in now.
                                              (45 come)

   He _____ to talk to you now.
         (46 want)

D: OK, Mom. Bye.

Uses of Tenses

Simple Present Tense	
General truths	Americans **speak** English. Oranges **grow** in Florida.
Regular activity, habit	I always **speak** English in class. I sometimes **eat** in the cafeteria. I **visit** my parents every Friday.
Customs	Americans **shake** hands. Japanese people **bow.**
Place of origin	Miguel **comes** from El Salvador. Marek **comes** from Poland.
With nonaction verbs	She **has** a new car. I **like** the U.S. You **look** great today.

Present Continuous (with action verbs only)	
Now	We **are reviewing** now. I **am looking** at page 181 now.
A long action in progress at this general time	Dan **is learning** about American customs. He **is studying** English.
A descriptive state	She **is wearing** shorts. He **is sitting** near the door. The teacher **is standing.**

1. Include *be* with a continuous tense.

   is
   He ⌃working now.

2. Use the correct word order in a question.

   are you
   Where ~~you're~~ going?
   don't you
   Why ~~you don't~~ like New York?

3. Don't use the present continuous with a nonaction verb.

   has
   She ~~is having~~ her own computer.

4. Use the -*s* form when the subject is *he*, *she*, or *it*.

   has   *s*
   He ~~have~~ a new car. He like ⌃to drive.

5. Don't use *be* with a simple present-tense verb.

   I'~~m~~ need a new computer.

6. Use *do* or *does* in a simple present-tense question.

   does   *live*
   Where ~~lives~~ your mother ⌃?

7. Don't use the -*s* form after *does*.

   Where does he take~~s~~ the bus?

Review the Editing Advice for the simple present tense on pages 68–69.

LESSON 6 TEST / REVIEW

PART 1 Find the mistakes with the underlined words and correct them. Not every sentence has a mistake. If the sentence is correct, write *C*.

EXAMPLES
She's ~~owning~~ *owns* a new bike now.
I'm not studying math this semester.   *C*

1. Why you aren't listening to me?

2. Usually I'm go home after class.

3. I think that he's having trouble with this lesson.

4. She's thinking about her family now.

5. Does she needs help with her homework?

6. What kind of car do you have?

7. What he's studying now?

8. Does he has any children?

9. He's wearing jeans now.

10. My teacher speak English well.

11. I'm speak my native language at home.

12. The baby sleeping now.

13. When begins summer?

14. Where does your family lives?

PART 2 This is a conversation between two students, Alicia (A) and Teresa (T), who meet in the school library. Fill in the blanks with the simple present or the present continuous form of the verb in parentheses ( ).

T: Hi, Alicia.

A: Hi, Teresa. What ___are you doing___ here?
(example: you/do)

T: I _____ for a book on American geography. What
(1 look)
about you?

A: I _____ a book. _____ to go for
(2 return)   *(3 you/want)*
a cup of coffee?

T: I can't. I _____(4 wait)_____ for my friend. We _____(5 work)_____

on a geography project together, and we _____(6 need)_____ to

finish it by next week.

A: _____(7 you/like)_____ your geography class?

T: Yes. I especially _____(8 like)_____ the teacher, Bob. He's a

handsome young man. He's very casual. He always

_____(9 wear)_____ jeans and a T-shirt to class. He

_____(10 have)_____ an earring in one ear.

A: That _____(11 seem)_____ very strange to me.

I _____(12 think)_____ that teachers in the U.S. are very informal.

How _____(13 Bob/teach)_____ the class? By lecturing?

T: No. We _____(14 usually/work)_____ in small groups, and he

_____(15 help)_____ us by walking around the classroom.

A: _____(16 he/give)_____ hard tests?

T: No. He _____(17 not/believe)_____ in tests.

A: Why _____(18 he/not/believe)_____ in tests?

T: He _____(19 think)_____ that students get too nervous during a test.

He _____(20 say)_____ it's better to work on projects. This week

we _____(21 work)_____ on city maps.

A: That _____(22 sound)_____ interesting.

T: Why _____(23 you/ask)_____ me so many questions about my teacher?

A: I _____ about taking a geography course next
      (24 think)

semester.

T: Bob's very popular. Be sure to register early because his classes

always _____ quickly. Oh. I _____
          (25 fill)   *(26 see)*

my friend now. She _____ toward us. I have to go now.
                        (27 walk)

A: Good luck on your project.

T: Thanks. Bye.

PART 3 Fill in the blanks with the negative form of the underlined word.

EXAMPLE Teresa <u>is</u> in the library. She _____*isn't*_____ at home.

1. Alicia <u>wants</u> to go for a cup of coffee. Teresa _____ to
   go for a cup of coffee.

2. Teresa is <u>looking</u> for a book. Alicia _____ for a book.

3. They <u>are talking</u> about school. They _____ about the
   news.

4. They <u>have</u> time to talk now. They _____ time for a cup
   of coffee.

5. Students in the geography class <u>work</u> in small groups.

   They _____ alone.

6. Alicia's teacher <u>gives</u> tests. Teresa's teacher _____ tests.

7. Teresa is <u>waiting</u> for a friend. Alicia _____ for a friend.

8. The teacher <u>seems</u> strange to Alicia. He _____ strange
   to Teresa.

9. Alicia is <u>returning</u> a book. Teresa _____ a book.

PART 4 Read each sentence. Then write a *yes/no* question about the
words in parentheses ( ). Write a short answer.

EXAMPLE Teresa is looking for a book. (a geography book)
         Is she looking for a geography book? Yes, she is.

1. Bob likes projects. (tests)

   _____

2. Alicia has time now. (Teresa)

   _____

3. They are talking about their classes. (their teachers)

   _____

4. Bob wears jeans to class. (ever / a suit)

   _____

5. Alicia wants to go for coffee. (Teresa)

   _____

6. American teachers seem strange to Alicia. (to Teresa)

   _____

7. Teresa is working on a geography project. (Alicia)

   _____

PART 5 Read each sentence. Then write a question with the words in parentheses ( ). An answer is not necessary.

EXAMPLE Bob is popular. (Why)
   Why is he popular?
   _____

1. Bob sounds interesting. (Why)

   _____

2. Bob doesn't like tests. (Why)

   _____

3. Teresa and her friend are working on a project. (What kind of project)

   _____

4. Teresa studies in the library. (How often)

   _____

5. Teresa is looking for a book. (What kind)

   _____

6. Teresa is waiting for her friend. (Why)

   _____

7. Her classmates aren't writing a term paper. (Why)

   _____

Classroom *Activities*

1. Think of a place (cafeteria, airport, train station, bus, playground, church, opera, movie theater, laundry, office at this school, kindergarten classroom, restaurant, department store, etc.). Pretend you are at this place. Write three or four sentences to tell what people in this place are doing. Other students will guess where you are.

   EXAMPLE   People are walking fast.
   People are carrying suitcases.
   People are standing in long lines.
   They're buying tickets.
   Guess: Are you at the airport?

2. Pretend you are calling from your cell phone. You are telling your family where you are. Fill in the blanks to tell what you and other people are doing. Then find a partner and see how many of your sentences match your partner's sentences.

   a. I'm at the supermarket. I'm _____.
      Do you need anything while I'm here?

   b. I'm in my car. I'm _____.

   c. I'm in the school library. I'm _____.

      People _____ me to be quiet because

      I'm _____ to you on my cell phone.

   d. I'm in a taxi. I'm on my way home. I'm _____

      you to let you know that _____.

   e. I'm at the bus stop. I _____ for the bus,
      but it's late. I don't want you to worry.

   f. I'm at a shoe store. I _____.

   g. I'm at the playground with the kids. The kids _____

      _____.

   h. I'm at the movies. I can't talk now because the movie _____

      _____.

   i. I'm in the bedroom. I have to talk softly because my roommate

      _____.

   j. I'm in class now. I can't talk. The teacher _____

      _____.

3. In a small group or with the entire class, discuss behaviors that are strange to you. What American behaviors are not polite in your native culture?

Go to the school cafeteria, student union, or other crowded place. Sit there for a while and look for unusual behaviors. Write down some of the unusual things you see. Report back to the class.

Find the Web site of a college in this city. Answer the following questions:

1. Where is it?

2. What's the tuition?

3. Does this college have evening classes?

4. Does this college have more than one location?

5. Does it have a graduate program?

6. Does it have dormitories?

7. Does it have ESL classes?

8. When is the next registration?

9. What are the vacation days?

 Additional Activities at **http://elt.heinle.com/gic**

GRAMMAR

Future Tenses—*Will* and *Be Going To*
Comparison of Tenses

CONTEXT: Weddings

Planning for a Wedding
Jason and Katie—Starting a Married Life

PLANNING FOR A WEDDING

Before You Read

1. In your native culture, what kind of gifts do people give to a bride and groom?

2. Are weddings expensive in your native culture?

Read the following article. Pay special attention to future-tense verbs.

Karyn and Steve are engaged now and are planning their wedding. They need a lot of time to plan. They**'re going to graduate** from college next year, and the wedding **will take** place a year and a half after they graduate from college. They **will need** time to choose a photographer, invitations, a place for the reception,[1] a wedding dress, flowers, rings, a wedding cake, entertainment, and more. The wedding **is going to be** very expensive. In addition to paying for the wedding and reception, they **will need** to rent a

limousine and pay for a rehearsal dinner and a honeymoon. They **are going to invite** about 250 people, including many friends and relatives from out of town. They **are going to pay** for the hotel rooms for their grandparents, aunts, and uncles. It **is going to take** a lot of time and energy to plan for the wedding.

Before their wedding, they **will register** for gifts. They **will go** to stores and select the gifts they want to receive. When guests go to the stores, they **will choose** a gift from this list. This way, Karyn and Steve **are going to receive** exactly what they want. They **won't receive** duplicate presents. About six or seven weeks before the wedding, they **will send** out their invitations. After they return from their honeymoon in Hawaii, they **are going to send** thank-you cards to all the guests.

Who**'s going to pay** for all this? After they graduate, they **will work** and **save** money for their dream wedding. But their parents **are going to help** too. Like many young couples, they **will have** credit card debt for years after the wedding. This is in addition to college debt.

[1] A *reception* is a party after a wedding.

Average Wedding Cost in the U.S.
(2003) = $22,000

Typical Costs

Wedding dress = $800
Engagement ring = $3,500
Flowers = $1,000
Reception = $11,000
Invitations = $500

Mr. and Mrs. David K. Smith
and
Mr. and Mrs. John H. Gilbert
invite you to join in the marriage
of their children
Karyn Ann
and
Steven James
Saturday, March 26
Three O'Clock
St. Luke's Church
Westford, New York

7.1 | Future with *Will*

Examples				Explanation
Subject	*Will*	Verb	Complement	We use *will* + the base form for the future tense. *Will* doesn't have an -*s* form.
They	**will**	**rent**	a limousine.	
There	**will**	**be**	a reception.	
The bride	**will**	**wear**	a white dress.	

They'll register for gifts.
She'll buy a white dress.
He'll rent a tuxedo.
It'll take them a long time to plan for the wedding.
				We can make a contraction with the subject pronoun and *will*.
				    I will = I'll It will = It'll
				    You will = You'll We will = We'll
				    He will = He'll They will = They'll
				    She will = She'll

They **will not receive** duplicate presents. They **won't pay** for everything. Their parents will help them.				Put *not* after *will* to form the negative. The contraction for *will not* is *won't*.
I will **always** love you. I will **never** leave you. We will **probably** give money as a gift.				You can put an adverb (*always, never, probably, even*) between *will* and the main verb.

EXERCISE 1 Fill in the blanks with an appropriate verb in the future tense. Practice *will*.

EXAMPLE Karyn and Steve's wedding _____*will be*_____ in a church.

1. They _____ 250 guests.

2. The wedding _____ expensive.

3. They _____ to Hawaii on their honeymoon.

4. They _____ debt for many years after the wedding.

5. Guests _____ presents that the bride and groom want.

6. The bride and groom _____ a limousine.

7. Their parents _____ them pay for the wedding.

7.2 | Future with *Be Going To*

Examples					Explanation
Subject	Be	Going To	Verb	Complement	Use *is/am/are* + *going to* + the base form for the future tense.
I	am	going to	buy	a gift.	We can make a contraction with the subject pronoun and *is, am, are:*
You	are	going to	attend	the wedding.	**I'm** going to buy a gift.
They	are	going to	send	invitations.	We can make a contraction with a singular noun + *is:*
The bride	is	going to	wear	a white dress.	The **bride's** going to wear a white dress.

Examples	Explanation
They **are not going to graduate** this year. Their parents **aren't going to pay** for everything.	To make a negative statement, put *not* after *is/am/are*.
They **are going to go** on a honeymoon. OR They **are going** on a honeymoon.	When the main verb is *to go*, we often delete it.
They **are probably going** to open their gifts at home. They **are always going** to remember their wedding day.	We can put an adverb (*always, never, probably, even*) between *is, am, are* and *going*.

Pronunciation Notes:
1. In informal speech, *going to* before another verb often sounds like "gonna." We don't write "gonna."
2. We only pronounce "gonna" before a verb. We don't pronounce "gonna" in the following sentence: They are going to Hawaii.
Listen to your teacher pronounce the sentences in the above boxes.

EXERCISE **2** Fill in the blanks with an appropriate verb in the future tense.
Practice *be going to*.

EXAMPLE They _____are going to send_____ thank-you cards to the guests.

1. Musicians _____ at the wedding.

2. A professional photographer _____ pictures.

3. There _____ a lot of people at the wedding.

4. The bride _____ a white dress.

5. The wedding _____ a lot of money.

6. They _____ wedding debt and college debt for many years.

7. The wedding cake _____ very expensive.

7.3 | Choosing *Will* or *Be Going To*

Examples	Explanation
I think the newlyweds **will** be very happy together. I think the newlyweds **are going to** be very happy together.	For a prediction, we can use either *will* or *be going to*.
The wedding **will** be in a church. The wedding **is going to** be in a church. They **will** send out 250 invitations. They **are going to** send out 250 invitations.	For a simple fact about the future, we can use either *will* or *be going to*.
I **will** always love you. I **will** never leave you.	For a promise, use *will*.
A: What gift are you planning to give your cousin for the wedding? B: I don't know. Maybe I'**ll** just give money.	Use *will* when you don't have a previous plan, but you decide what to do at the time of speaking.
A: This gift box is heavy. B: I'**ll** carry it for you.	When you offer to help someone, use *will*.
They **are going to** get married on May 6. I **am going to** buy a gift. Guests **are going to** come from out of town.	When we have a previous plan to do something, we usually use *be going to*. *I'm **going** to buy a gift.* = *I'm **planning** to buy a gift.*

EXERCISE **3**   ABOUT YOU Tell if you have plans to do these things or not.
Use *be going to.*

EXAMPLE   meet a friend after class.
I'm (not) going to meet a friend after class.

1. get something to eat after class
2. watch TV tonight
3. eat dinner at home tonight
4. go to the library this week
5. go shopping for groceries this week
6. stay home this weekend
7. take a vacation this year
8. move (to a different apartment) this year
9. buy a car this year

EXERCISE **4**   ABOUT YOU Tell if you predict that these things are going to
happen or not in this class. Use *be going to.*

EXAMPLE   we / finish this lesson today
We are going to finish this lesson today.

1. the teacher / give a test soon
2. the test / be hard
3. most students / pass the test
4. I / pass the test
5. the teacher / give everyone an A
6. my English / improve
7. we / finish this book by the end of the semester
8. the next test / cover the future tense
9. we / have a party at the end of the semester

EXERCISE **5**   Fill in the blanks to complete these statements. Use *be going to.*

EXAMPLE   I don't understand the meaning of a word. ___I'm going to look it up in___
my dictionary.

1. It's hot in here. I _____ a window.
2. It's too noisy in this house. I can't study. I _____ the library.
3. She's hungry. She _____ dinner now.
4. My mother in Poland always worries about me. I _____
_____ her that I'm fine.

5. We don't have any milk in the house. When I go out shopping, I

_____ some milk.

6. She plans to be a doctor. She _____ medical school next year.

7. I'm not happy with my job. I _____ and look for another one.

8. I _____ next week. Here's my new address.

9. My parents miss me very much. They _____ next month to visit for three weeks.

10. There's a great new movie at the Garden Theater. My friends and

I _____ tomorrow night. Do you want to go with us?

EXERCISE **6**   Tell if you predict that these things will happen or not in the next 50 years. Use *will*. You may work with a partner or in a small group.

EXAMPLE   people / have more free time
I think people won't have more free time. They will spend more time at their jobs and less time with their families.

1. there / another world war

2. the economy of the U.S. / get worse

3. people in the U.S. / have fewer children

4. Americans / live longer

5. health care / improve

6. cars / use solar energy[2]

7. divorce / increase

8. crime / get worse

9. people / get tired of computers

10. technology / continue to grow

EXERCISE 7 Some friends of yours are going to have a birthday soon, and you want to buy them a present or do something special for them. What will you buy or do for these people?

EXAMPLE Maria's birthday is in the winter.
I'll buy her a sweater.   OR   I'll take her skiing.

1. Bill loves to go fishing.

2. Tina loves to eat in restaurants.

3. Carl needs a new radio.

4. Jim has a new CD player.

5. Lisa loves the beach in the summer.

6. Tom loves movies.

EXERCISE 8 A man is proposing marriage to a woman. He is making promises. Fill in the blanks to complete these statements.

EXAMPLE I _____*will be*_____ a good husband to you.

1. I love you very much. I (always) _____ you.

2. I want to make you happy. I _____ everything I can to make you happy.

3. I don't have a lot of money, but I _____ and try to make money.

4. We _____ children, and I _____ a good father to them.

5. We _____ old together.

6. We _____ best friends and take care of each other.

7. You are the only woman for me. I (not) _____ at another woman.

---

[2] *Solar energy* comes from the sun.

EXERCISE **9**   Offer to help in these situations using *will* + an appropriate verb.

EXAMPLE   **A:** I have to move next Sunday. It's so much work.

   B: *Don't worry. I'll help you pack.*

1. **A:** My hands are full. I need to open the door.

   B: _____

2. **A:** I need stamps, but I have no time to go to the post office.

   B: I'm going to the post office. _____

3. **A:** I cook every night. I'm tired of cooking.

   B: Take a break. _____ tonight.

4. **A:** I don't have experience with computers. I have to write my composition on the computer.

   B: Come to my house after class. _____

5. **A:** I always drive when we go to the country. I'm tired.

   B: No problem. _____ this time.

6. **A:** Let's go out to dinner tonight.

   B: I can't. I don't have any money.

   A: That's okay. _____

7. **A:** I can't pay my phone bill. I'm not working now and don't have much money.

   B: Don't worry. _____. You can pay me back next month.

8. **A:** The phone's ringing and I'm eating a sandwich. My mouth is full.

   B: Finish your lunch. _____

7.4 | Questions with *Be Going To*

Compare Affirmative Questions and Statements

Wh-Word	Be	Subject	Be	Going To + Base Form	Complement	Short Answer
		You	are	going to send	a gift.	
	Are	you		going to send	money?	No, I'm not.
What	are	you		going to send?		Towels.
		Who	is	going to send	money?	Her uncle is.
		She	is	going to wear	a white dress.	
	Is	she		going to wear	white shoes?	Yes, she is.
		Who	is	going to wear	a tuxedo?	The groom is.

Compare Negative Questions and Statements

Wh-Word	Be + n't	Subject	Be + n't	Going To + Base Form	Complement
		You	aren't	going to attend	the wedding.
Why	aren't	you		going to attend?	

EXERCISE 10 ABOUT YOU Ask another student a *yes/no* question with *are you going to* about a time later today. Then ask a *wh-* question with the words in parentheses ( ) whenever possible.

EXAMPLE listen to the radio (when)

A: Are you going to listen to the radio tonight?
B: Yes, I am.

A: When are you going to listen to the radio?
B: After dinner.

1. watch TV (what show)

2. listen to the radio (when)

3. read the newspaper (what newspaper)

4. go shopping (why)

5. take a shower (when)

6. eat dinner (with whom) OR (who . . . with)

7. call someone (whom)

8. check your e-mail (when)

9. do your homework (when)

EXERCISE 11 Ask another student a *yes/no* question with *be going to* and the words given. Then ask a *wh-* question with the words in parentheses ( ) whenever possible.

EXAMPLE study another English course after this one (which course)

A: Are you going to study another English course after this one?
B: Yes, I am.

A: Which course are you going to study?
B: I'm going to study level 4.

1. stay in this city (why)

2. study something new (what)

3. look for a job (when)

4. get an A in this course (what grade)

5. buy a computer (why) (what kind)

6. visit other American cities (which cities)

7. transfer to another school (why) (which school)

7.5 | Questions with *Will*

Compare Affirmative Questions and Statements

Wh-Word	Will	Subject	Will	Base Form	Complement	Short Answer
		The wedding	will	begin	soon.	
	Will	the wedding		begin	in 15 minutes?	Yes, it will.
When	will	the wedding		begin?		At 8 o'clock.
		Who	will	begin	the wedding?	The groom will.

Compare Negative Questions and Statements

Wh-Word	Won't	Subject	Won't	Base Form	Complement
		The groom	won't	pay	for the whole wedding.
Why	won't	the groom		pay	for the whole wedding?

EXERCISE 12 Fill in the blanks with the correct form of the verb in ( ).
Use *will* for the future.

1. **A:** I don't have time to shop for a wedding gift, and the wedding is tomorrow.

   B: What _____*will you do*_____?
   (example: you/do)

   A: I _____ a check.
   (probably/send)

2. **A:** What time _____?
   (the wedding/start)

   B: The invitation says it _____ at 5:30 p.m., but
   (start)

   usually weddings don't start exactly on time.

3. **A:** Where _____?
   (the wedding/be)

   B: It'll be in a hotel.

4. **A:** What _____ to the wedding?
   (you/wear)

   B: I don't know. I _____ my blue suit. Oh. I just
   (probably/wear)

   remembered my blue suit is dirty. I _____ time
   (not/have)

   to take it to the cleaners. I _____ wear my gray suit.
   (have to)

5. **A:** How many people _____ the wedding?
   (attend)

   B: About 200 people _____ the wedding.
   (attend)

6. **A:** What kind of food _____ at the reception?
   (they/serve)

   B: There _____ a choice of chicken or fish.
   (be)

7. **A:** Do you think the bride and groom _____ happy
   (be)

   together?

   B: Yes, I think they _____. They love each other
   (be)

   very much.

8. A: I'm going to a store to check the wedding registry.

   B: I _____ with you.

(go)

   A: It's late. The store _____ closed by the time we

(probably/ be)

   arrive. I _____ tomorrow morning instead.

(go)

9. A: How long _____?

(the wedding/last)

   B: The ceremony _____ about a half hour. Then

(probably/last)

   there's a dinner. People _____ for hours after

(probably/stay)

   the dinner to dance.

10. A: _____ for their

(the bride and groom/leave)

   honeymoon immediately?

   B: Probably not. They _____ tired after the

(be)

   wedding. They _____ the next day.

(probably/leave)

EXERCISE 13 In this conversation, fill in the blanks using the words in parentheses ( ). Choose *will* or *be going to* for the future tenses. In some cases, both answers are possible.

A: I'm so excited. My sister ___*is going to get*___ married

(example: get)

next year.

B: Why are *you* so excited?

A: I'm going to be a bridesmaid.

B: How many bridesmaids _____?

(1 she/have)

A: Three—her two best friends and I.

B: What kind of dresses _____ ?

(2 the bridesmaids/wear)

A: All the bridesmaids _____ blue dresses,

(3 wear)

but each one _____ her own style.

(4 choose)

B: _____ in your church?

(5 the wedding/be)

A: No, it isn't. It's going to be outdoors, in a garden. After that, there

_____ a dinner at a restaurant.

(6 be)

B: Why _____ to get married?

(7 they/wait)

A: They're both in college now, and they want to get married after they finish college.

B: Where _____ after they get married?

(8 live)

A: Probably here for a while. But then they _____

(9 look)

for jobs in the Boston area.

B: How many people _____ to the wedding?

(10 invite)

A: It _____ a big wedding because we have a large

(11 be)

family, and so does her boyfriend, Joe. They _____

(12 invite)

about 400 people.

B: Wow! The wedding _____ expensive.

(13 be)

Who _____ for it?

(14 pay)

A: Our parents and Joe's parents _____. They

(15 pay)

_____ the cost 50/50. A lot of relatives

(16 split)

and friends _____ here from out of town.

(17 come)

B: Where _____?

(18 they/stay)

A: In hotels.

B: It's _____ expensive for the guests too. They

(19 be)

_____ pay for their flights,

(20 have to)

hotels, and a wedding gift.

A: I know. But they want to come. Of course, some people

_____ because it _____ too

(21 not come)   *(22 be)*

expensive for them.

7.6 | Future Tense + Time/*If* Clause[3]

Time or *If* Clause (Simple Present Tense)	Main Clause (Future Tense)	Explanation
After they **graduate**,	they **are going to work.**	The sentences on the left have two clauses, a time or *if* clause and a main clause.
Before they **get** married,	they **are going to send** out invitations.	
When they **return** from the honeymoon,	they **will send** thank-you cards.	We use the *future* only in the main clause; we use the *simple present tense* in the time/*if* clause.
If their grandparents **come** from out of town,	they **will pay** for their hotel.	

Main Clause (Future Tense)	Time or *If* Clause (Simple Present Tense)	Explanation
They **are going to work**	after they **graduate.**	We can put the main clause before the time/*if* clause.
Their grandparents **will stay** in a hotel	if they **come.**	

Punctuation Note:
If the time/*if* clause comes before the main clause, we use a comma to separate the two parts of the sentence. If the main clause comes first, we don't use a comma.

Compare:

If I get an invitation, I'll go to the wedding.

I'll go to the wedding if I get an invitation.

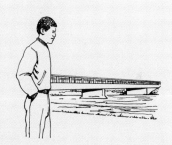

Usage Note:
There is a proverb that means "I will decide when I need to decide." The proverb is:

I'll cross that bridge when I get to it.

---

[3] A clause is a group of words that has a subject and a verb. Some sentences have more than one clause.

EXERCISE 14 This is an old fable.[4] It's the story of a young lady. She is carrying a pail of milk to the market. As she walks there, she thinks about what she will do with the money that the milk will bring. Fill in the blanks with the correct form of the verb to complete this story.

EXAMPLE When I _____*sell*_____ this milk, I _____*will buy*_____ some eggs.
                    (sell)   (buy)

1. When the eggs _____, I _____
                        (hatch)   (have)

   many chickens.

2. I _____ the chickens when they _____
        (sell)   (be)

   big.

3. When I _____ the chickens, I _____
              (sell)   (have)

   money to buy a pretty new dress.

4. I _____ to a party when I _____
        (go)   (have)

   my new dress.

5. All the young men _____ me when I
                            (notice)

   _____ the dress.
        (wear)

6. When the men _____ how pretty I am, they
                      (see)

   _____ to marry me.
        (want)

Suddenly the young woman drops the milk pail and all the milk spills.

What lesson does this story try to teach us?

EXERCISE 15 ABOUT YOU Complete each statement.

EXAMPLES When this class is over, _____*I'll go home.*_____

When this class is over, _____*I'm going to get something to eat.*_____

1. When this semester is over, _____

2. When this class is over, _____

3. When I get home today, _____

4. When I graduate (or finish my courses at this school), _____

_____

---

[4] A *fable* is an old story. It usually teaches us a lesson, called a moral.

5. When I return to my country / become a citizen, _____

6. When I retire, _____

7. When I speak English better, _____

EXERCISE 16 ABOUT YOU Complete each statement.

EXAMPLES   If I drink too much coffee, _____ *I won't sleep tonight.* _____

If I drink too much coffee, _____ *I'm going to feel nervous.* _____

1. If I practice English, _____

2. If I don't study, _____

3. If I don't pay my rent, _____

4. If I pass this course, _____

5. If we have a test next week, _____

6. If the teacher is absent tomorrow, _____

7. If I find a good job, _____

EXERCISE 17 On the first day of class, a teacher is explaining the course to the students. Fill in the blanks to complete this conversation between a teacher (T) and her students (S).

T: In this course, you _____ *are going to study* _____ English grammar. You
                       (example: study)

_____ a few short compositions. Tomorrow,
           (1 write)

I _____ you a list of assignments. Do you
         (2 give)

have any questions about this course?

S: Yes. How many tests _____?
                              (3 have)

T: You will have 14 tests, one for each lesson in the book. If you're

absent from a test, you can make it up.[5] If you _____
                                                    (4 not take)

the test, you _____ an F on that test.
                    (5 get)

S: _____ us about the tests ahead of time?
        (6 tell)

T: Oh, yes. I'll always tell you about a test a few days before.

---

[5] If you are absent on the day of a test, the teacher expects you to take it at a later time.

S: When _____ the midterm exam?
(7 give)

T: I'm going to give you the midterm exam in April.

S: _____ very hard?
(8 be)

T: If you _____ for the test, it won't be hard.
(9 study)

S: What _____ in this course?
(10 study)

T: You'll study verb tenses, count and noncount nouns, and comparison of adjectives.

S: _____ everything in this book?
(11 finish)

T: Yes, I think we'll finish everything.

S: _____ over?
(12 be)

T: The semester will be over[6] in June. Tomorrow I _____
(13 give)

you a course outline with all this information.

EXERCISE 18 Write two questions to ask your teacher about this course.

EXAMPLES *Will there be a test on this lesson?*

When will you give us the next test?

_____

_____

EXERCISE 19 A young woman (A) is going to leave her country to go to the U.S. Her friend (B) is asking her questions. Fill in the blanks to complete this conversation.

A: I'm so happy! I'm going to the U.S.

B: When *are you going to leave?*
(example: leave)

A: I'm going to leave next month.

B: So soon? _____ anything
(1 buy)

before you _____?
(2 leave)

---

[6] To *be over* means to be finished.

A: Yes. I'm going to buy warm clothes for the winter. I hear the winter there is very cold.

B: Where _____ ?
 (3 be)

A: I'll be in Ann Arbor, Michigan.

B: Where _____ ?
 (4 live)

A: I'm not sure. When I _____ there,
 (5 get)

I _____ where to live.
 (6 decide)

B: _____ in the U.S.?
 (7 work)

A: No, I'm not going to work. I have a scholarship. I'm going to study at the University of Michigan.

B: What _____ ?
 (8 study)

A: I'm going to study to be a computer analyst.

B: When _____ to our country?
 (9 return)

A: I _____ when I _____ .
 (10 return) *(11 graduate)*

B: When _____ ?
 (12 you/graduate)

A: In four years.

B: That's a long time! _____ me?
 (13 miss)

A: Of course, I'll miss you.

B: _____ to me?
 (14 write)

A: Of course. I _____ to you when I _____
 (15 write) *(16 find)*

a place to live.

EXERCISE 20

A young Korean woman and her fiancé, Kim, are planning to get married. Her friend is asking her questions about her plans. Fill in the blanks to complete this conversation.

A: I'm getting married!

B: That's wonderful! Congratulations. _____Are you going to have_____ a big
    (example: have)

    wedding?

A: No, we're going to have a small wedding. We _____
    (1 invite)

    about 50 people.

B: Where _____?
    (2 be)

A: It'll be at St. Peter's Church. We _____ a reception
    (3 have)

    at a Korean restaurant after the wedding.

B: _____ a wedding dress?
    (4 buy)

A: No, I _____ my sister's dress for the
    (5 use)

    wedding. Then, for the reception, I _____
    (6 wear)

    a traditional Korean dress.

B: Where _____ after you get married?
    (7 live)

A: For a few years, we _____ with Kim's
    (8 live)

    parents. When Kim _____ college and
    (9 finish)

    _____ a job, we _____
    (10 get)   *(11 get)*

    our own apartment.

B: You're going to live with your in-laws? I can't believe it.

A: In my country, it's common. My in-laws are very nice.

    I'm sure it _____ a problem.
    (12 not/be)

    We _____ children right away.
    (13 not/have)

B: _____ here for the wedding?
    (14 come)

A: No, my parents aren't going to come. But a month after the wedding,

    we _____ a trip to Korea,
    (15 take)

    and Kim can meet my parents there.

B: _____ married?
(16 get)

A: On May 15. I hope you'll be able to attend. We _____
(17 send)

you an invitation.

B: I _____ glad to attend.
_(18 be)_

JASON AND KATIE—STARTING A MARRIED LIFE

Before You Read

1. Do you think life is hard for newlyweds? In what way?

2. In your community, do parents help their children after they get married?

 Read the following article. Pay special attention to verb tenses: simple present, present continuous, and future.

Jason and Katie are newlyweds. The wedding is over, the honeymoon was great, the gifts are opened, and their life as a married couple **is beginning.** They **are learning** that they have many responsibilities as a married couple.

Katie **works** as a nurse full-time. She **doesn't work** in a hospital. She **goes** to people's homes and **helps** them there. Jason **isn't working** now. He's still **attending** college. He's in his last year. He**'s studying** to be a lawyer. After classes every day, he **studies** at home or **goes** to the law library at his college. He**'s going to graduate** next June. When he **graduates,** he **will have** to take a special exam for lawyers. If he **passes** it, he**'ll get** a good job and **make**

(continued)

good money. But when he **starts** to work, he**'ll have** to pay back student loans. For now, they**'re** both **living** on Katie's salary.

Katie and Jason **are saving** money little by little. They**'re planning** to buy a house in a suburb some day. They **are** also **thinking** about having two children in the future. But they want to be financially stable before they **have** children. Their parents sometimes **offer** to help them, but they **don't want** to depend on their parents. Because Jason is so busy with his studies and Katie is so busy with her job, they rarely **go** out. Staying at home **helps** them save money.

7.7 | Comparison of Tenses

Uses	
Examples	**Explanation**
	Use the **simple present tense:**
a. Katie **works** as a nurse. Jason **studies** law. Lawyers **make** a lot of money in the U.S.	a. with facts
b. Grown children **don't like** to depend on their parents.	b. with customs
c. Jason **goes** to the library almost every day.	c. with habits and regular activities
d. Jason and Katie **have** a lot of responsibilities now.	d. with nonaction verbs
e. When Jason **graduates,** he will look for a job.	e. in a time clause or an *if* clause when talking about the future
	Use the **present continuous tense:**
a. I **am reviewing** verb tenses now.	a. with an action in progress now, at this moment
b. Jason and Katie **are saving** money to buy a house. They **are planning** to move to a suburb.	b. with a long-term action that is in progress; it may not be happening at this exact moment
	Use *will* for the **future:**
a. Katie thinks Jason **will be** a good lawyer.	a. with predictions
b. The law exam **will be** in March.	b. with facts
c. "I**'ll always** love you, Katie," says Jason.	c. with promises
d. "I**'ll help** you in the kitchen," says Katie.	d. with an offer to help
e. What will you do next year? I**'ll** cross that bridge when I get to it.	e. when you don't have a previous plan; when you decide what to do at the time of speaking
	Use *be going to* for the **future:**
a. I think they **are going to have** a wonderful life.	a. with predictions
b. For many years, they **are going to receive** bills for student loans.	b. with facts
c. Jason **is going to look** for a job next year.	c. with plans

Forms

Simple Present Tense	Present Continuous Tense
Jason **studies** law.	They **are saving** money to buy a house.
He **doesn't study** medicine.	They **aren't saving** to buy a new car.
Does he **study** every day?	**Are** they **saving** for a vacation?
Yes, he **does.**	No, they **aren't.**
Where **does** he **study?**	How **are** they **saving** money?
Why **doesn't** he **study** medicine?	Why **aren't** they **saving** to buy a car?
Who **studies** medicine?	Who **is saving** money?

Future with *Will*	Future with *Be Going To*
Jason **will graduate** next year.	They **are going to buy** a house.
He **won't graduate** this year.	They **aren't going to buy** a new car.
Will he **graduate** in January?	**Are** they **going to buy** a house in the city?
No, he **won't.**	No, they **aren't.**
When **will** he **graduate?**	Where **are** they **going to buy** a house?
Why **won't** he **graduate** in January?	Why **aren't** they **going to buy** a house in the city?
Who **will graduate** in January?	Who **is going to buy** a house?

EXERCISE 21 Fill in the blanks with the correct tense and form of the verb in parentheses ( ).

EXAMPLE   Jason _____*is going to graduate*_____ next year.
(graduate)

1. He _____ a good job when he _____.
   (have)   (graduate)

2. He _____ in the library.
   (often/study)

3. Jason and Katie _____ out.
   (rarely/go)

4. They _____ their money now.
   (save)

5. They _____ about buying a house.
   (think)

6. They _____ it's better to live in a suburb.
   (think)

EXERCISE 22 Fill in the blanks with the negative form of the underlined verb.

EXAMPLE They <u>are</u> young. They _____*aren't*_____ old.

1. They <u>have</u> an apartment now. They _____ a house.

2. They <u>want</u> children, but they _____ children right now.

3. Katie <u>is working</u>. Jason _____ now. He's going to school.

4. They <u>depend</u> on each other. They _____ on their parents.

5. Jason <u>will graduate</u> in June. He _____ in January.

EXERCISE 23 Read each statement. Then write a *yes/no* question with the words in parentheses ( ). Write a short answer.

EXAMPLE Katie <u>works</u> as a nurse. (in a hospital)
Does she work in a hospital? No, she doesn't. _____

1. Jason <u>is</u> a student. (Katie)

_____

2. Jason <u>is attending</u> college now. (Katie)

_____

3. Jason <u>will have</u> a job. (a good job)

_____

4. They <u>are thinking</u> about buying a house. (about having children)

_____

5. They <u>are going to have</u> children. (five children)

_____

EXERCISE 24 Read each statement. Then write a *wh-* question about the words in parentheses ( ). An answer is not necessary.

EXAMPLE Katie <u>works</u> as a nurse. (Where)
Where does she work as a nurse?

1. They <u>are saving</u> their money. (why)

2. They <u>don't want</u> to depend on their parents. (why)

3. Jason <u>will make</u> good money. (when)

4. Jason <u>wants</u> to be a lawyer. (why)

5. Katie <u>isn't going to work</u> when her children are small. (why)

6. Jason <u>will pay</u> back his student loans. (when)

7. They <u>don't go</u> out very much. (why)

8. Jason <u>is attending</u> college. (what college)

9. He <u>is going to graduate</u>. (when)

10. Jason <u>isn't earning</u> money now. (who)

11. Someone <u>wants</u> to help them. (who)

12. They <u>are learning</u> about responsibilities. (how)

1. Future patterns with *will*

AFFIRMATIVE:	He **will buy** a car.
NEGATIVE:	He **won't buy** a used car.
YES/NO QUESTION:	**Will** he **buy** a new car?
SHORT ANSWER:	Yes, he **will**.
WH- QUESTION:	When **will** he **buy** a car?
NEGATIVE QUESTION:	Why **won't** he **buy** a used car?
SUBJECT QUESTION:	Who **will buy** a car?

2. Future patterns with *be going to*

AFFIRMATIVE:	He **is going to buy** a car.
NEGATIVE:	He **isn't going to buy** a used car.
YES/NO QUESTION:	**Is** he **going to buy** a new car?
SHORT ANSWER:	Yes, he **is**.
WH- QUESTION:	When **is** he **going to buy** a car?
NEGATIVE QUESTION:	Why **isn't** he **going to buy** a used car?
SUBJECT QUESTION:	Who **is going to buy** a car?

3. Uses of *be going to* and *will*

Use	Will	Be Going To
Prediction	You **will become** rich and famous.	You **are going to become** rich and famous.
Fact	The sun **will set** at 6:32 p.m. tonight	The sun **is going to set** at 6:32 p.m. tonight.
Plan		I**'m going to buy** a new car next month.
Promise	I **will help** you tomorrow.	
Offer to help	A: I can't open the door. B: I**'ll open** it for you.	
No previous plan	A: I need to go to the store. B: I**'ll go** with you.	

4. Review the simple present tense and the present continuous tense on page 181.

EDITING ADVICE

1. Don't use *be* with a future verb.

   I will ~~be~~ go.

2. Use *be* in a future sentence that has no other verb.

> *be*
> He will ˰angry.

> *be*
> There will ˰a party soon.

3. Don't combine *will* and *be going to*.

> *is*
> He ~~will~~ going to leave.   OR   *He will leave.*

4. Don't use the present tense for a future action.

> *'ll*
> I'm going home now. I ˰see you later.

5. Don't use the future tense after *when* or *if*.

> When they ~~will~~ go home, they will watch TV.

6. Use a form of *be* with *going to*.

> *is*
> He ˰going to help me.

7. Use *to* after *going*.

> *to*
> I'm going ˰study on Saturday.

8. Use correct word order for questions.

> *aren't you*
> Why ~~you aren't~~ going to eat lunch?

LESSON 7 TEST / REVIEW

PART 1 Find the mistakes with the underlined words and correct them. Not every sentence has a mistake. If the sentence is correct, write *C*.

EXAMPLES
> *am*
> I ~~will~~ going to buy a newspaper.
> If you're too tired to cook, I'll do it.   *C*

1. When <u>you will</u> write your composition?

2. We <u>will be buy</u> a new car soon.

3. Will you going to eat dinner tonight?

4. When he will leave, he will turn off the light.

5. I going to take a vacation soon.

6. Is he going to use the computer?

7. They're going graduate soon.

8. I will happy when I will know more English.

9. I'm going on vacation. I will going to leave next Friday.

10. I'll write you a letter when I arrive.

11. There will a test soon.

12. I'll help you tomorrow.

PART 2   Fill in the blanks with *will* or a form of *be + going to*. In some cases, both answers are possible.

EXAMPLES   I believe the next president ___*will*___ OR ___*is going to*___ be a Democrat.

You can't move your piano alone. I _____*'ll*_____ help you do it.

1. We _____ eat in a new restaurant tomorrow. Do you want to go with us?

2. My friend is planning her wedding. She _____ invite 150 guests to her wedding.

3. I promise I _____ clean my room tomorrow.

4. If you come to work late every day, you _____ lose your job.

5. You don't know anything about computers? Come to my house.

I _____ teach you.

6. The teacher _____ give a test next Friday.

7. Next week we _____ begin Lesson Eight.

8. Mother: Please call me when you arrive.

Daughter: Don't worry, Mom. I _____ call you as soon as I arrive.

9. We're planning a picnic, but I think it _____ rain tomorrow.

PART 3 Fill in the blanks with the negative form of the underlined word.

> **EXAMPLE** She <u>will get</u> married in church. She _____won't get_____ married at home.

1. She <u>is going to invite</u> all her relatives. She _____ all her friends.

2. He <u>will wear</u> a tuxedo. He _____ a suit.

3. I <u>am going to buy</u> a gift. I _____ dishes.

4. I'<u>ll help</u> you tomorrow. I _____ you today.

5. You <u>are going to meet</u> my parents. You _____ my brothers.

PART 4 Read each statement. Then write a *yes/no* question about the words in parentheses ( ). Write a short answer.

> **EXAMPLE** She <u>will write</u> a letter. (a postcard) (no)
> *Will she write a postcard? No, she won't.*

1. They <u>will send</u> a gift. (money) (no)

   _____

2. You'<u>re going to invite</u> your friends. (relatives) (yes)

   _____

3. They <u>are going to receive</u> gifts. (open the gifts) (yes)

   _____

4. They <u>will need</u> things for their kitchen. (for their bathroom) (yes)

   _____

5. There <u>will be</u> a party after the wedding. (food at the party) (yes)

   _____

PART 5 Read each statement. Then write a question with the words in parentheses ( ). No answer is necessary.

> **EXAMPLE** I'<u>m going to buy</u> something. (What)
> *What are you going to buy?*

1. They <u>will use</u> the money. (How)

   _____

2. I'm going to send a gift. (What kind of gift)

   _____

3. They will thank us. (When)

   _____

4. They're going to get married. (Where)

   _____

5. They aren't going to open the gifts at the wedding. (Why)

   _____

6. There will be a lot of people at the wedding. (How many people)

   _____

7. Some people will give money. (Who)

   _____

TEST ON COMPARISON OF TENSES

PART 1 Read the following letter. Fill in the blanks with the simple present, the present continuous, or the future tense.

Dear Judy,

   Please excuse me for not writing sooner. I rarely _____*have*_____
   (example: have)

time to sit and write a letter. My husband _____ on his
                                            (1 work)

car now, and the baby _____. So now I
                      (2 sleep)

_____ a few free moments.
   (3 have)

   I _____ a student now. I _____
        (4 be)   (5 go)

to Kennedy College twice a week. The school _____ a
                                             (6 be)

few blocks from my house. I usually _____ to school,
                                     (7 walk)

but sometimes I _____ . My mother usually
                (8 drive)

_____ the baby when I'm in school. This semester
   (9 watch)

I _____ English and math. Next semester
     (10 study)

I _____ a computer course. I _____
      (11 take)   (12 think)

knowledge about computers _____ me find a good job.
                           (13 help)

When the semester _____ over, we _____
(14 be)   (15 go)

to Canada for vacation. We _____ my husband's sister.
(16 visit)

She _____ in Montreal. We _____
(17 live)   (18 spend)

Christmas with her family this year. When we _____ to
(19 get)

Montreal, I _____ you a postcard.
(20 send)

Please write and tell me what is happening in your life.
Love,
Barbara

PART 2 Fill in the blanks with the negative form of the underlined verb.

EXAMPLE   Barbara's a student. She _____ isn't _____ a teacher.

1. She's <u>writing</u> a letter now. She _____ a composition.

2. Her mother sometimes <u>takes</u> care of her baby. Her father _____
_____ care of her baby.

3. They're <u>going to visit</u> her husband's sister. They _____
_____ her mother.

4. She <u>goes</u> to Kennedy College. She _____ to Truman
College.

5. Barbara and her husband <u>live</u> in the U.S. They _____
in Canada.

6. Her family <u>will go</u> to Montreal. They _____ to
Toronto.

PART 3 Read each statement. Then write a *yes/no* question with the words
in parentheses ( ). Write a short answer, based on the letter.

EXAMPLE   Barbara's studying English. (math)
Is she studying math? Yes, she is.

1. The baby's sleeping. (her husband)
_____

2. She sometimes drives to school. (ever/walk to school)
_____

3. She's going to take a computer course next semester. (a math class)
_____

4. She'll go to Canada. (Montreal)

   _____

5. She's going to send Judy a postcard. (a letter)

   _____

6. She sometimes writes letters. (write a letter/now)

   _____

7. Her sister-in-law lives in Canada. (in Toronto)

   _____

PART 4 Read each statement. Then write a *wh-* question with the words in parentheses ( ). Write an answer, based on the letter.

EXAMPLE She goes to college. (Where)

A: *Where does she go to college?*

B: *She goes to Kennedy College.*

1. Her baby's sleeping. (What/her husband/do)

   A: _____

   B: _____

2. She's taking two courses this semester. (What courses)

   A: _____

   B: _____

3. Someone watches her baby. (Who)

   A: _____

   B: _____

4. She's going to take a course next semester. (What course)

   A: _____

   B: _____

5. They'll go on vacation for Christmas. (Where)

   A: _____

   B: _____

6. Her husband's sister lives in another city. (Where/she)

A: _____

B: _____

7. She doesn't usually drive to school. (Why)

A: _____

B: _____

EXPANSION ACTIVITIES

Classroom Activities

1. Check (✓) the activities that you plan to do soon. Find a partner. Ask your partner for information about the items he or she checked off. Report something interesting to the class about your partner's plans.

   EXAMPLE   ___✓___ move
   When are you going to move?
   Why are you going to move?
   Are your friends going to help you?
   Are you going to rent a truck?
   Where are you going to move to?

   a. _____ get married

   b. _____ go back to my country

   c. _____ spend a lot of money

   d. _____ write a letter

   e. _____ buy something (a computer, a DVD player, a TV, an answering machine, etc.)

   f. _____ go to a party

   g. _____ have a job interview

   h. _____ transfer to another college

   i. _____ become a citizen

   j. _____ eat in a restaurant

2. Role-play the following characters. Practice the future tense.

   a. Fortune-teller and young woman. The woman wants to know her future.

   b. Man proposing marriage to a woman. The man is making promises.

   c. Teenager and parents. The teenager wants to go to a party on Saturday night.

   d. Politician and voter. The politician wants votes.

   e. Landlord and a person who wants to rent an apartment. The person wants to know what the landlord will do to fix up the apartment.

3. What are your concerns and plans for the future? Write one or two sentences (statements or questions) for each of the categories in the box below. Then find a partner. Discuss your concerns and plans with your partner.

Job/Career	*Where will I work if I lose my present job?*
Money	
Learning English	
Home	
Family and children	
Health	
Fun and recreation	
Other	

4. Imagine that you are going to buy a gift for someone in the following circumstances. What gift would you buy? Find a partner and compare your list of gifts to your partner's list.

a. a friend in the hospital after surgery _____

b. a couple with a new baby _____

c. a nephew graduating from high school _____

d. a friend getting married for the second time _____

e. a friend moving into a new apartment _____

f. a family that invites you to dinner at their house _____

Talk About it

1. In a small group or with the entire class, talk about gift-giving customs in your native culture. What kind of gifts do people give for weddings? How much money do they spend? Do newlyweds open presents at the wedding? Do they send thank-you cards? What kind of gifts do people give for other occasions?

2. Once a couple marries, both people often work. Sometimes only the man or only the woman works. In your native culture, does a woman ever support a man financially? Discuss.

Outside Activity

Use the third classroom activity above to interview an American about his or her concerns about the future. What is he or she worried about?

Internet Activity

Find a bridal or wedding registry on the Internet. What kind of gifts can a couple register for? What are the prices?

Additional Activities at http://elt.heinle.com/gic

GRAMMAR

The Simple Past Tense

CONTEXT: Flying

The Wright Brothers—Men with a Vision
Charles Lindbergh and Amelia Earhart
Robert Goddard

Before You Read

1. Do you like to travel by airplane? Why or why not?

2. What are the names of some famous inventors?

Wilbur Wright, 1867–1912; Orville Wright, 1871–1948

Read the following article. Pay special attention to simple past-tense verbs.

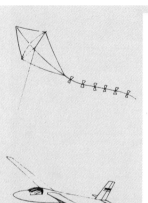

Over 100 years ago, people only **dreamed** about flying. The Wright brothers, Wilbur and Orville, **were** dreamers who **changed** the world.

Wilbur Wright **was** born in 1867 and Orville **was** born in 1871. In 1878, they **received** a paper flying toy from their father. They **started** to think about the possibility of flight. They **played** with kites and **studied** everything they could about glider planes.

When they were older, they **started** a bicycle business in Dayton, Ohio. They **used** the bicycle shop to design their airplanes. They **studied** three aspects of flying: lift, control, and power. In 1899, they **constructed** their first flying machine—a kite made of wood, wire, and cloth. It **had** no pilot.

Because of wind, it was difficult to control. They **continued** to study aerodynamics.[1] Finally Wilbur **designed** a small machine with a gasoline engine. Wilbur **tried** to fly the machine, but it **crashed.** They **fixed** it and **flew** it for the first time on December 17, 1903, with Orville as the pilot. The airplane **remained** in the air for twelve seconds. It **traveled** a distance of 120 feet. It **weighed** over 600 pounds. This historic flight **changed** the world. However, only four newspapers in the U.S. **reported** this historic moment.

The Wright brothers **offered** their invention to the U.S. government, but the government **rejected**[2] their offer at first. The government **didn't believe** that these men **invented** a flying machine. Finally, President Theodore Roosevelt **investigated** their claims and **offered** the inventors a contract to build airplanes for the U.S. Army.

December 17, 2003 **marked** 100 years of flight. There **was** a six-day celebration at Kitty Hawk, North Carolina, the location of the first flight. A crowd of 35,000 people **gathered** to see a replica[3] of the first plane fly. The cost to recreate the plane **was** $1.2 million. However, it **rained** hard that day and the plane **failed** to get off the ground.

You can now see the Wright brothers' original airplane in the Air and Space Museum in Washington, D.C.

8.1 | The Simple Past Tense of Regular Verbs

Examples	Explanation
The Wright brothers **started** a bicycle business in Ohio. They **dreamed** about flying. They **designed** an airplane. The president **offered** them a contract.	To form the simple past tense of regular verbs, we add *-ed* to the base form. **Base Form** **Past Form** start start**ed** dream dream**ed** design design**ed** offer offer**ed** The past form is the same for all persons.
The Wright brothers **wanted** *to fly.* They **continued** *to study* about flying.	The verb after *to* does **not** use the past form.
The Wright brothers **invented** the airplane over 100 years **ago.** We **celebrated** the one-hundredth anniversary of flight a few years **ago.**	We often use *ago* in sentences about the past. *Ago* means *before now.*

[1]*Aerodynamics* is the branch of mechanics that deals with the motion of air and its effect on things.
[2]*Reject* means not accept.
[3]A replica is a copy of an original.

EXERCISE 1 Underline the past tense verbs in the following sentences.

EXAMPLE The Wright brothers <u>lived</u> in Dayton, Ohio.

1. Their father worked as a Christian minister.
2. The boys learned mechanical things quickly.
3. They loved bicycles.
4. They opened the Wright Cycle Company repair shop, where they repaired bicycles.
5. They started to produce their own bicycle models.
6. They used the bike shop to build airplane parts.
7. They succeeded in flying the first airplane in 1903.
8. Wilbur died nine years later, of typhoid.[4]
9. Orville lived to be 76 years old.

8.2 | Spelling of the Past Tense of Regular Verbs

Rule	Base Form	Past Form
Add -ed to most regular verbs.	start rain	start**ed** rain**ed**
When the base form ends in e, add -d only.	die live	die**d** live**d**
When the base form ends in a consonant + y, change y to i and add -ed.	carry study	carr**ied** stud**ied**
When the base form ends in a vowel + y, add -ed. Do not change the y.	stay enjoy	stay**ed** enjoy**ed**
When a one-syllable verb ends in a consonant-vowel-consonant, double the final consonant and add -ed.	stop hug	stop**ped** hug**ged**
Do not double a final w or x.	fix show	fix**ed** show**ed**
When a two-syllable verb ends in a consonant-vowel-consonant, double the final consonant and add -ed only if the last syllable is stressed.	occúr permít	occur**red** permit**ted**
When the last syllable of a two-syllable verb is not stressed, do not double the final consonant.	ópen óffer	open**ed** offer**ed**

[4]*Typhoid* is a serious infection causing a fever and often death.

EXERCISE 2 Write the past tense of these regular verbs. (Accent marks show you where a word is stressed.)

EXAMPLES learn _____learned_____ clap _____clapped_____

love _____loved_____ lísten _____listened_____

1. play _____
2. study _____
3. decide _____
4. want _____
5. like _____
6. show _____
7. look _____
8. stop _____
9. háppen _____
10. carry _____

11. enjoy _____
12. drag _____
13. drop _____
14. start _____
15. follow _____
16. prefér _____
17. like _____
18. mix _____
19. admít _____
20. devélop _____

8.3 | Pronunciation of *-ed* Past Forms

Pronunciation	Rule	Examples	
/t/	Pronounce /t/ after voiceless sounds: /p, k, f, s, š, č/	jump—jumped cook—cooked cough—coughed	kiss—kissed wash—washed watch—watched
/d/	Pronounce /d/ after voiced sounds: /b, g, v, đ, z, ž, ǰ, m, n, ŋ, l, r/ and all vowels.	rub—rubbed drag—dragged love—loved bathe—bathed use—used massage—massaged charge—charged	name—named learn—learned bang—banged call—called care—cared free—freed
/əd/	Pronounce /əd/ after /d/ or /t/ sounds.	wait—waited hate—hated want—wanted	add—added decide—decided

EXERCISE 3 Go back to Exercise 2 and pronounce the base form and past form of each verb.

EXERCISE 4 Fill in the blanks with the past tense of the verb in parentheses ( ). Use the correct spelling.

EXAMPLE The Wright brothers __received__ a flying toy from their father.
                        (receive)

1. They _____ with kites.
                        (play)

2. They _____ about flying.
                        (dream)

3. They _____ everything they could about flying.
                        (study)

4. They _____a bicycle business.
                        (start)

5. They _____ the bicycle shop to design airplanes.
                        (use)

6. They _____ to fly their first plane in 1899.
                        (try)

7. Their first plane _____ .
                        (crash)

8. They _____ it.
                        (fix)

9. In 1903, their plane _____ in the air for 12 seconds.
                        (stay)

10. They _____ their invention to the U.S. government.
                        (offer)

11. The government _____ to offer them a contract.
                        (decide)

12. Wilbur Wright _____ in 1912.
                        (die)

13. Orville Wright _____ for many more years.
                        (live)

14. Their invention _____ the world.
                        (change)

CHARLES LINDBERGH AND AMELIA EARHART

1. When was the first time you traveled by airplane?
2. Do you recognize the people in these photos?

Charles Lindbergh, 1902–1974

Amelia Earhart, 1897–1937

 Read the following article. Pay special attention to the past-tense forms of *be*.

At the beginning of the twentieth century, flight **was** new. It **was** not for everyone. It **was** only for the brave and adventurous. Two adventurers **were** Charles Lindbergh and Amelia Earhart.

Charles Lindbergh loved to fly. He **was** born in 1902, one year before the Wright brothers' historic flight. In 1927, a man offered a $25,000 reward for the first person to fly from New York to Paris nonstop. Lindbergh **was** a pilot for the United States Mail Service at that time. He wanted to win the prize. He became famous because he **was** the first person to fly alone across the Atlantic Ocean. His plane **was** in the air for 33 hours. The distance of the flight **was** 3,600 miles. There **were** thousands of people in New York to welcome him home. He **was** an American hero. He **was** only 25 years old.

Another famous American aviator[5] **was** Amelia Earhart. She **was** the first woman to fly across the Atlantic Ocean alone. She **was** 34 years old. Americans **were** in love with Earhart. In 1937, however, she **was** on a flight around the world when her plane disappeared somewhere in the Pacific Ocean. No one really knows what happened to Earhart.

[5] *Aviator* means pilot.

8.4 | Past Tense of *Be*

The verb *be* has two forms in the past: *was* and *were*.

Examples			Explanation
Subject	*Was*	Complement	
I	**was**	interested in the story.	*I, he, she, it,* singular subject → *was*
Charles	**was**	a pilot too.	
He	**was**	brave.	
Amelia	**was**	a pilot.	
She	**was**	popular.	
The airplane	**was**	new in 1903.	
It	**was**	in the air for 12 seconds.	
Subject	*Were*	Complement	
We	**were**	interested in the story.	*We, you, they,* plural subject → *were*
You	**were**	in class yesterday.	
Amelia and Charles	**were**	brave.	
They	**were**	heroes.	
There	*Was*	Singular Subject	
There	**was**	a celebration in 2003.	*There + was +* singular noun
There	*Were*	Plural Subject	
There	**were**	thousands of people.	*There + were +* plural noun
Charles **was not** the first person to fly. We **were not** at the 2003 celebration.			To make a negative statement, put *not* after *was* or *were*.
I **wasn't** here yesterday. You **weren't** in class yesterday.			The contraction for *was not* is *wasn't.* The contraction for *were not* is *weren't.*

EXERCISE **5** Fill in the blanks with *was* or *were.*

EXAMPLE Lindbergh and Earhart ___were___ very famous.

1. The Wright brothers _____ the inventors of the airplane.

2. The first airplane _____ in the air for 12 seconds.

3. Lindbergh and Earhart _____ aviators.

4. There _____ thousands of people in New York to welcome Lindbergh home.

5. Earhart _____ the first woman to fly across the Atlantic Ocean.

6. I _____ interested in the story about Earhart and Lindbergh.

7. _____ you surprised that Earhart was a woman?

8. Lindbergh _____ in Paris.

9. We _____ happy to read about flight.

10. There _____ a celebration of 100 years of flight in 2003.

11. There _____ thousands of people at the celebration.

8.5 | Uses of *Be*

Examples	Explanation
Lindbergh **was** an aviator.	Classification of the subject
Lindbergh **was** brave.	Description of the subject
Lindbergh **was** in Paris.	Location of the subject
Earhart **was** from Kansas.	Place of origin of the subject
She **was** born in 1897.	With *born*
There **were** thousands of people in New York to welcome Lindbergh.	With *there*
Lindbergh **was** 25 years old in 1927.	With age

EXERCISE 6 Read each statement. Then write a negative statement with the words in parentheses ( ).

EXAMPLE The Wright brothers were inventors. (Earhart and Lindbergh)

Earhart and Lindbergh weren't inventors.

1. The train was common transportation in the early 1900s. (the airplane)

_____

2. Earhart was from Kansas. (Lindbergh)

_____

3. Lindbergh's last flight was successful. (Earhart's last flight)

_____

4. Lindbergh's plane was in the air for many hours. (the Wright brothers' first plane)

_____

5. The Wright brothers were inventors. (Earhart)

_____

6. There were a lot of trains 100 years ago. (planes)

_____

7. Lindbergh was born in the twentieth century. (the Wright brothers)

_____

8. The 1903 flight at Kitty Hawk was successful. (the 2003 flight)

_____

8.6 | Questions with *Was/Were*

Examples	Explanation
Was the first flight long? 　No, it **wasn't**. **Was** the first flight successful? 　Yes, it **was**. **Were** the Wright brothers inventors? 　Yes, they **were**.	*Yes/No Questions* 　*Was/were* + subject . . . ? Answer with a short answer, containing a pronoun + *was, wasn't, were, weren't*.
Were there a lot of people at the 100 year celebration? 　Yes, there **were**. **Was** there a lot of rain that day? 　Yes, there **was**.	In a question with *there*, use *there* + *was/were* in the short answer.
How long **was** the first flight? Where **was** the first flight?	*Wh- Questions* 　*Wh-* word + *was/were* + subject . . . ?
Why **wasn't** Amelia successful? Why **weren't** you there?	*Negative Questions* 　*Why* + *wasn't/weren't* + subject . . . ?
Who **was** with Earhart when she disappeared? How many people **were** in the airplane?	*Subject Questions* 　*Who* + *was* . . . ? 　*How many* . . . + *were* . . . ?

Compare statements and questions

Affirmative Statements and Questions

Wh- Word	Was/Were	Subject	Was/Were	Complement	Short Answer
		Amelia	was	born before 1903.	
	Was	she		born in the U.S.?	Yes, she was.
When	was	she		born?	In 1897.
		Charles and Amelia	were	famous.	
	Were	they		inventors?	No, they weren't.
		Someone	was	with Amelia.	
		Who	was	with Amelia?	A copilot.
		Many people	were	at the celebration of flight.	
		How many people	were	at the celebration?	Thousands.

Negative Statements and Questions

Wh- Word	Wasn't/Weren't	Subject	Wasn't/Weren't	Complement
		Air travel	wasn't	safe 100 years ago.
Why	wasn't	it		safe?
		The Wright brothers	weren't	afraid of flying.
Why	weren't	they		afraid?

The Simple Past Tense **233**

EXERCISE **7**   Read each statement. Then write a *yes/no* question with the words in parentheses ( ). Give a short answer.

EXAMPLE   The Wright brothers were inventors. (Lindbergh)

Was Lindbergh an inventor? No, he wasn't.

1. The airplane was an important invention. (the telephone)

2. Thomas Edison was an inventor. (the Wright brothers)

3. Amelia Earhart was American. (Lindbergh)

4. Travel by plane is common now. (100 years ago)

5. There were telephones 100 years ago. (airplanes)

6. You are in class today. (yesterday)

7. I was interested in the story about the aviators. (you)

8. I wasn't born in the U.S. (you)

EXERCISE **8**   ABOUT YOU Interview a classmate who is from another country.

1. Where were you born?
2. Were you happy or sad when you left your country?
3. Who was with you on your trip to the U.S.?
4. Were you happy or sad when you arrived in the U.S.?
5. What was your first impression of the U.S.?
6. Were you tired when you arrived?
7. Who was there to meet you?
8. How was the weather on the day you arrived?

EXERCISE **9**   Read each statement. Then write a *wh-* question with the words in parentheses ( ). Answer the question.

EXAMPLE   Lindbergh was very famous. (why)

A: *Why was Lindbergh famous?*

B: *He was one of the first aviators.*

1. Lindbergh was a hero. (why)

   A: _____

   B: _____

2. Lindbergh was American. (what nationality/Earhart)

   A: _____

   B: _____

3. Earhart was 34 years old when she crossed the ocean. (Lindbergh)

   A: _____

   B: _____

4. Lindbergh was a famous aviator. (who/the Wright brothers)

   A: _____

   B: _____

5. Lindbergh was born in 1902. (Earhart) (answer: 1897)

   A: _____

   B: _____

6. The Wright brothers were famous. (why)

   A: _____

   B: _____

7. The flight at Kitty Hawk in 2003 wasn't successful. (why)

   A: _____

   B: _____

EXERCISE **10**   Fill in the blanks with the correct past-tense form of *be*. Add any other necessary words.

A: I tried to call you last weekend. I ____was____ worried about you.
                                         (example)

B: I _____ home. I _____ out of town.
       (1 not)   *(2)*

A: Where _____(3)_____?

B: In Washington, D.C.

A: _____(4)_____ alone?

B: No, I _____(5)_____.
I was with my brother.

A: _____(6)_____ expensive?

B: No. Our trip wasn't expensive at all.

A: Really? Why _____(7)_____ expensive?

B: The flight from here to Washington _____(8)_____ cheap. And we

stayed with some friends in their apartment. They _____(9)_____

very helpful. They showed us a lot of beautiful places in Washington.
But my favorite place was the Air and Space Museum.

A: _____(10)_____ a lot of people at the museum?

B: Yes, there were. It _____(11)_____ very crowded. But it _____(12)_____

wonderful to see the Wright brothers' airplane and the airplane that

Lindbergh used when he crossed the Atlantic. Also it _____(13)_____

interesting to see the spacecraft of the astronauts too. We _____(14 not)_____

bored for one minute in that museum.

A: How long _____(15)_____ your flight to Washington?

B: It _____(16)_____ only 2 hours and 15 minutes from here. We don't think

about flying as anything special anymore. But just a little over

100 years ago, flight _____(17)_____ just a dream of two brothers.

Can you believe it? There _____(18)_____ only 66 years between the first

flight in 1903 and the trip to the moon in 1969!

A: That's amazing!

8.7 | Simple Past Tense of Irregular Verbs—An Overview

Examples	Explanation
I **came** to the U.S. by plane. My flight **took** six hours. I **felt** happy when I arrived.	Many verbs are irregular in the past tense. An irregular verb does not use the *-ed* ending.

ROBERT GODDARD

Before You Read

1. Did you ever see the first moon landing in 1969?

2. Are you interested in astronauts and rockets?

Robert Goddard with early rocket

Apollo 11 on the moon

 Read the following article. Pay special attention to past-tense verbs.

firecracker

Robert Goddard **was** born in 1882. When he **was** a child, he **became** interested in firecrackers and **thought** about the possibility of space travel. He later **became** a physics professor at a university. In his free time, he **built** rockets and **took** them to a field, but they **didn't fly.** When he **went** back to his university after his failed attempts, the other professors **laughed** at him.

(continued)

In 1920, Goddard **wrote** an article about rocket travel. He **believed** that one day it would be possible to go to the moon. When the *New York Times* **saw** his article, a reporter **wrote** that Goddard **had** less knowledge about science than a high school student. Goddard **wanted** to prove that the *New York Times* **was** wrong.

In 1926, he **built** a ten-foot rocket, **put** it into an open car, and **drove** to his aunt's nearby farm. He **put** the rocket in a field and **lit** the fuse. Suddenly the rocket **went** into the sky. It **traveled** at 60 mph to an altitude of 41 feet. Then it **fell** into the field. The flight **lasted** 2½ seconds, but Goddard **was** happy about his achievement. Over the years, his rockets **grew** to 18 feet and **flew** to 9,000 feet in the air. No one **made** fun of him after he was successful.

When Goddard **died** in 1945, his work **did not stop.** Scientists **continued** to build bigger and better rockets. In 1969, when the American rocket Apollo 11 **took** the first men to the moon, the *New York Times* **wrote:** "The *Times* regrets[6] the error."

1920	Goddard **published** a paper on rockets.
1926–1939	Goddard **built** and **flew** rockets.
1944	Germany **used** the first rockets in World War II.
1957	The Russians **sent** up their first satellite, Sputnik 1.
1958	The Americans **sent** up their first satellite, Explorer 1.
1961	Yuri Gagarin, a Russian, **became** the first person in space.
1961	Alan Shepard **became** the first American in space.
1969	The United States **put** the first men on the moon.
2004	A spacecraft on Mars **sent** color photos to Earth.

Mars Rover

[6]*Regret* means to be sorry for.

8.8 | List of Irregular Past Tense Verbs[7]

Verbs with No Change	
bet—bet	hurt—hurt
cost—cost	let—let
cut—cut	put—put
fit—fit	quit—quit
hit—hit	shut—shut

Final *d* Changes to *t*	
bend—bent	send—sent
build—built	spend—spent
lend—lent	

Verbs with a Vowel Change

feel—felt	lose—lost	bring—brought	fight—fought
keep—kept	mean—meant[8]	buy—bought	teach—taught
leave—left	sleep—slept	catch—caught	think—thought
break—broke	steal—stole	begin—began	sing—sang
choose—chose	speak—spoke	drink—drank	sink—sank
freeze—froze	wake—woke	ring—rang	swim—swam
dig—dug	spin—spun	drive—drove	shine—shone
hang—hung	win—won	ride—rode	write—wrote
blow—blew	grow—grew	bleed—bled	meet—met
draw—drew	know—knew	feed—fed	read—read[9]
fly—flew	throw—threw	lead—led	
sell—sold	tell—told	find—found	wind—wound
shake—shook	mistake—mistook	lay—laid	pay—paid
take—took		say—said[10]	
tear—tore	wear—wore	bite—bit	hide—hid
		light—lit	
become—became	eat—ate	fall—fell	hold—held
come—came			
give—gave	lie—lay	run—ran	see—saw
forgive—forgave		sit—sat	
forget—forgot	get—got	stand—stood	
shoot—shot		understand—understood	

Miscellaneous Changes

be—was/were	go—went	hear—heard
do—did	have—had	make—made

[7]For an alphabetical list of irregular verbs, see Appendix D.
[8]There is a change in the vowel sound. *Meant* rhymes with *sent.*
[9]The past form of *read* is pronounced like the color *red.*
[10]*Said* rhymes with *bed.*

EXERCISE 11   Fill in the blanks with the past tense of one of the words from the box below.

fly	think	drive	be	fall
write	put	✓become	see	

EXAMPLE   Goddard ___became___ interested in rockets when he was a child.

1. He _____ a professor of physics.

2. People _____ that space travel was impossible.

3. Goddard _____ his first rocket in a car and _____ to his aunt's farm.

4. The rocket _____ for 2¹/₂ seconds and then it _____ to the ground.

5. Goddard never _____ the first moon landing.

6. The *New York Times* _____ about their mistake 49 years later.

EXERCISE 12   Fill in the blanks with the past tense of the verb in parentheses ( ).

EXAMPLE   The Wright brothers' father ___gave___ them a flying toy.
                                               (give)

1. They _____ a dream of flying.
          (have)

2. They _____ interested in flying after seeing a flying toy.
          (become)

3. They _____ many books on flight.
          (read)

4. They _____ bicycles.
          (sell)

5. They _____ the first airplane.
          (build)

6. At first they _____ problems with wind.
          (have)

7. They _____ some changes to the airplane.
          (make)

8. They _____ for the first time in 1903.
   (fly)

9. Only a few people _____ the first flight.
   (see)

10. President Theodore Roosevelt _____ about their airplane.
    (hear)

11. The airplane was an important invention because it _____
    (bring)

    people from different places closer together.

12. Thousands of people _____ to North Carolina for the 100th
    (go)

    anniversary of flight.

8.9 | Negative Forms of Past Tense Verbs

Compare affirmative (A) and negative (N) statements with past-tense verbs.

Examples	Explanation
A. Lindbergh **returned** from his last flight. N. Earhart **didn't return** from her last flight.	For the negative past tense, we use *didn't* + the base form for ALL verbs, regular and irregular.
A. The Wright brothers **flew** in their airplane. N. Goddard **didn't fly** in his rocket.	**Compare** returned—didn't return flew—didn't fly built—didn't build put—didn't put
A. Goddard **built** rockets. N. He **didn't build** airplanes.	
A. The Russians **put** a woman in space in 1963. N. The Americans **didn't put** a woman in space until 1983.	**Remember:** *Put* and a few other past-tense verbs are the same as the base form.

EXERCISE 13 Fill in the blanks with the negative form of the underlined words.

EXAMPLE   Goddard believed in space flight. Other people ___*didn't believe*___ in space flight.

1. In 1926 his rocket flew. Before that time, his rockets

   _____ .

2. He wanted to build rockets. He _____ to build airplanes.

3. In 1920, a newspaper wrote that he was foolish. The newspaper _____ about the possibility of rocket travel.

4. The first rocket stayed in the air for $2\frac{1}{2}$ seconds. It

   _____ in the air for a long time.

5. Goddard thought his ideas were important. His colleagues

   _____ his ideas were important.

6. Goddard saw his rockets fly. He _____ rockets go to the moon.

7. A rocket went to the moon in 1969. A rocket _____ to the moon during Goddard's lifetime.

8. In 1957, the Russians put the first man in space. The Americans

   _____ the first man in space.

9. In 1969, the first Americans walked on the moon. Russians

   _____ on the moon.

10. The Wright brothers dreamed about flying. They

    _____ about rockets.

11. They sold bicycles. They _____ cars.

12. Their 1903 airplane had a pilot. Their first airplane

    _____ a pilot.

13. The Wright brothers built the first airplane. They

    _____ the first rocket.

14. The Wright brothers wanted to show their airplane to the U.S.

    government. The government _____ to see it at first.

EXERCISE 14 ABOUT YOU If you are from another country, fill in the blanks with the affirmative or negative form of the verb in parentheses to tell about the time before you came to the U.S. Add some specific information to tell more about each item.

EXAMPLES I _____studied_____ English before I came to the U.S.
                        (study)

I studied with a private teacher for three months.

OR

I _____didn't study_____ English before I came to the U.S.
                        (study)

I didn't have enough time.

1. I _____ my money for dollars before I came to
       (exchange)
   the U.S.

2. I _____ a passport.
       (get)

3. I _____ for a visa.
       (apply)

4. I _____ English.
       (study)

5. I _____ some things (house, furniture, etc.).
       (sell)

6. I _____ goodbye to my friends.
       (say)

7. I _____ an English dictionary.
       (buy)

8. I _____ a clear idea about life in the U.S.
       (have)

9. I _____ afraid about my future.
       (be)

10. I _____ to another country first.
       (go)

11. I _____ English well.
       (understand)

12. I _____ a lot about Americans.
       (know)

EXERCISE 15 If you come from another city or country, tell if these things happened or didn't happen after you moved to this city. Add some specific information to tell more about each item.

EXAMPLE find an apartment
I found an apartment two weeks after I arrived in this city.
OR
I didn't find an apartment right away. I lived with my cousins for two months.

1. find a job
2. register for English classes
3. rent an apartment
4. buy a car
5. get a Social Security card

6. go to the bank
7. visit a museum
8. see a relative
9. buy clothes
10. get a driver's license

EXERCISE 16 ABOUT YOU Tell if you did or didn't do these things in the past week. Add some specific information to tell more about each item.

EXAMPLE go to the movies
I went to the movies last weekend with my brother. We saw a great movie.
OR
I didn't go to the movies this week. I didn't have time.

1. receive a letter
2. write a letter
3. go to the library
4. do laundry
5. buy groceries
6. use a phone card

7. buy a magazine
8. work hard
9. look for a job
10. rent a DVD
11. send an e-mail
12. read a newspaper

8.10 | Questions with Past Tense Verbs

Yes/No Questions and Short Answers

Examples	Explanation

Did Goddard **invent** the rocket?
    Yes, he **did.**
Did Goddard **live** to see man land on the moon?
    No, he **didn't.**
Did Lindbergh **fly** across the ocean alone?
    Yes, he **did.**
	Did + subject + base form . . . ?
	
	Use the base form for both regular and irregular verbs.
	Short Answers
	    Yes, + subject pronoun + did.
	    No, + subject pronoun + didn't.

Wh- Questions

Wh- Questions When **did** Lindbergh **cross** the ocean? How **did** Earhart's **plane** disappear? When **did** Goddard **become** a professor?	*Wh- word + did + subject + base form . . . ?*
Negative Questions Why **didn't** the Wright brothers' first plane **fly?** Why didn't Earhart **return?**	*Why + didn't + subject + base form . . . ?*

Compare affirmative statements and questions

Wh- Word	Did	Subject	Verb	Complement	Short Answer
		Goddard	studied	physics.	
	Did	he	study	hard?	Yes, he did.
When	did	he	study	physics?	In the beginning of the twentieth century.
		Lindbergh	flew	across the Atlantic.	
	Did	he	fly	alone?	Yes, he did.
Why	did	he	fly	alone?	Because he was brave.

Compare negative statements and questions

Wh- Word	Didn't	Subject	Verb	Complement
		Goddard	didn't see	the rocket go to the moon.
Why	didn't	he	see	the rocket go to the moon?
		Amelia	didn't return	from her last trip.
Why	didn't	she	return?	

EXERCISE 17 ABOUT YOU Use these questions to ask another student about the time when he or she lived in his or her native country.

1. Did you study English in your country?
2. Did you live in a big city?
3. Did you live with your parents?
4. Did you know a lot about the U.S.?
5. Were you happy with the political situation?
6. Did you finish high school?
7. Did you own a car?
8. Did you have a job?
9. Did you think about your future?
10. Were you happy?

EXERCISE 18 Read each statement. Write a *yes/no* question about the words in parentheses ( ). Write a short answer.

EXAMPLE The Wright brothers had a dream. (Goddard) (yes)
Did Goddard have a dream? Yes, he did.

1. Wilbur Wright died in 1912. (his brother) (no)

   _____

2. The Wright brothers built an airplane. (Goddard) (no)

   _____

3. Earhart loved to fly. (Lindbergh) (yes)

   _____

4. Lindbergh crossed the ocean. (Earhart) (yes)

   _____

5. Lindbergh worked for the U.S. Mail Service. (Earhart) (no)

   _____

6. Lindbergh became famous. (Earhart) (yes)

   _____

7. Earhart disappeared. (Lindbergh) (no)

   _____

8. Lindbergh was born in the twentieth century. (Earhart) (no)

   _____

9. Lindbergh won money for his first flight. (the Wright brothers) (no)

   _____

10. People didn't believe the Wright brothers at first. (Goddard) (no)

    _____

11. The Wright brothers dreamed about flight. (Goddard) (yes)

    _____

12. The Russians sent a rocket into space in 1957. (the Americans) (no)

    _____

13. The Russians put a man in space in 1961. (Americans) (yes)

    _____

14. Americans saw the first moon landing. (Goddard) (no)

    _____

EXERCISE 19   Fill in the blanks with the correct words.

EXAMPLE   What kind of engine _did the first airplane have?_ _____
The first airplane had a gasoline engine.

1. Where _____?
   The Wright brothers built their plane in their bicycle shop.

2. Why _____?
   The first plane crashed because of the wind.

3. Why _____ difficult to control?
   The plane was difficult to control because of the wind.

4. Why _____ the first flight in 1903?
   Newspapers didn't report it because they didn't believe it.

5. Where _____?
   Lindbergh worked for the U.S. Mail Service.

6. Why _____?
   He crossed the ocean to win the prize money.

7. How much money _____?
   He won $25,000.

8. How old _____ when he crossed the ocean?
   Lindbergh was 25 years old when he crossed the ocean.

9. Where _____?
   His plane landed in Paris.

10. When _____?
    Lindbergh died in 1974.

11. Where _____?
    Earhart was born in Kansas.

12. Where _____?
    She disappeared in the Pacific Ocean.

13. Why _____?
    Nobody knows why Earhart didn't return.

14. Who _____ with?
    Earhart was with a copilot.

15. When _____?
    The first man walked on the moon in 1969.

16. Why _____ the first moon landing?
    Goddard didn't see the first moon landing because he died in 1945.

EXERCISE 20 Read each statement. Then write a question with the words in parentheses ( ). Answer with a complete sentence. (The answers are at the bottom of the page.)

EXAMPLE The Wright brothers were born in the nineteenth century. (Where)
Where were they born? They were born in Ohio.

1. The Wright brothers were born in the nineteenth century. (When/Lindbergh)

   _____

2. Their father gave them a toy. (What kind of toy)

   _____

3. They had a shop. (What kind of shop)

   _____

4. They designed airplanes. (Where)

   _____

5. They flew their first plane in North Carolina. (When)

   _____

6. The first plane stayed in the air for a few seconds. (How many seconds)

   _____

7. The U.S. government didn't want to see the airplane at first. (Why)

   _____

8. The Wright brothers invented the airplane. (What/Goddard)

   _____

9. Goddard took his rocket to his aunt's farm. (Why)

   _____

10. People laughed at Goddard. (Why)

    _____

ANSWERS TO EXERCISE 20:
(1) 1902, (2) a flying toy, (3) a bicycle shop, (4) in their bicycle shop, (5) in 1903, (6) 12 seconds, (7) they didn't believe it, (8) the rocket, (9) to see if it would fly, (10) they didn't believe him (they thought he was a fool)

EXERCISE 21 ABOUT YOU Check (✓) all statements that are true for you. Then read aloud one statement that you checked. Another student will ask a question with the words in parentheses ( ). Answer the question.

EXAMPLES ___✓___ I did my homework. (where)

B: Where did you do your homework?
A: I did my homework in the library.

___✓___ I got married. (when)

B: When did you get married?
A: I got married six years ago.

1. _____ I graduated from high school. (when)

2. _____ I studied biology. (when)

3. _____ I bought an English dictionary. (where)

4. _____ I left my country. (when)

5. _____ I came to the U.S. (why)

6. _____ I brought my clothes to the U.S. (what else)

7. _____ I rented an apartment. (where)

8. _____ I started to study English. (when)

9. _____ I chose this college. (why)

10. _____ I found my apartment. (when)

11. _____ I needed to learn English. (when)

12. _____ I got married. (when)

EXERCISE 22 ABOUT YOU Check (✓) which of these things you did when you were a child. Make an affirmative or negative statement about one of these items. Another student will ask a question about your statement.

EXAMPLE _____ I attended public school.

A: I didn't attend public school.
B: Why didn't you attend public school?
A: My parents wanted to give me a religious education.

1. _____ I participated in a sport.
2. _____ I enjoyed school.
3. _____ I got good grades in school.
4. _____ I got an allowance.[11]
5. _____ I lived with my grandparents.
6. _____ I took music lessons.
7. _____ I had a pet.
8. _____ I lived on a farm.
9. _____ I played soccer.
10. _____ I studied English.
11. _____ I had a bike.
12. _____ I thought about my future.

8.11 | Questions About the Subject

Examples			Explanation
Subject	Verb	Complement	When we ask a question about the subject, we use the past-tense form, not the base form. We don't use *did* in the question.
Someone	invented	the rocket.	
Who	invented	the rocket?	
			Compare
Some people	laughed	at Goddard.	What **did** the Wright Brothers **invent?**
How many people	laughed	at Goddard?	Who **invented** the airplane?
Something	happened	to Amelia's plane.	Why **did** people **laugh** at Goddard?
What	happened	to Amelia's plane?	Who **laughed** at Goddard?
			When **did** the accident **happen?**
			What **happened?**

[11]An *allowance* is money children get from their parents, usually once a week.

EXERCISE 23   Choose the correct words to answer these questions about the subject. (The answers are at the bottom of the page.)

EXAMPLE   Who invented the airplane? ((The Wright brothers,) Goddard, Lindbergh)

1. Which country sent the first rocket into space? (the U.S., China, Russia)

2. Who walked on the moon in 1969? (an American, a Russian, a Canadian)

3. Who sent up the first rocket? (The Wright brothers, Goddard, Lindbergh)

4. Who disappeared in 1937? (Earhart, Goddard, Lindbergh)

5. Who won money for flying across the Atlantic Ocean? (Earhart, Lindbergh, Goddard)

6. Which president showed interest in the Wright brothers' airplane? (T. Roosevelt, Lincoln, Wilson)

7. Which newspaper said that Goddard was a fool? (*Chicago Tribune, Washington Post, New York Times*)

EXERCISE 24   Read one of the *who* questions below. Someone will volunteer an answer. Then ask the person who answered "I did" a related question.

EXAMPLES   A: Who went to the bank last week?
B: I did.

A: Why did you go to the bank?
B: I went there to buy a money order.

1. Who brought a dictionary to class today?

2. Who drank coffee this morning?

3. Who wrote a composition last night?

4. Who watched TV this morning?

5. Who came to the U.S. alone?

6. Who made a long distance call last night?

7. Who studied English before coming to the U.S.?

8. Who bought a newspaper today?

ANSWERS TO EXERCISE 23:
(1) Russia, (2) an American, (3) Goddard, (4) Earhart, (5) Lindbergh, (6) T. Roosevelt, (7) *New York Times*

EXERCISE 25 *Combination Exercise* Fill in the blanks in this conversation between two students about their past.

A: I _____was born_____ in Mexico. I _____
(example: born)   (1 come)

to the U.S. ten years ago. Where _____ born?
                                        (2 be)

B: In El Salvador. But my family _____ to Guatemala
                                          (3 move)

when I _____ ten years old.
              (4 be)

A: Why _____ to Guatemala?
                              (5 move)

B: In 1998 we _____ our home.
                        (6 lose)

A: What _____?
                  (7 happen)

B: A major earthquake _____ my town. Luckily,
                                  (8 hit)

my family was fine, but the earthquake _____
                                                (9 destroy)

our home and much of our town. We _____
                                          (10 go)

to live with cousins in Guatemala.

A: How long _____ in Guatemala?
                      (11 stay)

B: I stayed there for about three years. Then I _____
                                                        (12 come)

to the U.S.

A: What about your family? _____ to the U.S. with you?
                                      (13 come)

B: No, they _____ until I _____ a job,
                      (14 wait)   (15 find)

_____ my money, and _____
          (16 save)   (17 bring)

them here later.

A: My parents _____ with me either. But my older
(18 not/come)

brother did. I _____ to go to school as soon as I
(19 start)

_____.
(20 arrive)

B: Who _____ you while you were in school?
(21 support)

A: My brother _____.
(22)

B: I _____ to school right away because I
(23 not/go)

_____ to work. Then I _____
(24 have) *(25 get)*

a grant and _____ to go to City College.
(26 start)

A: Why _____ City College?
(27 choose)

B: I chose it because it has a good ESL program.

A: Me, too.

SUMMARY OF LESSON 8

The Simple Past Tense

1. *Be*

I He She It	was in Paris.	We You They	were in Paris.
There was a problem.		There were many problems.	

AFFIRMATIVE:	He **was** in Poland.	They **were** in France.
NEGATIVE:	He **wasn't** in Russia.	They **weren't** in England.
YES/NO QUESTION:	**Was** he in Hungary?	**Were** they in Paris?
SHORT ANSWER:	No, he **wasn't**.	No, they **weren't**.
WH- QUESTION:	Where **was** he?	When **were** they in France?
NEGATIVE QUESTION:	Why **wasn't** he in Russia?	Why **weren't** they in Paris?
SUBJECT QUESTION:	Who **was** in Russia?	How many people **were** in France?

2. Other Verbs

	Regular Verb *(work)*	Irregular Verb *(buy)*
AFFIRMATIVE:	She **worked** on Saturday.	They **bought** a car.
NEGATIVE:	She **didn't work** on Sunday.	They **didn't buy** a motorcycle.
YES/NO QUESTION:	**Did** she **work** in the morning?	**Did** they **buy** an American car?
SHORT ANSWER:	Yes, she **did.**	No, they **didn't.**
WH- QUESTION:	Where **did** she **work?**	What kind of car **did** they **buy?**
NEGATIVE QUESTION:	Why **didn't** she **work** on Sunday?	Why **didn't** they **buy** an American car?
SUBJECT QUESTION:	Who **worked** on Sunday?	How many people **bought** an American car?

EDITING ADVICE

1. Use the base form, not the past-tense form, after *to*.

           buy
I wanted to ~~bought~~ a new car.

2. Review the spelling rules for adding *-ed*, and use correct spelling.

    studied
I ~~studyed~~ for the last test.

    dropped
He ~~droped~~ his pencil.

3. Use the base form after *did* or *didn't*.

        know
She didn't ~~knew~~ the answer.

          come
Did your father ~~came~~ to the U.S.?

4. Use correct word order in a question.

        your mother go
Where did ~~go your mother~~?

      did your sister buy
What ~~bought your sister~~?

5. Use *be* with *born*. (Don't add *-ed* to *born*.) Don't use *be* with *died*.

        was born
Her grandmother ~~borned~~ in Russia.

She ~~was~~ died in the U.S.

    was
Where ~~did~~ your grandfather born?

    did
Where ~~was~~ your grandfather died?

6. Check your list of verbs for irregular verbs.

      brought
I ~~bringed~~ my photos to the U.S.

      saw
I ~~seen~~ the accident yesterday.

7. Use *be* with an age.

      was
My grandfather ~~had~~ 88 years old when he died.

8. Don't confuse *was* and *were*.

      were
Where ~~was~~ you yesterday?

9. Don't use *did* in a question about the subject.

      took
Who ~~did take~~ my pencil?

LESSON 8 TEST/REVIEW

PART 1 Find the mistakes with the underlined words, and correct them. Not every sentence has a mistake. If the sentence is correct, write *C*.

              was
EXAMPLES Lindbergh ~~were~~ famous.
Lindbergh <u>was born</u> in 1902. *C*

1. Lindbergh <u>decided to flew</u> across the Atlantic.

2. The first plane <u>stay</u> in the air for 12 seconds.

3. When <u>Lindbergh crossed</u> the ocean?

4. Earhart <u>borned</u> in 1897.

5. Who <u>invented</u> the first rocket?

6. When <u>did Goddard invented</u> the rocket?

7. When <u>was Goddard died</u>?

8. When <u>was Goddard born</u>?

9. Lindbergh <u>won</u> $25,000.

10. Thousands of people <u>seen</u> Lindbergh in Paris.

11. Lindbergh <u>had</u> 25 years old when he made his historic flight.

12. Who <u>did walk</u> on the moon in 1969?

13. How many people <u>walked</u> on the moon?

14. Earhart <u>didn't returned</u> from her flight across the Pacific.

15. The Wright brothers' father <u>gave</u> his sons a flying toy.

16. Goddard's colleagues <u>didn't believed</u> him.

17. The first rocket flight <u>lasted</u> $2\frac{1}{2}$ seconds.

18. When <u>landed men</u> on the moon?

19. What <u>happened</u> to Earhart's plane?

20. Who <u>saw</u> the first moon landing?

PART 2 Write the past tense of each verb.

EXAMPLES live _____*lived*_____ feel _____*felt*_____

1. eat	_____	11. drink	_____
2. see	_____	12. build	_____
3. get	_____	13. stop	_____
4. sit	_____	14. leave	_____
5. hit	_____	15. buy	_____
6. make	_____	16. think	_____
7. take	_____	17. run	_____
8. find	_____	18. carry	_____
9. say	_____	19. sell	_____
10. read	_____	20. stand	_____

PART 3 Fill in the blanks with the negative form of the underlined verb.

EXAMPLE Lindbergh <u>worked</u> for the U.S. Mail Service. Earhart
_____*didn't work*_____ for the U.S. Mail Service.

1. There <u>were</u> trains in 1900. There _____ any airplanes.

2. The Wright brothers <u>flew</u> a plane in 1903. They _____ a plane in 1899.

3. Charles Lindbergh <u>was</u> an aviator. He _____ a president.

4. The Wright brothers <u>invented</u> the airplane. They _____ _____ the telephone.

5. Wilbur Wright <u>died</u> of typhoid fever. He _____ in a plane crash.

6. Lindbergh <u>went</u> to Paris. Earhart _____ to Paris.

7. Lindbergh <u>came</u> back from his flight. Earhart _____ back from her last flight.

8. Goddard <u>was born</u> in the nineteenth century. He _____ in the twentieth century.

9. Goddard <u>built</u> a rocket. He _____ an airplane.

10. Goddard <u>became</u> a physics professor. He _____ a pilot.

PART 4 Read each statement. Write a *yes/no* question about the words in parentheses ( ). Write a short answer.

EXAMPLE   Lindbergh crossed the ocean. (Earhart) (yes)
           Did Earhart cross the ocean? Yes, she did.

1. Wilbur Wright became famous. (Orville Wright) (yes)

   _____

2. Lindbergh was an aviator. (Goddard) (no)

   _____

3. Lindbergh flew across the Atlantic Ocean. (Earhart) (yes)

   _____

4. Lindbergh was born in the U.S. (Goddard) (yes)

   _____

5. Goddard wrote about rockets. (the Wright brothers) (no)

   _____

6. The Russians sent a man into space. (the Americans) (yes)

   _____

7. Goddard died in 1945. (Wilbur Wright) (no)

   _____

8. The U.S. put men on the moon in 1969. (Russia) (no)

   _____

9. People laughed at Goddard's ideas in 1920. (in 1969) (no)

   _____

10. Goddard thought about rockets. (about computers) (no)

    _____

PART 5 Write a *wh-* question about the words in parentheses ( ). It is not necessary to answer the questions.

EXAMPLE The Wright brothers became famous for their first airplane. (why / Lindbergh)

Why did Lindbergh become famous?

1. Earhart was born in 1897. (when / Lindbergh)

   _____

2. Thomas Edison invented the phonograph. (what / the Wright brothers)

   _____

3. Thomas Edison invented the phonograph. (who / the airplane)

   _____

4. Lindbergh crossed the ocean in 1927. (when / Earhart)

   _____

5. Lindbergh got money for his flight. (how much)

   _____

6. Earhart wanted to fly around the world. (why)

   _____

7. Many people saw Lindbergh in Paris. (how many people)

   _____

8. Goddard's colleagues didn't believe his ideas. (why)

   _____

9. Wilbur Wright died in 1912. (when / Orville Wright)

   _____

10. A president examined Goddard's ideas. (what)

    _____

Classroom Activities

1. In a small group or with the entire class, interview a foreign student about his or her first experiences in the U.S.

    EXAMPLES   Where did you live when you arrived?
    Who picked you up from the airport?
    Who helped you in the first few weeks?
    What was your first impression of the U.S.?

2. Find a partner from another country to interview. Ask questions about the circumstances that brought him or her to the U.S. and the conditions of his or her life after he or she arrived. Write your conversation. Use Exercise 25 as your model.

    EXAMPLE   A: When did you leave your country?
    B: I left Ethiopia five years ago.
    A: Did you come directly to the U.S.?
    B: No. First I went to Sudan.
    A: Why did you leave Ethiopia?

3. **Game:** Who and When

    Part A. On left side of the page, there are questions about famous people. On the right side of the page are some names of famous people. Work with a partner and see how many you can match. (You can find the answers on page 262.) The first one has been done for you.

    a. Who invented the rocket?   4
    b. Who discovered America?
    c. Who painted the Mona Lisa?
    d. Who wrote *Romeo and Juliet*?
    e. Who was the first person to walk on the moon?
    f. Who was the first person in space?
    g. Which president freed the slaves?
    h. Who composed *The Magic Flute*?
    i. Who invented the phonograph?
    j. Who was the first president of the U.S.?
    k. Who became president after Reagan and before Clinton?
    l. Who invented the telephone?

    1. Leonardo da Vinci
    2. Yuri Gagarin
    3. William Shakespeare
    4. Robert Goddard
    5. Thomas Edison
    6. George Washington
    7. George Bush
    8. Pablo Picasso
    9. Alexander Graham Bell
    10. Johann Sebastian Bach
    11. Christopher Columbus
    12. Neil Armstrong
    13. Wolfgang Mozart
    14. Abraham Lincoln

Part B. Take each question from Part A and write a question using *when*. Try to guess the answer by choosing one of the years given. (You can find the answers on page 262.)

EXAMPLE   When did Goddard invent the rocket?

a. 1903	1914	(1926)	1935
b. 1215	1385	1492	1620
c. 1325	1503	1625	1788
d. 1596	1675	1801	1865
e. 1957	1960	1969	1972
f. 1957	1960	1969	1970
g. 1834	1850	1865	1899
h. 1623	1688	1699	1791
i. 1877	1899	1902	1920
j. 1620	1724	1789	1825
k. 1985	1989	1990	1992
l. 1845	1877	1910	1935

4. Finish these statements five different ways. Then find a partner and compare your sentences to your partner's sentences. Did you have any sentences in common?

EXAMPLE   When I was a child, *I didn't like to do my homework.*

When I was a child, *my parents gave me a bicycle for my tenth birthday.*

When I was a child, *my nickname was "Curly."*

a. When I was a child, _____

_____

_____

_____

_____

b. Before I came to the U.S., _____

_____

_____

_____

_____

Outside Activities

1. Interview an American about a vacation he or she took. Find out where he or she went, with whom, for how long, and other related information.

2. Interview an American about a famous person he or she admires. Ask what this famous person did.

1. Using the Internet, find out something about one of the following famous people. What did he or she do? When did he or she do it? When was he or she born? Is he or she still alive? If not, when did he or she die?

   a. Marie Curie
   b. Alexander Fleming
   c. Thomas Edison
   d. Alexander Graham Bell
   e. Bill Gates
   f. Henry Ford
   g. Jonas Salk
   h. Edwin Hubble
   i. Enrico Fermi
   j. John Von Neumann
   k. Leo Baekeland
   l. Ian Wilmut

2. Find a Web site with information about the 2004 landing on Mars. Find a picture of Mars.

3. Find a Web site with information about the 2003 anniversary of the Wright brothers' first flight. What events took place?

Additional Activities at http://elt.heinle.com/gic

ANSWERS TO CLASSROOM ACTIVITY 3:
Part A: b = 11, c = 1, d = 3, e = 12, f = 2, g = 14, h = 13, i = 5, j = 6, k = 7, l = 9
Part B: a = 1926, b = 1492, c = 1503, d = 1596, e = 1969, f = 1957, g = 1865, h = 1791, i = 1877, j = 1789, k = 1989, l = 1877

GRAMMAR

Infinitives
Modals
Imperatives

CONTEXT: Smart Shopping

Getting the Best Price
Getting a Customer's Attention
Smart Shopping: Coupons, Rain Checks, and Rebates
The Customer Service Counter

9.1 | Infinitives—An Overview

Examples	Explanation
I want **to go** shopping. I need **to buy** a new DVD player. It's important **to compare** prices. It's not hard **to be** a good shopper.	An infinitive is *to* + the base form: *to go, to buy, to compare, to be*

GETTING THE BEST PRICE

Before You
Read

1. Do you like to shop for new things such as TVs, DVD players, computers, microwave ovens?

2. Do you try to compare prices in different stores before you buy an expensive item?

 Read the following article. Pay special attention to infinitives.

Are you planning **to buy** a new TV, digital camera, or DVD player? Of course you want **to get** the best price. Sometimes you see an item you like at one store and then go to another store **to compare** prices. If you find the same item at a higher price, you probably think it is necessary **to go** back to the first store **to get** the lower price. But it usually isn't. You can simply tell the salesperson in the second store that you saw the item at a better price somewhere else. Usually the salesperson will try **to match**[1] the other store's price. However, you need **to prove** that you can buy it cheaper elsewhere.[2] The proof can be an advertisement from the newspaper. If you don't have an ad, the salesperson can call the other store **to check** the price. The salesperson doesn't want you **to leave** the store without buying anything. He wants his store **to make** money. Some salespeople are happy **to call** the other store **to check** the price.

What happens if you buy something and a few days later see it cheaper at another store? Some stores will give you the difference in price for a limited period of time (such as 30 days). It's important **to keep** the receipt **to show** when you bought the item and how much you paid.

Every shopper wants **to save** money.

[1] To *match* a price means to give you an equal price.
[2] *Elsewhere* means somewhere else, another place.

9.2 | Verbs Followed by an Infinitive

We often use an infinitive after certain verbs.

Examples				Explanation
Subject	Verb	Infinitive	Complement	We use an infinitive after these verbs:
I	plan	**to buy**	a camera.	begin hope prefer
We	want	**to get**	the best price.	continue like promise
You	need	**to be**	a smart shopper.	decide love start
She	likes	**to save**	money.	expect need try
				forget plan want
They	want	**to buy**	a DVD player.	An infinitive never has an ending. It never shows tense. Only the first verb has an ending or shows tense.
We	wanted	**to buy**	a new TV.	
He	is planning	**to buy**	a microwave oven.	*Wrong:* He wanted to *bought* a new TV.

Pronunciation Notes:

1. In informal speech, *want to* is pronounced "wanna." Listen to your teacher pronounce these sentences:

   I *want to* buy a DVD.

   Do you *want to* go shopping with me?

2. In other infinitives, we often pronounce *to* like "ta" or "da" (after a vowel sound) or "a" (after a "d" sound). Listen to your teacher pronounce these sentences:

   Do you like to watch movies at home? ("ta")

   I plan to buy a new DVD player. ("ta")

   Try to get the best price. ("da")

   We decided to buy a digital camera. ("a")

   I need to compare prices. ("a")

EXERCISE 1   Circle the correct verb form to complete each sentence.

EXAMPLE   She wants (*buy*, (*to buy*,) *buys*) a new microwave oven.

1. I'm planning (*shop*, *shopping*, *to shop*) for a wide-screen TV.
2. I decided (*to spend*, *to spent*, *spent*) about $500.
3. I'm trying (*get*, *to get*, *to getting*) the best price.
4. The saleswoman forgot (*gave*, *to give*, *to gave*) me her business card.
5. Did you decide (*to buy*, *to bought*, *bought*) a DVD player?
6. You need (*be*, *to be*, *are*) a smart shopper.

EXERCISE **2**   ABOUT YOU Make a sentence about yourself with the words given. Use an appropriate tense. You may find a partner, and compare your sentences to your partner's sentences.

EXAMPLES   like / eat

I like to eat pizza.

learn / speak

I learned to speak German when I was a child.

try / find

I'm trying to find a bigger apartment.

1. love / go

_____

2. like / play

_____

3. need / have

_____

4. expect / get

_____

5. want / go

_____

6. plan / buy

_____

7. need / understand

_____

8. not need / have

_____

9. try / learn

_____

EXERCISE 3 ABOUT YOU Ask a question with the words given in the present tense. Another student will answer.

EXAMPLE like / travel

A: Do you like to travel?
B: Yes, I do.   OR   No, I don't.

1. expect / pass this course

2. plan / graduate soon

3. plan / transfer to another college

4. like / read

5. like / study grammar

6. try / understand Americans

7. try / learn idioms

8. expect / leave this country

EXERCISE 4 ABOUT YOU Ask a question with "Do you want to . . . ?" and the words given. Another student will answer. Then ask a *wh-* question with the words in parentheses ( ) whenever possible.

EXAMPLE buy a car (why)

A: Do you want to buy a car?
B: Yes, I do.   OR   No, I don't.

A: Why do you want to buy a car?
B: I don't like public transportation.

1. take a computer course next semester (why)

2. move (why) (when)

3. leave this country (why) (when)

4. get a job/get another job (what kind of job)

5. become an American citizen (why)

6. transfer to a different school (why)

7. take another English course next semester (which course)

8. learn another language (which language)

9. review the last lesson (why)

9.3 | *It* + *Be* + Adjective + Infinitive

We often use an infinitive with sentences beginning with an impersonal *it*.

Examples				Explanation
It	*Be (+ n't)*	Adjective	Infinitive Phrase	An infinitive can follow these adjectives:
It	is	important	**to save** your receipt.	dangerous hard good
It	is	easy	**to shop.**	possible difficult expensive
It	isn't	necessary	**to go** back to the first store.	impossible easy fun
				important necessary

EXERCISE 5   Complete each statement.

EXAMPLE   It's expensive to own *a big car*. _____

1. It's important to learn _____

2. It's hard to pronounce _____

3. It's hard to lift _____

4. It's necessary to have _____

5. It's easy to learn _____

6. It's hard to learn _____

7. It isn't necessary to know _____

EXERCISE 6   Complete each statement with an infinitive phrase.

EXAMPLE   It's easy *to ride a bike.* _____

1. It's fun _____

2. It's impossible _____

3. It's possible _____

4. It's necessary _____

5. It's dangerous _____

6. It's hard _____

7. It isn't good _____

8. It isn't necessary _____

9.4 | *Be* + Adjective + Infinitive

We often use an infinitive after certain adjectives.

Examples				Explanation
Subject	*Be*	Adjective	Infinitive Phrase	We can use an infinitive after these adjectives:
I	am	ready	**to buy** a camera.	
The salesman	is	glad	**to help** you.	happy afraid lucky
He	is	prepared	**to make** a sale.	sad prepared proud
				glad ready

EXERCISE 7 Fill in the blanks.

EXAMPLE   I'm lucky *to be in the U.S.*

1. Americans are lucky _____

2. I'm proud _____

3. I'm happy _____

4. I'm sometimes afraid _____

5. I'm not afraid _____

6. Are the students prepared _____

7. Is the teacher ready _____

EXERCISE 8 ABOUT YOU Answer the following questions. (You may work with a partner and ask and answer with your partner.)

1. Are you happy to be in this country?

2. Is it important to know English or another language in your country?

3. Are you afraid to make a mistake when you speak English?

4. Is it possible to find a job without knowing any English?

5. Is it easy to learn English grammar?

6. Is it important to wear a seat belt when you are a passenger in a car?

7. Is it necessary to have a computer?

8. Were you sad to leave your country?

9. Are you prepared to have a test on this lesson?

9.5 | Using an Infinitive to Show Purpose

Examples	Explanation
I went to a store **to buy** a digital camera. I went to a second store **to compare** prices. The saleswoman called the first store **to check** the price.	We use an infinitive to show the purpose of an action. Do not use *for* to show purpose. *Wrong:* I went to a store *for buy* a digital camera.
I use a digital camera **to** e-mail photos to my friends. I use a digital camera **in order to** e-mail photos to my friends.	*To* for purpose is the short form of *in order to*.

EXERCISE 9 Fill in the blanks to show purpose.

EXAMPLE I bought a phone card to *call my friends.* _____

1. I use my dictionary to _____
2. At the end of a concert, people applaud to _____
3. He went to an appliance store to _____
4. She worked overtime to _____
5. I bought the Sunday newspaper to _____
6. You need to show your driver's license to _____
7. You can use a hammer to _____
8. Some people join a health club to _____
9. On a computer, you use the mouse to _____
10. When you return an item to a store, take your receipt to _____
   _____

EXERCISE 10 Fill in the blanks to complete this conversation.

A: Do you want to see my new digital camera?
B: Wow. It's so small. Does it take good pictures?

A: Absolutely. I use this camera _____*to take*_____ all my pictures
                                  (example)

now. I never use my old one anymore.
B: Aren't digital cameras expensive?

A: Not anymore. I went online _____ prices. Then I
                                        (1)

went to several stores in this city _____ the best price.
                                                          (2)

B: Do you take a lot of pictures?

A: Oh, yes. And I put them on my computer _____
(3)

them by e-mail to my family back home.

B: Do you ever make prints of your pictures?

A: Of course. I bought some high-quality glossy paper

_____ prints for my family album.
(4)

B: I still like my old camera.

A: But you have to take the film to a photo place and then you have to

wait _____ if the pictures are good or not. With my
(5)

digital camera, I can see immediately if the pictures are good.

B: Is it hard to use the camera?

A: At first I had to read the manual carefully _____
(6)

how to take good pictures and transfer them to my computer.
But now it's easy. I'll take a picture of you. Smile.

B: My eyes are closed in the picture. Take another picture of me.

A: OK. This one's better. But I don't like the background. I can push this

button _____ the background. It's too dark. I can
(7)

push this button _____ the color brighter.
(8)

B: Which button do you push _____ me more handsome?
(9)

Before You
Read

1. Do you try free samples of food in supermarkets?

2. Do you ever go to the movies early in the day to get a cheaper ticket?

 Read the following article. Pay special attention to objects before an infinitive.

Stores use several techniques to get your business. Did you ever go to a food store and see someone giving away free samples? Many supermarkets **encourage you to buy** a product by giving you a free sample. They think that if you try this product, maybe you will buy it. Often they encourage you even more by giving you a coupon for the product.

Sometimes a store will advertise two for the price of one. This is a marketing technique to get your interest. After you come into the store for the sale item, the manager **wants you to do** the rest of your shopping there, too.

Movie theaters will lower their price in the early hours. This is because most people don't think of going to a movie early in the day. Both you and the movie theater benefit when you take advantage of the reduced price. You help fill the theater and get a cheap ticket in return.

Another way to get customer attention is with good service. Sometimes as you're leaving a store, a salesperson may ask you, "Do you **want me to take** this out to your car for you?" There is no extra charge for such service.

With so much competition between businesses, owners and managers have to use all kinds of techniques to get our attention and **encourage us to shop** at their store and return often.

9.6 | Object Before an Infinitive

Examples	Explanation
They **like you to try** the free sample. Do you **want me to carry** this out to your car for you? They **want us to do** all our shopping in one store. I **expect salespeople to be** courteous. I **expect them to be** helpful, too.	After *like, want, need, expect,* and *encourage,* we can use a noun or object pronoun (*me, you, him, her, it, us, them*) + an infinitive.

EXERCISE 11 Circle the correct words in parentheses ( ) to complete each conversation.

CONVERSATION 1

Salesman: Do you want ((me,) I) (*to help, help*) you find something?

                (example)   *(1)*

Mother: Yes. We could use your help. Our daughter wants (*we, us*)

                                                                  (2)

(*bought, to buy*) her a new cell phone. We don't know which

  (3)

plan to buy.

Salesman: How many minutes a month does she talk on the phone?

Mother: She never stops talking on the phone. I want (*her to use,*

                                                    (4)

that she use) it just for emergencies, but she chats with her

friends all the time.

Salesman: Here's a plan I want (*you to consider, that you consider*).

                                             (5)

It has unlimited calls at night and on weekends.

Mother: You don't understand. We want (*her, she*) to use the phone

                                                   (6)

less, not more.

CONVERSATION 2

Man: I'm going to buy a digital camera on Saturday. I need

(*that you, you to*) come with me.

    (1)

Friend: Why? How do you want (*that I, me to*) help you?

                               (2)

Man: You already have a digital camera, so you can give me advice.

CONVERSATION 3

Husband: Oh, look. There's free food over there. Do you want

(*me to get, that I get*) you a little hotdog?
   (1)

Wife: No. They just want (*us, we*) to spend our money on things
                              (2)

we don't need.

CONVERSATION 4

Grocery Clerk: Excuse me, miss. You have a lot of bags. Do you want

(*me, I*) (*to help, helping*) you take them to your car?
 (1)   (2)

Shopper: Thanks. My husband's in the car. I wanted (*him, he*)
                                                        (3)

(*to help, helped*) me, but he hates shopping. He prefers
 (4)

to wait in the car. Besides, he has a bad back, and I

don't want (*that he, him to*) lift anything. We're having a
           (5)

dinner party on Saturday and we invited 20 guests, but I . . .

Grocery Clerk: Uh, excuse me. I hear my boss calling me. He needs me

now (*to give, giving*) him some help.
    (6)

EXERCISE 12   Fill in the blanks with an object pronoun and the infinitive of the word in parentheses ( ).

EXAMPLE   **A:** What should we do for homework?

            B: I'd like _____*you to write*_____ a composition about shopping.
                                       (write)

1. **A:** Do you want the teacher to explain the grammar again?

     B: Yes. And I want _____ more slowly.
                                   (speak)

2. **A:** Do your parents want you to be more independent?

     B: Yes. They want _____ how to drive.
                                   (learn)

3. **A:** Do you expect your parents to buy you a car?

     B: No, but I expect _____ my insurance.
                                   (pay for)

4. **A:** Do you need my help on Saturday?

     B: Yes. I need _____ some of my furniture
                                 (move)

           into the basement.

5. **A:** Where's your girlfriend?

     B: I don't know. I expected _____ here
                                  (be)

           two hours ago, but she's always late.

6. **A:** Our teacher gives so much homework. He expects _____
              _____ one composition a week.
                                 (write)

     B: And he doesn't want _____ late
                                   (come)

           to class. If we come ten minutes late, he marks us absent.

7. **A:** Did your brother go on the trip with you?

     B: No, he didn't. We wanted _____,
                                  (go)

           but he needed to stay home.

9.7 | Overview of Modals

List of Modals	Facts About Modals

can
could
should
will
would
may
might
must
	1. Modals are different from other verbs because they don't have an *-s, -ed,* or *-ing* ending.
	    He **can** compare prices. (NOT: He *cans*)
	2. Modals are different from other verbs because we don't use an infinitive after a modal.[3] We use the base form.
	    Compare:
	        He **wants to buy** a digital camera.
	        He **might buy** a digital camera.
	3. To form the negative, put *not* after the modal.
	        You **should not** throw away the receipt.
	        Hurry! These prices **may not** last.
	4. Some verbs are like modals in meaning: *have to, be able to*
	        You **must** return the item within 30 days. = You **have to** return the item within 30 days.
	        He **can't** get a credit card. = He **is not able to** get a credit card.

Compare Affirmative Statements and Questions

Wh- Word	Modal	Subject	Modal	Base Form	Complement	Short Answer
		You	should	buy	a new TV.	
	Should	you		buy	a DVD player?	No, you shouldn't.
What	should	you		buy?		
		Who	should	buy	a new TV?	
		She	can	compare	prices.	
	Can	she		compare	prices online?	Yes, she can.
How	can	she		compare	prices online?	
		Who	can	compare	prices?	

Compare Negative Statements and Questions

Wh- Word	Modal	Subject	Modal	Base Form	Complement
		He	shouldn't	buy	a digital camera.
Why	shouldn't	he		buy	a digital camera?

[3] Exception: *ought to. Ought to* means *should.*

Before You **Read**

1. Do you see coupons in magazines and newspapers? Do you use them?

2. Do you see signs that say "rebate" on store products? Do you see signs that say "Buy one, get one free"?

MANUFACTURER'S COUPON	DO NOT DOUBLE	EXPIRES 12/12/07

Save 50¢

Tony T's
Homemade
Pizza Sauce

CONSUMER: Limit one coupon per purchase.
RETAILER: Please redeem for face value as specified. Any other use constitutes fraud.
Cash value: 1/100 cent.

4677000072

GTG
Good Time Grocery   No. 7942

Rain Check

Date _____

Item _____ Item size _____

Item quantity _____ Item Price _____ Discount _____

Coupon UPC _____ Expiration _____

Good toward similar item of equal or lesser value

Authorization _____

Read the following article. Pay special attention to modals and related expressions.

Do you ever receive coupons in the mail? Manufacturers often send coupons to shoppers. They want people to try their products. If you always use the same toothpaste and the manufacturer gives you a coupon for a different toothpaste, you **might** try the new brand.[4] Coupons have an expiration date. You **should** pay attention to this date because you **cannot** use the coupon after this date.

Stores have weekly specials. But there is usually a limit. If you see a sign that says, "Eggs, 69¢ a dozen. Limit 2," this means you **can** only buy two dozen at this price. If you see a sign that says, "3 for $1.00," you **don't have to** buy three items to get the special price. If you buy only one, you **will** pay 34¢.

What **should** you do if a store has a special but you **can't** find this item on the shelf? If this item is sold out, you **can** go to the customer service desk and ask for a rain check. A rain check allows you to buy this item at the sale price even after the sale is over. A rain check usually has an expiration date. You **must** buy this item by the expiration date if you want to receive the sale price.

If you see a sign that says "rebate," this means that you **can** get money back from the manufacturer. You **have to** mail the proof of purchase and the cash register receipt to the manufacturer to prove that you bought this product. Also you **have to** fill out a small form. The manufacturer **will** return some money to you. It **may** take six to eight weeks to receive this money.

These sales techniques help manufacturers get your attention, but they also help you save money.

---

[4] The brand is the company name.

Rebate Form

_____

Name   Address

_____

City/State   Zip   Phone

Product Name: _____
Size/Weight: _____
Price: _____
Store where Purchased: _____
Date of Purchase: _____
Proof of Purchase attached: yes / no

9.8 | Can

Examples	Explanation
I **can** find many ways to save money. I **can** explain how to use a rebate.	Ability
If you use coupons, you **can** save money. If the item is sold out, you **can** get a raincheck.	Possibility
The sign says, "Eggs 69¢. Limit 2." You **can** only buy two cartons of eggs at the special price. You **can** return an item within 30 days.	Permission
I can't afford to eat in a restaurant every day. **Can** you **afford** to buy lobster?	*Can afford to* means have enough money to buy something.
You **cannot** buy more than the limited quantity. You **can't** use a coupon after the expiration date.	The negative of *can* is *cannot*. The contraction is *can't*.

Pronunciation Notes:

1. In affirmative statements, we usually pronounce *can* /kən/. In negative statements, we pronounce *can't* /kænt/. Sometimes it is hard to hear the final **t**, so we must pay attention to the vowel sound and the stress to hear the difference between *can* and *can't*. Listen to your teacher pronounce these sentences:

   I *can* gó. /kən/

   I *cán't* go. /kænt/

2. In a short answer, we pronounce *can* /kæn/.

   Can you help me later?

   Yes, I *can*. /kæn/

EXERCISE 13 ABOUT YOU Fill in the blanks with *can* or *can't* to tell about your abilities.

EXAMPLES I ____can____ drive a car.

I ____can't____ fly a plane.

1. I _____ read without glasses.

2. I _____ speak Spanish.

3. I _____ drive a car.

4. I _____ play tennis.

5. I _____ sing well.

6. I _____ change a tire.

7. I _____ save money.

8. I _____ read the newspaper without a dictionary.

EXERCISE 14 ABOUT YOU Ask a question about a classmate's abilities with the words given. Another student will answer.

EXAMPLE speak Spanish

A: Can you speak Spanish?
B: Yes, I can. OR No, I can't.

1. write with your left hand
2. type without looking at the keyboard
3. use a computer
4. play chess
5. ski

6. play the piano
7. speak French
8. bake a cake
9. play the guitar
10. sew

EXERCISE 15 Write down one thing that you can do well. Share your answer with a partner or with the entire class.

_____

EXERCISE 16 These sentences are true about an American supermarket. Check (✓) which ones are true about a supermarket in another country.

1. _____ You can use coupons.

2. _____ You can sometimes buy two items for the price of one.

3. _____ You can cash a check.

4. _____ You can buy stamps.

5. _____ You can get money back from a manufacturer.

6. _____ You can pay by check or credit card.

7. _____ You can't bargain[5] for the price.

8. _____ You can return an item if you're not satisfied. You can get your money back.

9. _____ You can get free bags (paper or plastic).

10. _____ You can use a shopping cart. Small children can sit in the cart.

11. _____ If you have a small number of items, you can go to a special lane.

12. _____ You can shop 24 hours a day (in some supermarkets).

9.9 | Should

Examples	Explanation
You **should** use coupons to save money. What **should** I do if the item is sold out? You **should** compare prices before you buy.	We use *should* to give or ask for advice.
You **should not** waste your money. You **shouldn't** buy things you don't need.	The negative of *should* is *should not*. The contraction is *shouldn't*. We use the negative to give advice or a warning.

EXERCISE 17 If someone from another country is going to live in the U.S., what advice can you give him or her about shopping? Work with a partner to write six sentences of advice.

EXAMPLES *You should always look at the expiration date on a food product.*

You should shop for summer clothes in July and August. Summer clothes are cheapest at that time.

1. _____

2. _____

3. _____

4. _____

5. _____

6. _____

---

[5] To *bargain* for a price means to make an offer lower than the price the seller is asking.

EXERCISE 18   What should a person do about each of the following health problems? Write a sentence of advice for each one. (You may work with a partner.)

EXAMPLE   He has a headache.

He should take an aspirin and lie down.

1. He has a stomachache. _____

2. She has a cut. _____

3. He has a burn. _____

4. She has a cold. _____

5. He has a fever. _____

6. She has a toothache. _____

7. He's always nervous. _____

8. She has a backache. _____

EXERCISE 19   A father is giving his son advice. What advice do you think he is giving? Write sentences with *should*. (You may work with a partner.)

EXAMPLES   You eat hot dogs, fries, and colas all the time.

You should eat more fruits and vegetables.

You shouldn't eat so much junk food.

1. You spend too much time at the computer.

    _____

2. You always ask me for money.

    _____

3. You always wait until the last minute to study for a test.

    _____

4. Your hair is too long.

    _____

5. Your clothes look dirty.

    _____

6. You talk for hours on the phone with your friends.

    _____

7. You never clean your room. It's a mess!⁶

   _____

8. You never listen to your mother when she tells you something.

   _____

9. You want your driver's license, but you're not responsible.

   _____

EXERCISE 20 Check (✓) if you agree or disagree about what schoolchildren should or shouldn't do. Discuss your answers with the whole class or in a small group.

	I agree.	I disagree.
1. Children should go to a teacher when they have a family problem.		
2. They shouldn't play video games.		
3. They should select their own TV programs.		
4. They shouldn't trust all adults.		
5. They should always tell the truth.		
6. They should be responsible for taking care of younger sisters and brothers.		
7. They should select their own friends.		
8. They should always obey their parents and teachers.		
9. They should learn to use a computer.		
10. They should study a foreign language.		
11. They should help their parents with small jobs in the house.		

⁶ To be a *mess* means to be disorganized.

EXERCISE 21   Read each statement. Then ask a question with the word in parentheses ( ). Another student will answer.

EXAMPLE   The students should do the homework. (why)

A: Why should they do the homework?
B: It helps them understand the lesson.

1. The students should study the lessons. (why)
2. The teacher should take attendance. (when)
3. The students should bring their textbook to class. (what else)
4. I should study modals. (why)
5. We should register for classes early. (why)
6. The teacher should speak clearly. (why)
7. The students shouldn't talk during a test. (why)
8. We shouldn't do the homework in class. (where)
9. The teacher should announce a test ahead of time. (why)

9.10 | *Must*

Examples	Explanation
To get a rebate, you **must** send the proof of purchase. You **must** include your receipt.	We use *must* to talk about rules and laws. *Must* has a very official, formal tone.
You **must not** use the handicapped parking space if you don't have permission. The store **mustn't** sell a product after its expiration date.	For the negative, use *must not*. The contraction is *mustn't*. *Must not* and *cannot* are very close in meaning. You *must not* park in the handicapped space = You *cannot* park in the handicapped space.

EXERCISE 22 Here are some rules in a supermarket. Fill in the blanks with *must* or *must not*.

1. Employees in the deli department _____ wear a hairnet or a hat.

2. When employees use the washroom, they _____ wash their hands before returning to work.

3. Employees _____ touch food with their bare hands.

   They _____ wear plastic gloves.

4. The store _____ sell food after the expiration date.

5. Customers _____ take shopping carts out of the parking lot.

EXERCISE 23 Name something.

EXAMPLE Name something you must have if you want to drive.
You must have a license.

1. Name something you must do or have if you want to leave the country.

2. Name something you must not carry onto an airplane.

3. Name something you must not do in the classroom.

4. Name something you must not do during a test.

5. Name something you must not do or have in your apartment.

6. Name something you must do or have to enter an American university.

7. Name something you must do when you drive a car.

8. Name something you must not do when you drive a car.

9.11 | Have To

	Examples	Explanation
Affirmative	I don't have enough milk. I **have to** go shopping. If you want to return an item, you **have to** show a receipt.	*Have to* is similar in meaning to *must*. *Have to* is less formal. We use it for personal obligations.
Negative	A: The DVD player was cheaper in the first store. Let's go back there. B: You **don't have to** go back there. Just tell the salesperson, and she'll probably give you the same price. If you sample food in a supermarket, you **don't have to** buy it.	*Don't have to* means it's not necessary.

EXERCISE 24 Tell if you *have to* or *don't have to* do these things at this school. (Remember: *don't have to* means it's not necessary.)

EXAMPLES study before a test
I have to study before a test.

study in the library
I don't have to study in the library. I can study at home.

1. wear a suit to school
2. come to class on time
3. stand up to ask a question in class
4. do homework
5. notify the teacher if I'm going to be absent
6. call the teacher "professor"
7. raise my hand to answer
8. take a final exam
9. wear a uniform
10. buy my own textbooks

EXERCISE 25 Ask your teacher what he or she *has to* or *doesn't have to* do.

EXAMPLE work on Saturdays

A: Do you have to work on Saturdays?
B: Yes, I do. OR No, I don't.

1. take attendance
2. give students grades
3. call students by their last names
4. wear a suit
5. work in the summer
6. have a master's degree
7. work on Saturdays
8. come to this school every day

EXERCISE 26 If you are from another country, write four sentences about students and teachers in your country. Tell what they *have to* or *don't have to* do. Use the ideas from the previous exercises. You may share your sentences with a small group or with the class.

EXAMPLE   *In my country, a student has to wear a uniform.*

1. _____
2. _____
3. _____
4. _____

EXERCISE 27 Tell what Judy *has to* or *doesn't have to* do in these situations.

EXAMPLE   Judy has a coupon for cereal. The expiration date is tomorrow. She has to *use it by tomorrow or she won't get the discount* .

1. The coupon for cereal says "Buy 2, get 50¢ off." She has to

   _____ in order to get the discount.

2. Judy has no milk in the house. She has to _____
   more milk.

3. Eggs are on sale for 89¢, limit two. She has three cartons of eggs. She

   has to _____ one of the cartons of eggs.

4. She has a rebate application. She has to fill out the application if she

   wants to get money back. She also has to _____ the
   proof-of-purchase symbol and the receipt to the manufacturer.

5. She wants to pay by check. The cashier asks for her driver's license.

   She has to _____ .

6. She has 26 items in her shopping cart. She can't go to a lane that says

   "10 items or fewer." She has to _____ another lane.

9.12 | *Must* and *Have To*

In affirmative statements, *have to* and *must* are very **similar** in meaning. In negative statements, *have to* and *must* are very **different** in meaning.

	Examples	Explanation
Affirmative	If you wish to return an item, you **must** have a receipt. You **must** send the rebate coupon by October 1. You **have to** send the rebate coupon by October 1.	Use *must* or *have to* for rules. *Must* is more formal or more official, but we can use *have to* for rules too.
	I don't have any milk. I **have to** go to the store to buy some. I need to buy a lot of things. I **have to** use a shopping cart.	Use *have to* for personal obligations or necessities.
Negative	You **must not** park in the handicapped parking space. The store **must not** sell an item after the expiration date.	*Must not* shows that something is prohibited or against the law.
	The sign says, "3 for $1.00," but you **don't have to** buy three to get the sale price. You **don't have to** pay with cash. You can use a credit or debit card.	*Don't have to* shows that something is not necessary, that there is a choice.

EXERCISE 28 Fill in the blanks with *must not* or *don't have to*.

EXAMPLES You _____*must not*_____ take a shopping cart out of the parking lot.

We _____*don't have to*_____ shop every day. We can shop once a week.

1. If you sample a product, you _____ buy it.

2. If you have just a few items, you _____ use a shopping cart. You can use a basket.

3. If you have a lot of items in your shopping cart, you _____ _____ use the checkout that says "10 items or fewer."

4. You _____ park in the handicapped parking space if you don't have permission.

5. You _____ take your own bags to the supermarket. Someone will give you bags for your groceries.

9.13 | *Might/May* and *Will*

Examples	Explanation
I have a coupon for a new toothpaste. I **might** buy it. I **may** like it. A rebate check **might** take six to eight weeks.	*May* and *might* have the same meaning. They show possibility. Compare *maybe* (adverb) and *may* or *might* (modal verbs): *Maybe it will rain* tomorrow. It *may rain* tomorrow. It *might rain* tomorrow.
Those cookies taste great, but they **may not** be healthy for you. I **might not** have time to shop next week, so I'll buy enough for two weeks.	The negative of *may* is *may not*. The negative of *might* is *might not*. We do not make a contraction for *may not* and *might not*.
If the price is 3 for $1.00, you **will** pay 34¢ for one. If the sign says "Two for one," the store **will** give you one item for free.	*Will* shows certainty about the future.

EXERCISE 29   Tell what may or might happen in the following situations.

EXAMPLE   Meg needs to go shopping. She's not sure what her kids want. They might
_____want a new kind of_____ cereal.

1. She's not sure if she should buy the small size or the large size of
   cereal. The large size may _____ cheaper.

2. If she sends in the rebate form today, she might _____
   a check in four or five weeks.

3. The store sold all the coffee that was on sale. The clerk said, "We
   might _____ more coffee tomorrow."

4. Bananas are so expensive this week. If she waits until next week, the
   price may _____.

5. The milk has an expiration date of June 27. Today is June 27. She's
   not going to buy the milk because it might _____.

6. She's not sure what brand of toothpaste she should buy. She might
   buy the one she usually buys, or she might _____.

EXERCISE 30   Tell what *may* or *might* happen in the following situations.
If you think the result is certain, use *will*.

EXAMPLES   If you don't put money in a parking meter, _____you might get a_____

_____parking ticket._____

If you are absent from tests, _____you may not pass the course._____
If you don't pass the tests, _____you'll fail the course._____

1. If you drive too fast, _____

2. If you get a lot of tickets in one year, _____

3. If you don't water your plants, _____

4. If you don't take the final exam, _____

5. If you don't lock the door of your house, _____

6. If you eat too much, _____

7. If you work hard and save your money, _____

8. If the weather is nice this weekend, _____

9. If you park in the handicapped space without permission, _____

_____

9.14 | Making Requests

Examples	Explanation
Park over there. **Don't park** in the handicapped space. **Send** the rebate coupon soon. **Do not** wait.	We can use imperatives to make a request. The imperative is the base form of the verb. The subject is *you*, but we don't include *you* in the sentence. For a negative, put *don't (do not)* before the verb.
May I see your driver's license? **Could** you give me change for a dollar?	We also use modals to make requests. Modals give the request a more polite tone.

THE CUSTOMER SERVICE COUNTER

Before You
Read

1. Do you have a check-cashing card at a local supermarket?

2. Do you pay with cash when you shop in a supermarket?

Read the following conversation, first between two friends (A and B), and then between A and a customer service representative (C). Pay special attention to requests.

A: I need to cash a check.
B: **Let's go** to the customer service counter at Dominick's. Someone told me they have a check-cashing service there.
A: **Could** you drive?
B: **Why don't we** walk? It's not far.

. . . *At the customer service counter* . . .

C: **Can** I help you?
A: Yes. **I'd like** to cash a check.
C: Do you have a check-cashing card?
A: No, I don't.
C: Here's an application. Please **fill** it out.
A: I don't have a pen. **Could** I use your pen?
C: Here's a pen.
A: Thanks.

. . . A few minutes later . . .

A: Here's my application.

C: **May** I see your driver's license?

A: Here it is. Did I fill out the application correctly?

C: No. Please **don't write** in the gray box. You made another mistake, too. You wrote the day before the month. Please **write** the month before the day. For August 29, we write 8/29, not 29/8. **Why don't you fill out** another form? Here's a clean one.

A: Thanks.

. . . A few minutes later . . .

A: Here it is. **Could** you check to see if I filled it out right this time?

C: You forgot to sign your name. Please **sign** your name on the bottom line.

A: OK. **Could** you cash my check now?

C: I'm sorry, sir. We have to wait for approval. We'll send you your check-cashing card in the mail in a week to ten days. Can I help you with anything else?

A: Yes. **I'd like** to buy some stamps.

C: Here you are. Anything else?

A: No. That's it.

C: Have a nice day.

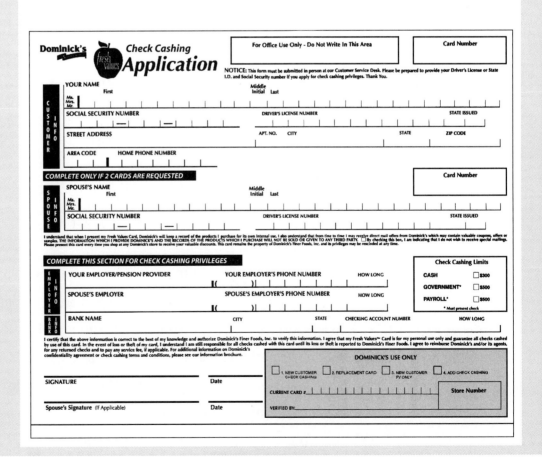

9.15 | Imperatives

Imperatives give instructions, warnings, and suggestions.

Examples	Explanation
Please **sign** your name at the bottom. **Write** the month before the day. **Be** careful when you fill out the application. **Don't write** in the gray box.	We use the imperative form to give instructions.
Stand at attention. **Don't move**! You're under arrest.	We use the imperative to give a command.
Watch out! There's a bee on your nose. **Don't move**.	We use the imperative to give a warning.
Always do your best. **Never give** up.	We use the imperative to give encouragement. We can put *always* and *never* before an imperative.
Have a nice day. **Make** yourself at home.	We use the imperative in certain conversational expressions.
Shut up! **Mind** your own business!	We use the imperative in some angry, impolite expressions.
Let's get an application for check cashing. **Let's not** make any mistakes.	*Let's* = *let us*. We use *let's* + the base form to make a suggestion. The negative form is *let's not*. *Let's* includes the speaker.

EXERCISE **31** Fill in the blanks with an appropriate imperative verb (affirmative or negative) to give instructions.

EXAMPLE   _____*Go*_____ to the customer service desk for an application.

1. _____ out the application in pen.

2. _____ a pencil to fill out an application.

3. _____ all the information in clear letters.

4. If you have a middle name, _____ your middle initial.

5. _____ anything in the box in the lower right corner.

6. If you are not married, _____ out the second part.

7. When you give your telephone number, always _____ your area code.

8. _____ your last name before your first name on this application.

9. _____ the application to a person at the customer service counter.

EXERCISE **32** Choose one of the activities from the following list (or choose a different one, if you like). Use imperatives to give instructions on how to do the activity. (You may work with a partner.)

EXAMPLE get from school to your house

Take the number 53 bus north from the corner of Elm Street. Ask the driver for a transfer. Get off at Park Avenue. Cross the street and wait for a number 18 bus.

1. hang a picture
2. change a tire
3. fry an egg
4. prepare your favorite recipe
5. hem a skirt
6. write a check
7. make a deposit at the bank
8. tune a guitar
9. get a driver's license
10. use a washing machine
11. prepare for a job interview
12. get from school to your house
13. get money from a cash machine (automatic teller)
14. do a search on the Internet
15. send a text message

EXERCISE **33** Work with a partner. Write a list of command forms that the teacher often uses in class. Read your sentences to the class.

EXAMPLES *Open your books to page 10.*

Don't come late to class.

1. _____
2. _____
3. _____

EXERCISE 34 Fill in the blanks with an appropriate verb to complete this conversation.

A: I need to cash a check.

B: We need to get some groceries. Let's _____*go*_____ to the
(example)

supermarket.

A: Do you want to drive there?

B: The supermarket is not so far. Let's _____.
(1)

A: It looks like rain.

B: No problem. Let's _____ an umbrella.
(2)

A: Let's _____. It's late and the stores will close soon.
(3)

B: Don't worry. This store is open 24 hours a day.

A: We're almost out of dog food. Let's _____ a
(4)

20-pound bag.

B: Let's not _____ then. I don't want to carry a
(5)

20-pound bag home. Let's _____ instead.
(6)

EXERCISE 35 Work with a partner. Write a few suggestions for the teacher or other students in this class. Read your suggestions to the class.

EXAMPLES *Let's review verb tenses.*

Let's not speak our native languages in class.

1. _____

2. _____

3. _____

4. _____

5. _____

6. _____

9.16 | Using Modals to Make Requests and Ask Permission

An imperative form may sound too strong in some situations. Modals can make a request sound more polite.

Examples	Explanation
Would / **Could** you cash my check, please?	We use these modals to make a request. These expressions are more polite than "Cash my check."
May / **Could** / **Can** I use your pen, please?	We use these modals to ask permission. These expressions are more polite than "Give me your pen."
I **would like** to cash a check. How **would** you **like** your change?	*Would like* has the same meaning as *want*. *Would like* is softer than *want*. The contraction of *would* after a pronoun is *'d*: *I'd* like to cash a check.
Why don't you fill out another form? **Why don't we** walk to the supermarket?	Use *why don't you . . . ?* and *why don't we . . . ?* to offer suggestions.
May / **Can** I help you?	Salespeople often use these expressions to offer help to a customer.

EXERCISE 36   Read the following conversation between a salesperson (S) and a customer (C) in an electronics store. Change the underlined words to make the conversation more polite. Change the punctuation if necessary.

        May I help you?

S: <u>What do you need?</u>
     (example)

C: I want to buy a new computer. <u>Show</u> me your latest models.
   (1)   *(2)*

S: <u>Do you want</u> to see the laptops or the desktops?
      (3)

C: <u>Show</u> me the desktops.
    (4)

S: This is one of our most popular desktops.

C: <u>Turn it on.</u>
    (5)

S: It *is* on. Just hit the space bar.

C: I don't know how much memory to buy.

S: How do you use your computer?

C: We like to play games and watch movies.

S: Then <u>buy</u> this computer, which has a lot of memory and speed.
$\qquad$ (6)

C: <u>Tell</u> me the price.
$\quad$ (7)

S: We have a great deal on this one. It's $1,299. If you buy it this week, you can get a $200 rebate from the manufacturer.

C: <u>Let me take</u> it home and try it out.
$\qquad$ (8)

S: No problem. If you're not happy with it, you can return it within 30

days and get your money back. <u>Do you want</u> to buy a service contract?
$\qquad$ (9)

C: What's that?

S: If you have any problem with the computer for the next two years, we will replace it for free. The contract costs $49.99.

C: <u>Let me see</u> the service contract.
$\qquad$ (10)

S: Here's a copy. Take this card to the customer service desk and someone will bring you your computer.

C: Thanks.

S: Have a nice day.

C: You, too.

1. **Imperatives**
   Sit down. **Don't** be late.

2. *Let's*
   Let's go to the movies. **Let's not** be late.

3. **Infinitive Patterns**
   He wants **to go.**
   It's necessary **to learn** English.
   I'm afraid **to stay.**
   I use coupons **to save** money.
   I want them **to help** me.

4. **Modals**

Modal	Examples	Explanation
can can't	He **can** speak English. An 18-year-old **can** vote. **Can** I borrow your pen? You **can't** park here. It's a bus stop. I **can't** help you now. I'm busy.	He has this ability. He has permission. I'm asking permission. It is not permitted. I am not able to.
should shouldn't	You **should** eat healthy food. You **shouldn't** drive if you're sleepy.	It's good advice. It's a bad idea.
may may not	**May** I borrow your pen? I **may** buy a new car. I **may not** be here tomorrow.	I'm asking permission. This is possible. This is possible.
might might not	It **might** rain tomorrow. We **might not** have our picnic.	This is possible. This is possible.
must must not	A driver **must** have a license. I'm late. I **must** hurry. You **must not** drive without a license.	This is a legal necessity. This is a personal necessity. This is against the law.
will will not	The manufacturer **will** send you a check. You **will not** receive the check right away.	This is in the future.
would would like	**Would** you help me move? I **would like** to use your pen.	I'm asking a favor. I want to use your pen.
could	**Could** you help me move?	I'm asking a favor.
have to not have to	She **has to** leave. She **doesn't have to** leave.	It's necessary. It's not necessary.

1. Don't use *to* after a modal.

   I must ~~to~~ go.

2. Use *to* between verbs.

   They like _∧play. *[to]*

3. Always use the base form after a modal.

   He can swims.

   She can't ~~driving~~ the car. *[drive]*

4. Use the base form in an infinitive.

   He wants to goes.

   I wanted to worked.

5. We can introduce an infinitive with *it* + an adjective.

   _∧Is important to get exercise. *[It i]*

6. Don't put an object between the modal and the main verb.

   She can ~~the lesson understand~~. *[understand the lesson]*

7. Use the correct word order in a question.

   Why ~~you can't~~ stay? *[can't you]*

8. Use an infinitive after some adjectives.

   I'm happy _∧meet you. *[to]*

   It's necessary _∧have a job. *[to]*

9. Use *not* after *let's* to make a negative.

   Let's ~~don't~~ go to the party. *[not]*

10. Use *don't* to make a negative imperative.

    ~~Not~~ come home late. *[Don't]*

11. Use *to*, not *for*, to show purpose.

~~for~~ *to*
We went to the theater ~~for~~ see a play.

12. Use the object pronoun and an infinitive after *want*, *expect*, *need*, etc.

him to close
I want ~~he closes~~ the door.

LESSON 9 TEST /REVIEW

PART 1 Find the ***grammar*** mistakes with the underlined words and correct them. Not every sentence has a mistake. If the sentence is correct, write *C*.

EXAMPLES You should ~~to~~ study more.
I don't have to work on Saturday.   *C*

1. I need cash a check.

2. What I can do for you?

3. I'm afraid to walk alone at night.

4. She has to leave early today.

5. We wanted to went home early last night.

6. Is necessary to have a car.

7. You must to go to court next week.

8. She can English speak very well.

9. Don't to walk so fast.

10. What I must do to get a driver's license?

11. He should study harder.

12. We want learn English quickly.

13. My brother can speaks English very well.

14. It's impossible learn English in one month.

15. She likes to swim in the ocean.

16. Let's don't make a lot of noise. Dad is sleeping.

Infinitives; Modals; Imperatives   **299**

17. I was glad <u>to met</u> him yesterday.

18. <u>Don't worry</u>. Everything will be fine.

19. She went to the school <u>for talk</u> to her daughter's teacher.

20. You <u>should looking</u> for a new job.

21. The teacher always says, "<u>Not</u> talk during a test."

22. I use spell check <u>to checking</u> my spelling.

23. My parents want <u>I graduate</u> from college.

PART 2 Fill in the first blank with *to* or nothing (*X*). Then write the negative form in the second blank.

EXAMPLES I'm ready _____*to*_____ study Lesson 10.

I _____*'m not ready to study*_____ Lesson 11.

You should _____*X*_____ drive carefully.

You _____*shouldn't drive*_____ fast.

1. I need _____ learn English. I _____ Polish.

2. You must _____ stop at a red light. You _____ on the highway.

3. The teacher expects _____ pass most of the students. She _____ all of the students.

4. We want _____ study grammar. We _____ literature.

5. The teacher has _____ give grades. He _____ an A to everyone.

6. We might _____ have time for some questions later. We _____ time for a discussion.

7. It's important _____ practice American pronunciation now.

It _____ British pronunciation.

8. It's easy _____ learn one's native language.

It _____ a foreign language.

9. Let's _____ speak English in class. _____ our native languages in class.

10. Please attend the meeting. _____ be here at six o'clock,

please. _____ late.

PART 3 Change each sentence to a question.

EXAMPLES I'm afraid to drive.

Why *are you afraid to drive?*

He can help you.

When *can he help me?*

1. You should wear a seat belt.

Why _____

2. I want to buy some grapes.

Why _____

3. He must fill out the application.

When _____

4. She needs to drive to New York.

When _____

5. You can't park at a bus stop.

Why _____

6. It's necessary to eat vegetables.

Why _____

7. She has to buy a car.

Why _____

8. They'd like to see you.

When _____

PART 4 This is a phone conversation between a woman (W) and her mechanic (M). Choose the correct words to fill in the blanks.

W: This is Cindy Fine. I'm calling about my car.

M: I _____*can't*_____ hear you. _____
      (example: can't, may not)   (1 could, might)

you speak louder, please?

W: This is Cindy Fine. Is my car ready yet?

M: We're working on it now. We're almost finished.

W: When _____ I pick it up?
          (2 would, can)

M: It will be ready by four o'clock.

W: How much will it cost?

M: $375.

W: I don't have that much money right now. _____
(3 Can, Might)

I pay by credit card?

M: Yes. You _____ use any major credit card.
(4 may, might)

Later, at the mechanic's shop:

M: Your car's ready, ma'am. The engine problem is fixed. But you

_____ replace your brakes. They're not so good.
(5 may, should)

W: _____ do it right away?
(6 Do I have to, May I)

M: No, you _____ do it immediately, but you
(7 must not, don't have to)

_____ do it within a month or two. If you don't do
(8 would, should)

it soon, you _____ have an accident.
(9 may, would)

W: How much will it cost to replace the brakes?

M: It _____ cost about $200.
(10 would, will)

W: I _____ like to make an appointment to take care
(11 will, would)

of the brakes next week. _____ I bring my car in
(12 Can, Will)

next Monday?
M: Yes, Monday is fine. You _____ bring it in early
(13 could, should)

because we get very busy later in the day.
W: OK. See you Monday morning.

PART **5**   Decide if the sentences have the same meaning or different meanings. Write *S* for same, *D* for different.

EXAMPLES   Would you like to go to a movie? Do you want to go to a movie?   *S*
We will not go to New York. We should not go to New York.   *D*

1. You should go to the doctor. You can go to the doctor.

2. I may buy a new car. I must buy a new car.

3. Could you help me later? Would you help me later?

4. She must not drive her car. She doesn't have to drive her car.

5. She has to leave immediately. She must leave immediately.

6. We will have a test soon. We may have a test soon.

7. I can't go to the party. I might not go to the party.

8. You shouldn't buy a car. You don't have to buy a car.

9. May I use your phone? Could I use your phone?

10. He might not eat lunch. He may not eat lunch.

11. I should go to the doctor. I must go to the doctor.

12. I have to take my passport with me. I should take my passport with me.

PART 6 Circle the correct words to complete each sentence.

1. If you sample a product in a supermarket, you (*don't have to, shouldn't*) buy it.

2. If you have just a few items, you (*shouldn't, don't have to*) use a shopping cart. You (*can, must*) use a small basket.

3. You (*must, should*) use coupons to save money.

4. You (*shouldn't, don't have to*) pay with cash. You can use a credit card.

5. Salesperson to customer: (*May, Would*) I help you?

6. You (*must, should*) make a list before going shopping.

7. You (*don't have to, must not*) take your own bags to the supermarket. Bags are free.

8. Try this new pizza. You (*should, might*) like it.

9. You (*can't, shouldn't*) use coupons after the expiration date.

10. You (*must not, don't have to*) park in the handicapped parking space. It's against the law.

Classroom Activities

1. Imagine that a friend of yours is getting married. You are giving him or her advice about marriage. Write some advice for this person. (You may work with a partner or compare your advice to your partner's advice when you are finished.)

It's important	It's not important
It's important to be honest.	It's not important to do everything together.

2. Imagine that a friend of yours is going to travel to the U.S. You are giving him or her advice about the trip and life in the U.S. Write as many things as you can in each box. Then find a partner and compare your advice to your partner's advice.

It's necessary OR It's important OR You should	It's difficult OR You shouldn't
It's necessary to have a passport.	It's difficult to understand American English.

3. Working in a small group, write a list to give information to a new student or to a foreign student. If you need more space, use your notebook.

should or shouldn't	must or have to	don't have to	might or might not	can or can't
You should bring your transcripts to this college.				

4. With a partner, write a few instructions for one of the following situations.

   EXAMPLE using a microwave oven

   > You shouldn't put anything metal in the microwave.
   > You can set the power level.
   > You should rotate the dish in the microwave. If you don't, the food might not cook evenly.

   a. preparing for the TOEFL[7]

   b. taking a test in this class

   c. preparing for the driver's test in this state

5. Bring in an application. (Bring two of the same application, if possible.) It can be an application for a job, driver's license, license plate, apartment rental, address change, check-cashing card, rebate, etc. Work with a partner. One person will give instructions. The other person will fill it out.

6. Bring in ads from different stores. You can bring in ads from supermarkets or any other store. See what is on sale this week. Find a partner and discuss the products and the prices. Compare prices at two different stores, if possible. What do these products usually cost in your native country? Do you have all of these products in your native country?

Talk About it

Discuss: Do you use coupons, rebates, or rain checks? Why or why not?

Write About it

1. Write about the differences between shopping in the U.S. and in another country.

2. Imagine that a new classmate just arrived from another country. Write a composition giving advice about shopping in the U.S.

Internet Activities

1. Use the Internet to compare the prices of a product, such as a DVD player, TV, digital camera, or computer.

2. Use the Internet to find application forms. (Examples: change of address form from the post office; application for a checking account from a bank; application for a credit card; application for a frequent flyer program from an airline; motor vehicle registration form in your state)

Additional Activities at **http://elt.heinle.com/gic**

---

[7] The *TOEFL* is the Test of English as a Foreign Language.

LESSON

10

GRAMMAR
Count and Noncount Nouns
Quantity Words

CONTEXT: Nutrition and Health
A Healthy Diet
Eat Less, Live Longer

10.1 | Count and Noncount Nouns—An Overview

Nouns can be divided into two groups: count and noncount nouns.

Examples	Explanation

I eat four **eggs** a week.
I eat one **apple** a day.
Do you like **grapes?**
	Count nouns have a singular and plural form.
	    egg—eggs
	    apple—apples

I like **milk.** I drink **coffee** every day. Do you like **cheese?**	Noncount nouns have no plural form.

A HEALTHY DIET

Before You Read

1. What kind of food do you like to eat? What kind of food do you dislike?

2. What are some popular dishes from your country or native culture?

 Read the following article. Pay special attention to count and noncount nouns.

It is important to eat well to maintain good **health.** A healthy diet consists of a variety of **foods.**

You need carbohydrates. The best carbohydrates come from whole grain **bread, cereal,** and **pasta.** Brown **rice** is much healthier than white **rice. Sugar** is a carbohydrate too, but it has no real nutritional value.

Of course, you need **fruits** and **vegetables** too. But not all vegetables are equally good. **Potatoes** can raise the sugar in your **blood,** which can be a problem for people with diabetes. It is better to eat **carrots, broccoli, corn,** and **peas.**

You also need protein. Red **meat** is high in protein, but a diet with a lot of red **meat** can cause heart disease, diabetes, and cancer. Better sources of protein are **chicken, fish, beans**, **eggs,** and **nuts.** Some people worry that **eggs** contain too much **cholesterol.** (Cholesterol is a substance found in animal **foods.**) But recent studies show that eating one **egg** a day is not usually harmful and gives us other nutritional benefits.

Many **people** think that all **fat** is bad. But this is not true. The **fat** in **nuts** (especially **walnuts**) and **olive oil** is very healthy. The **fat** in **butter** and **cheese** is not good.

It is not clear how much **milk** and other dairy **products** an adult needs. It is true that dairy products are a good source of **calcium,** but a calcium supplement can give you what you need without the **fat** and **calories** of milk.

The best way to stay healthy is to eat the right kinds of food. Food **packages** have information about nutrition and calories. You should read the package to avoid artificial **ingredients** and high levels of **fat** and **sugar.** It is also important to control your weight and to exercise every day.

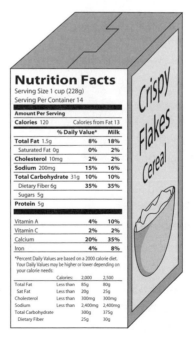

10.2 | Noncount Nouns

Noncount nouns fall into four different groups.

Group A: Nouns that have no distinct, separate parts. We look at the whole.

milk	air	meat
oil	pork	butter
water	cholesterol	poultry
coffee	paper	cheese
tea	soup	
yogurt	bread	

Group B: Nouns that have parts that are too small or insignificant to count.

rice	snow	hair
sugar	sand	grass
salt	corn	popcorn

Group C: Nouns that are classes or categories of things. The members of the category are not the same.

money (nickels, dimes, dollars)
food (vegetables, meat, spaghetti)
candy (chocolates, mints, candy bars)
furniture (chairs, tables, beds)
clothing (sweaters, pants, dresses)
mail (letters, packages, postcards)
fruit (cherries, apples, grapes)
makeup (lipstick, rouge, eye shadow)
homework (compositions, exercises, reading)

Group D: Nouns that are abstractions.

love	advice	happiness
life	knowledge	education
time	nutrition	experience
truth	intelligence	crime
beauty	unemployment	music
luck	patience	art
fun	noise	work
help	information	health

EXERCISE **1** Fill in the blanks with a noncount noun.

EXAMPLE Brown ____*rice*____ is healthier than white ____*rice*____.

1. Babies need a lot of _____, but adults don't.

2. Food from animals contains _____.

3. Children like to eat _____, but it's not good for their teeth.

4. Food packages have information about _____.

5. Some people put _____ in their coffee.

6. _____ is a good source of fat.

   _____ is not a good source of fat.

7. _____ contains caffeine. Don't drink it at night.

8. People with high blood pressure shouldn't put a lot of

   _____ on their food.

9. Soda and candy contain a lot of _____.

EXERCISE **2** Fill in the blanks with a noncount noun from the list on page 310.

EXAMPLE Students at registration need ____*information*____.

1. I get a lot of _____ every day in my mailbox.

2. In the winter, there is a lot of _____ in the northern parts of the U.S.

3. In the U.S., people eat _____ in a movie theater.

4. Students have to do _____ every day.

5. When you walk on the beach, you get _____ in your shoes.

6. Money doesn't buy _____.

7. Our parents often give us a lot of _____ about how to live our lives.

8. Some cities have a lot of _____. Many people are without jobs.

9. I need a quiet place to study. Can you study with

   _____ in the background?

10.3 | Count and Noncount Nouns

Examples	Explanation

I eat a lot of **rice** and **beans.**
 	
  rice = noncount noun
 	
  beans = count noun
	Count and *noncount* are grammatical terms, but they are not always logical. *Rice* is very small and is a noncount noun. *Beans* and *peas* are also very small, but they are count nouns.

a. He eats a lot of **fruit.** b. Oranges and lemons are **fruits** that contain Vitamin C. a. She bought a lot of **food** for the party. b. **Foods** that contain a lot of cholesterol are not good for you.	a. Use *fruit* and *food* as noncount nouns when you mean fruit and food in general. b. Use *fruits* and *foods* as count nouns when you mean kinds of fruit or categories of food.
a. Children like to eat **candy.** b. There are three **candies** on the table.	a. When you talk about candy in general, *candy* is noncount. b. When you look at individual pieces of candy, you can use the plural form.

EXERCISE 3 Fill in the blanks with the singular or plural form of the word in parentheses ( ). Use the singular for noncount nouns. Use the plural for count nouns.

EXAMPLE Add __*peas*__ to the soup. Then put in some __*salt*__ .
        (pea)   (salt)

1. Do you like to eat _____?
                          (fruit)

2. Oranges, grapefruits, and lemons are _____ that
                                            (fruit)

   have a lot of Vitamin C.

3. When children eat a lot of _____, they sometimes
                                  (candy)

   get sick.

4. Let's go shopping. There is no _____ in the house.
                                      (food)

5. Milk and eggs are _____ that contain cholesterol.
                        (food)

6. She's going to make _____ and
                          (rice)

   _____ for dinner.
      (bean)

10.4 | Describing Quantities of Count and Noncount Nouns

Examples	Explanation
She ate three **apples** today. He ate four **eggs** this week.	We can put a number before a count noun.
I ate two **slices of bread**. Please buy a **jar of olive oil**. She drank three **glasses of milk.**	We cannot put a number before a noncount noun. We use a unit of measure, which we can count.

Ways we see noncount nouns:

By Container	By Portion	By Measurement[1]	By Shape or Whole Piece	Other
a bottle of water a carton of milk a jar of pickles a bag of flour a can of soda (pop)[2] a bowl of soup a cup of coffee a glass of milk	a slice (piece) of bread a piece of meat a piece of cake a piece (sheet) of paper a slice of pizza a piece of candy a strip of bacon	a spoonful of sugar a scoop of ice cream a quart of oil a pound of meat a gallon of gasoline	a loaf of bread an ear of corn a piece of fruit a head of lettuce a candy bar a roll of film a tube of toothpaste a bar of soap	a piece of mail a piece of furniture a piece of advice a piece of information a work of art

EXERCISE **4** Fill in the blanks with a logical quantity for each of these noncount nouns.

EXAMPLES She bought _____*one pound of*_____ coffee.

She drank _____*two cups of*_____ coffee.

1. She ate _____ meat.

2. She bought _____ meat.

3. She bought _____ bread.

4. She ate _____ bread.

[1]For a list of conversions from the American system of measurement to the metric system, see Appendix G.
[2]Some Americans say "soda"; others say "pop."

5. She bought _____ rice.

6. She ate _____ rice.

7. She bought _____ sugar.

8. She put _____ sugar in her coffee.

9. She ate _____ soup.

10. She ate _____ corn.

11. She bought _____ gas for her car.

12. She put _____ motor oil into her car's engine.

13. She used _____ paper to do her homework.

14. She took _____ film on her vacation.

10.5 | A Lot Of, Much, Many

Use *many* for count nouns. Use *much* for noncount nouns. Use *a lot of* for both count and noncount nouns.

	Count (plural)	Noncount
Affirmative	He baked **many** cookies. He baked **a lot of** cookies.	He baked **a lot of** bread.
Negative	He didn't bake **many** cookies. He didn't bake **a lot of** cookies.	He didn't bake **much** bread. He didn't bake **a lot of** bread.
Question	Did he bake **many** cookies? Did he bake **a lot of** cookies? **How many** cookies did he bake?	Did he bake **much** bread? Did he bake **a lot of** bread? **How much** bread did he bake?

Language Notes:
1. *Much* is rarely used in affirmative statements. Use *a lot of* in affirmative statements.
2. When the noun is omitted (in the following case, *cookies*), use *a lot*, not *a lot of*.
   He baked a lot of cookies, but he didn't eat **a lot**.

EXERCISE 5 Fill in the blanks with *much*, *many*, or *a lot of*. In some cases, more than one answer is possible.

EXAMPLES She doesn't eat ___*much*___ pasta.

___*Many*___ American supermarkets are open 24 hours a day.

___*A lot of*___ sugar is not good for you.

1. In the summer in the U.S., there's _____ corn.
2. Children usually drink _____ milk.
3. _____ American people have an unhealthy diet.
4. I drink coffee only about once a week. I don't drink _____ coffee.
5. There are _____ places that sell fast food.
6. It's important to drink _____ water.
7. How _____ glasses of water did you drink today?
8. How _____ fruit did you eat today?
9. How _____ cholesterol is there in one egg?
10. It isn't good to eat _____ candy.

10.6 | A Few, A Little

	Examples	Explanation
Count	I bought **a few** bananas. She ate **a few** cookies. She drank **a few cups** of tea.	Use *a few* with count nouns or with quantities that describe noncount nouns (*cup, bowl, piece,* etc.).
Noncount	He ate **a little** meat. He drank **a little** tea.	Use *a little* with noncount nouns.

EXERCISE 6 Fill in the blanks with *a few* or *a little.*

EXAMPLES He has ___*a few*___ good friends.

He has ___*a little*___ time to help you.

1. Every day we study _____ grammar.
2. We do _____ exercises in class.
3. The teacher gives _____ homework every day.
4. We do _____ pages in the book each day.
5. _____ students always get an A on the tests.
6. It's important to eat _____ fruit every day.
7. It's important to eat _____ pieces of fruit every day.

8. I use _____ milk in my coffee.

9. I receive _____ mail every day.

10. I receive _____ letters every day.

10.7 | Some, Any, and A/An

	Singular Count	Plural Count	Noncount
Affirmative	I ate **a** peach. I ate **an** apple.	I ate **some** peaches. I ate **some** apples.	I ate **some** bread.
Question	Do you want **a** sandwich?	Do you want **any fries?** Do you need **some** napkins?	Do you want **any** salt? Do you need **some** ketchup?
Negative	I don't need **a** fork.	There aren't **any** potatoes in the soup. There are **no** potatoes in the soup.	There isn't **any** salt in the soup. There is **no** salt in the soup.

Language Notes:
1. We can use *any* or *some* for questions with plural or noncount nouns.
2. Use *any* after a negative verb. Use *no* after an affirmative verb.
   Wrong: I didn't eat *no* cherries.

EXERCISE **7** Fill in the blanks with *a*, *an*, *some*, or *any*. In some cases, more than one answer is possible.

EXAMPLE I ate ___*an*___ apple.

1. I ate _____ corn.

2. I didn't buy _____ potatoes.

3. Did you eat _____ watermelon?

4. I don't have _____ sugar.

5. There are _____ apples in the refrigerator.

6. There aren't _____ oranges in the refrigerator.

7. Do you want _____ orange?

8. Do you want _____ cherries?

9. I ate _____ banana.

10. I didn't eat _____ strawberries.

EXERCISE 8 Make a statement about people in this class with the words given and an expression of quantity. Practice count nouns.

EXAMPLES   Vietnamese student(s)
There are a few Vietnamese students in this class.

Cuban student(s)
There's one Cuban student in this class.

1. Polish student(s)
2. Spanish-speaking student(s)
3. American(s)
4. child(ren)
5. woman/women

6. man/men
7. teacher(s)
8. American citizen(s)
9. senior citizen(s)
10. teenager(s)

EXERCISE 9 Fill in the blanks with an appropriate expression of quantity. In some cases, more than one answer is possible. Practice noncount nouns.

EXAMPLE   Eggs have ___*a lot of*___ cholesterol.

1. You shouldn't eat so much red meat because meat has _____ fat.

2. Only animal products contain cholesterol. There is _____ cholesterol in fruit.

3. Diet colas use a sugar substitute. They don't have _____ sugar.

4. There is _____ sugar in a cracker, but not much.

5. Plain popcorn is healthy, but buttered popcorn has _____ fat.

6. Coffee has caffeine. Tea has _____ caffeine too, but not as much as coffee.

7. She doesn't drink _____ tea. She only drinks tea occasionally.

8. I usually put _____ butter on a slice of bread.

9. I'm going to put some sugar in my coffee. Do you want _____ sugar in your coffee?

10. My sister is a vegetarian. She doesn't eat _____ meat at all.

    She doesn't eat _____ fish or chicken either.

EXERCISE 10 ABOUT YOU Ask a question with *much* and the words given. Use *eat* or *drink*. Another student will answer. Practice noncount nouns.

EXAMPLES candy

A: Do you eat much candy?
B: No. I don't eat any candy.

fruit

A: Do you eat much fruit?
B: Yes. I eat a lot of fruit.

Eat
1. rice
2. fish
3. chicken
4. pork
5. bread
6. cheese

Drink
7. apple juice
8. lemonade
9. milk
10. tea
11. coffee
12. soda or pop

EXERCISE 11 ABOUT YOU Ask a question with "Do you have . . ." and the words given. Another student will answer. Practice both count and noncount nouns.

EXAMPLES American friends

A: Do you have any American friends?
B: Yes. I have a lot of American friends.

free time

A: Do you have any free time?
B: No. I don't have any free time.

1. money with you now
2. credit cards
3. bread at home
4. bananas at home
5. orange juice in your refrigerator
6. plants in your home
7. family pictures in your wallet
8. time to relax

EXERCISE 12 This is a conversation between a husband (H) and wife (W). Choose the correct word or words to fill in the blanks.

H: Where were you today? I called you from work

_____*many*_____ times, but there was no answer.
(examples: much, many)

W: I went to the supermarket today. I

bought _____ things.
(1 a little, a few)

H: What did you buy?

W: There was a special on coffee, so I bought _____
                                                    (2 a lot of, much)

coffee. I didn't buy _____ fruit because the prices
                        (3 any, no)

were very high.

H: How _____ money did you spend?
          (4 much, many)

W: I spent _____ money because of the coffee. I
              (5 much, a lot of)

bought ten 1-pound bags.

H: It took you a long time.

W: Yes. The store was very crowded. There were _____
                                                    (6 much, many)

people in the store. And there was _____ traffic at
                                        (7 a lot of, much)

that hour, so it took me _____ time to drive home.
                            (8 a lot of, much)

H: There's not _____ time to cook.
                  (9 much, many)

W: Maybe you can cook today and let me rest?

H: Uh . . . I don't have _____ experience. You do it
                            (10 much, no)

better. You have _____ experience.
                    (11 a lot of, much)

W: Yes. I have _____ because I do it all the time!
                  (12 a lot of, a lot)

EXERCISE 13   This is a conversation between a waitress (W) and a customer (C).
               Fill in the blanks with an appropriate quantity word. (In some
               cases, more than one answer is possible.)

W: Would you like ___*any (or some)*___ coffee, sir?
                        (example)

C: Yes, and please bring me _____ cream too. I don't
                                (1)

need _____ sugar. And I'd like a
          (2)

_____ of orange juice, too.
      (3)

A few minutes later:

W: Are you ready to order, sir?

C: Yes. I'd like the scrambled eggs with three _____
                                                    (4)

of bacon. And some pancakes, too.

—Breakfast Menu—

Eggs
  scrambled..............$2.50
  sunny side up..........$2.00
  hardboiled...............$1.00
Waffles.....................$3.50
French Toast..............$3.25
Pancakes
  plain.....................$3.50
  strawberry..............$4.50
  blueberry................$4.50

Side Orders
  bacon....................$1.50
  sausage.................$2.00
  home fries.............$1.50

W: Do you want _____ syrup with your pancakes?
(5)

C: Yes. What kind do you have?

W: We have _____ different kinds: strawberry, cherry,
(6)

blueberry, maple . . .

C: I'll have the strawberry syrup. And bring me _____
(7)

butter too.

After the customer is finished eating:

W: Would you like _____ dessert?
(8)

C: Yes. I'd like a _____ cherry pie. And put
(9)

_____ ice cream on the pie. And I'd like
(10)

_____ more coffee, please.
(11)

After the customer eats dessert:

W: Would you like anything else?

C: Just the check. I don't have _____ cash with me.
(12)

Can I pay by credit card?

W: Of course.

EAT LESS, LIVE LONGER

Before You Read

1. Do you think the American diet is healthy?

2. Do you see a lot of overweight Americans?

Read the follwing article. Pay special attention to *too much*, *too many*, and *a lot of*.

About 65 percent of Americans are overweight. The typical American consumes **too many** calories and **too much** fat and doesn't get enough exercise. Many American children are overweight too. Children spend **too much** time in front of the TV and not enough time getting exercise. Eighty percent of commercials during children's programs are for food products. In four hours of Saturday morning cartoons, there are over 200 ads for junk food.

Twenty-five percent of American pets are overweight too. Like their owners, they eat **too much** and don't get enough exercise.

There is evidence that eating fewer calories can help us live longer. Doctors studied the people on the Japanese island of Okinawa, who eat 40 percent less than the typical American. The Okinawan diet is low in calories and salt. Also Okinawans eat **a lot of** fruit, vegetables, and fish and drink **a lot of** green tea and water. Okinawa has **a lot of** people over the age of 100.

How can we live longer and healthier lives? The answer is simple: Eat less and exercise more.

10.8 | *A Lot Of* vs. *Too Much/Too Many*

Examples	Explanation
It is good to eat **a lot of** fruit. In Okinawa, there are **a lot of** people over the age of 100. I don't eat **a lot** in the morning.	*A lot (of)* shows a large quantity. It is a neutral term.
You shouldn't eat a lot of ice cream because it has **too many** calories. If you drink **too much** coffee, you won't sleep tonight.	*Too much* and *too many* show that a quantity is excessive and causes a problem. Use *too many* with count nouns. Use *too much* with noncount nouns.
If you eat **too much,** you will gain weight.	Use *too much* after verbs.

EXERCISE 14

 Circle the correct words to fill in this conversation between a mother (M) and her 12-year-old son (S).

M: I'm worried about you. You spend too (*much/* (*many*)) hours in front
(example)

of the TV. And you eat too (*much/many*) junk food and don't get
(1)

enough exercise. You're getting fat.

S: Mom. I know I watch (*a lot of/a lot*) TV, but I learn (*a lot/a lot of*)
*(2)**(3)*

from TV.

M: No, you don't. Sometimes you have (*a lot of/too much*) homework,
(4)

but you turn on the TV as soon as you get home from school.
I'm going to make a rule: No TV until you finish your homework.

S: Oh, Mom. You have too (*much/many*) rules.
(5)

M: That's what parents are for: to guide their kids to make the right

decisions. There are (*a lot of/too many*) things to do besides watching
(6)

TV. Why don't you go outside and play? When I was your age, we
played outside.

S: *"When I was your age."* Not again. You always say that.

M: Well, it's true. We had (*too much/a lot of*) fun outside, playing with
(7)

friends. I didn't have (*a lot of/too much*) toys when I was your age.
(8)

And I certainly didn't have video games or computer games. Also we

helped our parents (*a lot/too much*) after school. We cut the grass
(9)

and washed the dishes.

S: My friend Josh cuts the grass, throws out the garbage, and cleans the

basement once a month. His mom pays him (*too much/a lot of*)
(10)

money for doing it. Maybe if you pay me, I'll do it.

M: Not again. *"Josh does it. Josh has it. Why can't I?"* You always say
that. You're not Josh, and I'm not Josh's mother. I'm not going to pay
you for things you should do.

S: OK. Just tell me what to do, and I'll do it.

M: There are (*a lot of/too much*) leaves on the front lawn. Why don't
(11)

you start by putting them in garbage bags? And you can walk

Sparky. He's getting fat, too. He eats (*too much/too many*) and
(12)

sleeps all day. Both of you need more exercise.

EXERCISE 15 Fill in the blanks with *much* or *many*, and complete each statement.

EXAMPLE If I drink too ___much___ coffee, ___I won't be able to sleep tonight.___

1. If the teacher gives too _____ homework, _____

   _____

2. If I take too _____ classes, _____

   _____

3. If I eat too _____ candy, _____

   _____

4. If I'm absent too _____ days, _____

   _____

5. Too _____ cholesterol _____

   _____

10.9 | *Too Much/Too Many* vs. *Too*

Examples	Explanation
I don't eat ice cream because it's **too** fattening. He should lose weight. He's getting **too** fat.	Use *too* with adjectives and adverbs.
I don't eat ice cream because it has **too many** calories and **too much** fat.	Use *too much* and *too many* before nouns. Use *too many* with count nouns. Use *too much* with noncount nouns.

EXERCISE 16 Fill in the blanks with *too*, *too much*, or *too many*.

Situation A. Some students are complaining about the school cafeteria. They are giving reasons why they don't want to eat there.

EXAMPLE It's ___too___ noisy.

1. The food is _____ greasy.
2. There are _____ students. I can't find a place to sit.
3. The lines are _____ long.
4. The food is _____ expensive.
5. There's _____ noise.

Situation B. Some students are complaining about their class and school.

1. The classroom is _____ small.

2. There are _____ students in one class.

3. We have to write _____ compositions.

4. The teacher gives _____ homework.

5. There are _____ tests.

EXERCISE 17   ABOUT YOU Write a few sentences to complain about something: your apartment, your roommate, this city, this college, etc. Use *too*, *too much*, or *too many* in your sentences.

EXAMPLE   My roommate spends too much time in the bathroom in the morning. He's too messy.[3]

_____

_____

_____

EXERCISE 18   Fill in the blanks with *too*, *too much*, or *too many* if a problem is presented. Use *a lot of* if no problem is presented.

EXAMPLE   Most people can't afford to buy a Mercedes because it costs _too much_ money.

1. There are _____ noncount nouns in English.

2. "Rice" is a noncount noun because the parts are _____ small to count.

3. If this class is _____ hard for you, you should go to a lower level.

4. Good students spend _____ time doing their homework.

5. If you spend _____ time watching TV, you won't have time for your homework.

6. It takes _____ time to learn English, but you can do it.

7. Oranges have _____ vitamin C.

8. If you are on a diet, don't eat potato chips. They have _____ _____ calories and _____ fat.

9. Babies drink _____ milk.

10. If you drink _____ coffee, you won't sleep.

[3]A *messy* person does not put his or her things in order.

EXERCISE **19** *Combination Exercise.* A doctor (D) and patient (P) are talking. Fill in the blanks with an appropriate quantity word or unit of measurement to complete this conversation. (In some cases, more than one answer is possible.)

D: I'm looking at your lab results and I see that your cholesterol level

is very high. Also your blood pressure is _____*too*_____

(example)

high. Do you use _____ salt on your food?

(1)

P: Yes, Doctor. I love salt. I eat _____ potato chips and

(2)

popcorn.

D: That's not good. You're overweight, too. You need to lose 50 pounds. What do you usually eat?

P: For breakfast I usually grab _____ coffee and a

(3)

doughnut. I don't have _____ time for lunch, so I

(4)

eat _____ potato chips and drink

(5)

_____ soda while I'm working. I'm so busy that I

(6)

have _____ time to cook at all. So for dinner, I

(7)

usually stop at a fast-food place and get a burger and fries.

D: That's a terrible diet! How _____ exercise do

(8)

you get?

P: I never exercise. I don't have _____ time at all. I

(9)

own my own business and I have _____ work.

(10)

Sometimes I work 80 hours a week.

D: I'm going to give you an important _____ advice.

(11)

You're going to have to change your lifestyle.

P: I'm _____ old to change my habits.

(12)

Count and Noncount Nouns; Quantity Words   **325**

D: You're only 45 years old. You're _____ young to die.
(13)

And if you don't change your habits, you're going to have a heart attack. I'm going to give you a booklet about staying healthy. It has

_____ information that will teach you about diet
(14)

and exercise. Please read it and come back in six months.

SUMMARY OF LESSON 10

Words that we use before count and noncount nouns:

Word	Count (Singular) Example: *book*	Count (Plural) Example: *books*	Noncount Example: *tea*
the	X	X	X
a	X		
one	X		
two, three, etc.		X	
some (affirmatives)		X	X
any (negatives and questions)		X	X
a lot of		X	X
much (negatives and questions)			X
many		X	
a little			X
a few		X	

EDITING ADVICE

1. Don't put *a* or *an* before a noncount noun.

   some
   I want to give you ~~an~~ advice.

2. Noncount nouns are always singular.

   a lot of
   My mother gave me ~~many~~ advices.

   pieces of
   He received three ˄ mails today.

3. Don't use a double negative.

> He doesn't have ~~no~~ *any* time.   OR   *He has no time.*

4. Don't use *much* with an affirmative statement.

> UNCOMMON: There was much rain yesterday.
> COMMON: There was a lot of rain yesterday.

5. Use *a* or *an*, not *any*, with a singular count noun.

> Do you have ~~any~~ *a* computer?

6. Don't use *a* or *an* before a plural noun.

> She has ~~a~~ blue eyes.

7. Use the plural form for plural count nouns.

> He has a lot of friend*s*.

8. Omit *of* after *a lot* when the noun is omitted.

> In my country, I have a lot of friends, but in the U.S. I don't have a lot ~~of~~.

9. Use *of* with a unit of measure.

> I ate three pieces *of* bread.

10. Don't use *of* after *many, much, a few,* or *a little* if a noun follows directly.

> She has many ~~of~~ friends.
> He put a little ~~of~~ milk in his coffee.

11. Only use *too much/too many* if there is a problem.

> He has a good job. He earns ~~too much~~ *a lot of* money.

12. Don't use *too much* before an adjective or adverb.

> I don't want to go outside today. It's too ~~much~~ hot.

13. Don't confuse *too* and *to.*

> If you eat ~~to~~ *too* much candy, you'll get sick.

PART 1 Find the mistakes with the underlined words, and correct them. Not every sentence has a mistake. If the sentence is correct, write *C*.

EXAMPLES   My dog doesn't get enough exercise. He's too ~~much~~ fat.

You can be happy if you have a few good friends.   *C*

1. He doesn't have <u>no</u> money with him at all.

2. He's a lucky man. He has <u>too many</u> friends.

3. There are a lot of tall buildings in a big city. There aren't <u>a lot of</u> in a small town.

4. I don't have <u>much</u> time to help you.

5. A 14-year-old person is <u>too much</u> young to get a driver's license.

6. <u>A few</u> students in this class are from Pakistan.

7. I don't have <u>some</u> time to help you.

8. I don't have <u>any</u> car. I use public transportation.

9. Did we have <u>many</u> snow last winter?

10. <u>Many</u> people would like to have <u>a lot of</u> money in order to travel.

11. He doesn't have <u>any</u> time to study at all.

12. I'd like to help you, but I have <u>too many</u> things to do this week. Maybe I can help you next week.

13. She drinks <u>two cups of coffee</u> every morning.

14. I drink <u>four milks</u> a day.

15. He bought five <u>pounds sugar</u>.

16. <u>How much</u> bananas did you buy?

17. <u>How much</u> money did you spend?

18. This building doesn't have <u>a</u> basement.

19. I have <u>much</u> time to read because I'm on vacation now.

20. She gave me <u>a good advice</u>.

21. The piano is <u>too much</u> heavy. I can't move it.

22. I have <u>a lot of</u> CDs, probably over 200.

23. I don't have <u>much experience</u> with cars.

24. I can't help you now. I'm <u>to</u> busy.

25. There are <u>many of</u> books in the library.

26. I have <u>a little time</u>, so I can help you.

PART 2 Fill in the blanks with an appropriate measurement of quantity.

EXAMPLE   a ___*cup*___ of coffee

1. a _____ of soda   6. a _____ of advice

2. a _____ of sugar   7. a _____ of bread

3. a _____ of milk   8. a _____ of paper

4. a _____ of furniture   9. a _____ of meat

5. a _____ of mail   10. a _____ of soup

PART 3 Read the following composition. Choose the correct quantity word or indefinite article.

I had _____*some*_____ problems when I first came to the U.S.
(example: some, any, a little)

First, I didn't have _____ money.
(1 much, a, some)

_____ friends of mine lent me _____
(2 A few, A little, A few of)   *(3 some, a, any)*

money, but I didn't feel good about borrowing it.

Second, I couldn't find _____ apartment. I went to
(4 a, an, no)

see _____ apartments, but I couldn't afford
(5 some, a little, an)

_____ of them. For _____
(6 an, any, none)   *(7 a little, a few of, a few)*

months, I had to live with my uncle's family, but the situation wasn't good.

Third, I started to study English, but soon found

_____ job and didn't have _____
(8 a, any, some)   *(9 no, much, a few)*

time to study. As a result, I was failing my course.

However, little by little my life started to improve, and I don't need

_____ help from my friends and relatives anymore.
(10 no, some, much)

Classroom Activities

1. Make a list of unhealthy things that you eat. Make a list of things that you need to eat for a healthy diet.

Unhealthy things I eat	Things I should eat

2. These are some popular foods in the U.S. Put a check (✓) in the column that describes your experience of this food. Then find a partner and compare your list to your partner's list.

Food	I Like	I Don't Like	I Never Tried
pizza		✓	
hot dogs			
hamburgers			
tacos			
submarine sandwiches			
breakfast cereal			
peanut butter			
cheesecake			
tortilla chips			
potato chips			
popcorn			
chocolate chip cookies			
fried chicken			
pretzels			

3. Cross out the phrase that doesn't fit and fill in the blanks to make a true statement about the U.S. or another country. Find a partner and compare your answers.

EXAMPLE   People in _____Argentina_____ eat/~~don't eat~~

_____a lot of_____ meat.

a. People in _____ eat/don't eat

_____ natural foods.

b. People in _____ drink/don't drink

_____ tea.

c. People in _____ shop/don't shop for food every day.

d. People in _____ eat/don't eat in a movie theater.

e. People in _____ drink/don't drink

_____ bottled water.

Talk About it

1. Look at the dialogue that takes place in a restaurant on pages 319–320. Do you think this man is eating a healthy breakfast? Why or why not?

2. Americans often eat some of these foods for breakfast: cereal and milk, toast and butter or jelly, orange juice, eggs, bacon, coffee. Describe a typical breakfast for you.

3. Most American stores sell products in containers: bags, jars, cans, and so forth. How do stores in other countries sell products?

4. Do stores in other countries give customers bags for their groceries, or do customers have to bring their own bags to the store?

5. Some things are usually free in an American restaurant: salt, pepper, sugar, cream or milk for coffee, mustard, ketchup, napkins, water, ice, coffee refills, and sometimes bread. Are these things free in a restaurant in other countries?

6. The following saying is about food. Discuss the meaning. Do you have a similar saying in your native language?

You are what you eat.

Outside Activities

1. Bring to class a package of a food or drink you enjoy. Read the label for "Nutrition Facts." Look at calories, grams of fat, cholesterol, sodium, protein, vitamins, and minerals. Do you think this is a nutritious food? Why or why not?

2. Bring a favorite recipe to class. Explain how to prepare this recipe.

Write
About it

Describe shopping for food in the U.S. or in another country. You may include information about the following:

- packaging
- open market vs. stores
- self-service vs. service from salespeople
- shopping carts
- fixed prices vs. negotiable prices
- freshness of food

Internet
Activities

1. At a search engine, type in "nutrition." Find an interesting article. How does your diet compare?

2. Use the Internet to find a recipe for something you like to eat. Bring the recipe to class.

Additional Activities at http://elt.heinle.com/gic

GRAMMAR

Adjectives
Noun Modifiers
Adverbs

CONTEXT: Great Women

Helen Keller
Grandma Moses

Helen Keller (1882–1968)

1. Do you know of any special schools for handicapped people?

2. What kind of facilities or services does this school have for handicapped people?

Helen Keller
and Anne Sullivan

 Read the following article. Pay special attention to adjectives and adverbs.

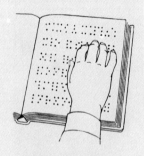

Did You Know?

In Washington, D.C., there is a special college for deaf students—Gallaudet University.

Do you know of anyone with a disability who did remarkable things? Helen Keller was a truly **remarkable** woman.

Helen Keller was a **healthy** baby. But when she was 19 months old, she had a **sudden** fever. The fever disappeared, but she became **blind** and **deaf.** Because she couldn't hear, it was difficult for her to learn to speak. As she grew, she was **angry** and **frustrated** because she couldn't understand or communicate with people. She became **wild**, throwing things and kicking and biting.

When Helen was seven years old, a teacher, Anne Sullivan, came to live with Helen's family. First, Anne taught Helen how to talk with her fingers. Helen was **excited** when she realized that things had names. Then Anne taught Helen to read by the Braille system. Helen learned these skills **quickly.** However, learning to speak was harder. Anne continued to teach Helen **patiently.** Finally, when Helen was ten years old, she could speak **clearly** enough for people to understand her.

Helen was very **intelligent.** She went to an institute for the blind, where she did very **well** in her studies. Then she went to college,[1] where she graduated with honors when she was 24 years old. Helen traveled **extensively** with Anne. She worked **tirelessly,** traveling all over America, Europe, and Asia to raise money to build schools for **blind** people. Her **main** message was that **handicapped** people are like everybody else. They want to live life **fully** and **naturally.** Helen wanted all people to be treated **equally.**

While she was in college, Helen wrote her first of many books, *The Story of My Life,* in 1903.

---

[1] In the U.S., the words *college* and *university* usually have the same meaning.

11.1 | Adjectives and Adverbs

Examples	Explanation
Helen was a **healthy** baby. She seemed **intelligent.** She became **blind.** Anne Sullivan was a **wonderful** teacher.	Adjectives describe nouns. We can use adjectives before nouns or after the verbs *be, become, look, seem,* and other sense-perception verbs.
Anne taught Helen **patiently.** Helen learned **quickly.** People want to live life **fully.**	Adverbs of manner tell how or in what way we do things. We form most adverbs of manner by putting *-ly* at the end of an adjective. Adverbs of manner usually follow the verb phrase.

EXERCISE 1 Decide if the underlined word is an adjective (*adj.*) or adverb (*adv.*).

EXAMPLES Helen was a healthy baby. *adj.*

We should respect all people equally. *adv.*

1. When Helen was angry, she threw things.

2. She seemed wild.

3. She was blind and deaf.

4. She learned to speak clearly.

5. She had a good teacher.

6. Anne was a patient woman.

7. Helen learned quickly.

8. Helen wanted to live life fully.

9. She was a remarkable woman.

11.2 | Adjectives

Examples	Explanation
Anne was a **patient** teacher. Helen was an **intelligent** person.	Adjectives describe nouns.
Anne was a **good** friend. I have many **good** friends.	Adjectives are always singular. *Wrong: goods friends*
Helen felt **frustrated** when she couldn't communicate. She was **excited** when she learned her first word. **Handicapped** people are like everybody else.	Some -ed words are adjectives: *married, divorced, excited, frustrated, handicapped, worried, finished, tired, crowded.*
Helen was a **normal, healthy** baby. Anne was a **patient, intelligent** teacher.	Sometimes we put two adjectives before a noun. We can separate the two adjectives with a comma.
Some people have an easy childhood. Helen had a hard **one.** Do you like serious stories or funny **ones?**	After an adjective, we can substitute a singular noun with *one* and a plural noun with *ones*.
Anne was **a kind teacher.** Anne was kind.	Only use an article before an adjective if a noun follows. *Wrong: Anne was a kind.*

EXERCISE **2** Fill in the blanks with an appropriate adjective. (Change *a* to *an* if the adjective begins with a vowel sound.)

EXAMPLES   When Helen couldn't communicate, she became _____ *wild* _____.

Helen was a *n interesting* _____ person.

1. Helen was a _____ baby.

2. Before Helen learned to communicate, she felt very

   _____.

3. She had a _____ life.

4. She wanted _____ treatment for blind people.

5. Helen had a _____ teacher.

6. Helen was a very _____ woman.

7. The story about Helen Keller was _____.

8. _____ people can read with the Braille method.

EXERCISE **3**   Fill in the blanks with an appropriate adjective. (Change *a* to *an* if
the adjective begins with a vowel sound.)

EXAMPLES   This is a _____*big*_____ class.

This is a _*n interesting*_____ class.

1. This classroom is _____.

2. The classrooms at this school are _____.

3. English is a _____ language.

4. This book is very _____.

5. We sometimes have _____ tests.

6. We read a _____ story about Helen Keller.

7. Did you learn any _____ words in the story?

EXERCISE **4**   ABOUT YOU Ask a question of preference with the words given.
Follow the example. Use *one* or *ones* to substitute for the noun.
Another student will answer.

EXAMPLES   an easy exercise / hard

A: Do you prefer an easy exercise or a hard one?
B: I prefer a hard one.

funny movies / serious

A: Do you prefer funny movies or serious ones?
B: I prefer funny ones.

1. a big city / small

2. an old house / new

3. a cold climate / warm

4. a small car / big

5. a soft mattress / hard

6. green grapes / red

7. red apples / yellow

8. strict teachers / easy

9. noisy children / quiet

10. used textbooks / new

11.3 | Noun Modifiers

Examples	Explanation
Helen learned to communicate using **sign** language. She wrote her **life** story.	We can use a noun to describe another noun.
a. Helen had a **college education.** b. Did she go to a **state college?**	When two nouns come together, the second noun is more general than the first. In sentence (a), *college* is a specific kind of education. In sentence (b), *college* is general and *state* is specific.
Helen lost her **eyesight** when she was a baby. When Helen was a ten-year-**old** child, she could finally speak. Helen learned **sign** language.	When two nouns come together, the first is always singular. *Eyesight* is sight of the eyes. A *ten-year-old child* is a child who is ten years old. *Sign language* is language that uses hand signs.

EXERCISE 5   Fill in the blanks by putting the two nouns in the correct order.

EXAMPLE   People need a ___*winter coat*___ in cold climates.
                          (coat/winter)

1. You have an important _____.
                          (phone/call)

2. Do you own a _____?
                  (phone/cell)

3. We use a _____ to paint the walls.
               (brush/paint)

4. If you want to drive, you need a _____.
                        (driver's/license)

5. Do you like to learn about _____?
                     (history/U.S.)

6. A married person usually wears a _____ on his or her left hand.
                       (wedding/ring)

7. Please put your garbage in the _____.
                     (can/garbage)

8. The college is closed during _____.
                    (vacation/winter)

9. There's a good _____ at 7 p.m.
                 (program/TV)

10. I'm taking a _____ this semester.
(course/math)

11. We like to visit the _____ on Saturdays.
(museum/art)

12. Does your father have a _____?
(college/education)

EXERCISE 6 Fill in the blanks. Make sure that the noun modifier is singular.

EXAMPLE A store that sells groceries is a ____*grocery store*____.

1. A store that sells books is a _____

2. A store that has departments is a _____

3. A department that sells shoes is a _____

4. Language that communicates with signs is _____

5. Glasses for eyes are _____

6. A pot for flowers is a _____

7. A garden of roses is a _____

8. A bill of five dollars is a _____

9. A child who is six years old is a _____

10. A vacation of two weeks is a _____

11. A brush for teeth is a _____

12. A man who is 6 feet tall is a _____

11.4 | Comparing Adverbs of Manner and Adjectives

An **adverb of manner** tells *how* we do something. It describes the verb (action) of the sentence. An **adjective** describes a noun.

Adjectives	Adverbs	Explanation
Anne was a **patient** teacher. Helen was a **quick** learner. She had a **clear** voice. She had a **full** life.	She taught **patiently.** She learned **quickly.** She spoke **clearly.** She lived life **fully.**	We form most adverbs of manner by putting *-ly* at the end of an adjective.
This is a **fast** car. I have a **late** class. We had a **hard** test. I have an **early** appointment.	He drives **fast.** I arrived **late.** I studied **hard.** I need to wake up **early.**	Some adjectives and adverbs have the same form.
Helen was a **good** student.	She did **well** in school.	The adverb *well* is completely different from the adjective form *good.*

Adverbs and Word Order	
Helen learned sign language **quickly.** Helen **quickly** learned sign language.	An adverb of manner usually follows the verb phrase. Or it can come before the verb. It cannot come between the verb and the object. *Wrong:* Helen learned *quickly* sign language.
Helen learned **very** quickly. She did **very** well in college.	You can use *very* before an adverb of manner.

EXERCISE **7**   Check (✓) if the sentence is true or false.

	True	False
1. Helen lost her hearing slowly.		✓
2. Anne taught Helen patiently.		
3. Helen learned quickly.		
4. Helen never learned to speak clearly.		
5. Helen didn't do well in college.		
6. Helen wanted deaf people to be treated differently from hearing people.		

11.5 | Spelling of -ly Adverbs

Adjective Ending	Examples	Adverb Ending	Adverb
y	easy lucky happy	Change y to i and add -ly.	eas**ily** luck**ily** happ**ily**
consonant + le	simple double comfortable	Drop the -e and add -ly.	simp**ly** doub**ly** comfortab**ly**
e	nice free brave	Just add -ly.	nice**ly** free**ly** brave**ly**

Language Note: There is one exception for the last rule: *true—truly*

EXERCISE 8 Write the adverb form of each adjective. Use correct spelling.

1. bad _____
2. good _____
3. lazy _____
4. true _____
5. nice _____
6. responsible _____
7. polite _____
8. fast _____
9. constant _____
10. terrible _____

EXERCISE 9 Fill in the blanks with the adverb form of the underlined adjective.

EXAMPLE He's a <u>careful</u> driver. He drives *carefully*_____.

1. She has a <u>beautiful</u> voice. She sings _____.
2. You are a <u>responsible</u> person. You always act _____.
3. You have <u>neat</u> handwriting. You write _____.
4. I'm not a <u>good</u> swimmer. I don't swim _____.
5. He is a <u>cheerful</u> person. He always smiles _____.
6. He is <u>fluent</u> in French. He speaks French _____.
7. You have a <u>polite</u> manner. You always talk to people _____.
8. Nurses are <u>hard</u> workers. They work _____.
9. She looks <u>sad</u>. She said goodbye _____.
10. You are a <u>patient</u> teacher. You explain the grammar _____.
11. My answers are <u>correct</u>. I filled in all the blanks _____.

EXERCISE 10 Tell how you do these things.

EXAMPLE   write
I write a composition carefully and slowly.

1. speak English
2. speak your native language
3. dance
4. walk
5. study
6. do your homework

7. drive
8. sing
9. type
10. work
11. dress for class
12. dress for a party

EXERCISE 11 Read the story of Helen Keller's teacher, Anne Sullivan. Find the mistakes with adjectives, adverbs, and noun modifiers in the underlined words. Correct them. Not all underlined words have a mistake. If the underlined words are correct, write *C*.

                                                         C
When Helen was a <u>small</u> child, she was a <u>blind</u> and <u>deaf</u>. She behaved <u>wild</u>.
                    (example)   *(example)*   *(1)*   *(2)*

When she was a seven-<u>years</u>-old child, her parents found a <u>wonderful</u>
                          (3)   *(4)*

teacher to work with her. The teacher's name was Anne Sullivan.

Anne was from a <u>poorly</u> immigrant family. She had a <u>terrible</u> life.
                              (5)   *(6)*

When she was a <u>child small</u>, she had a disease that left her almost blind.
                                      (7)

When she was eight <u>years</u> old, her mother died. A few years later, her
                                  (8)

father abandoned the family, and Anne went to live in an orphanage.

When she was fourteen years old, she could not see <u>clear</u> and she could
                                                                         (9)

not read. But she got the opportunity to go to a school for the blind. So at

the age of 14, she started <u>school elementary</u>. She was a <u>student very bright</u>
                                      (10)   *(11)*

and graduated from high school as the <u>top</u> student.
                                                          (12)

She heard about a job to teach a <u>blind</u> girl,
(13)

Helen Keller. Anne went to live with Helen's

family. Anne worked <u>patient</u> with Helen, showing
(14)

her that things had names. Within one month,

Helen learned <u>signs language</u>. After that, Helen
(15)

learned <u>quickly</u> and wanted to study in school.
(16)

Anne attended <u>classes college</u> with Helen,
(17)

spelling out the lectures and reading to her after

class. Helen graduated from college with honors.

Anne got <u>marry</u> in 1905, when Helen was 23. But it wasn't a <u>happy</u>
(18)   (19)

marriage, and Anne separated from her husband. She continued to help

Helen for the rest of her life. But her <u>sight eyes</u> became worse and she
(20)

became completely blind. She died in 1936. Helen lived until 1968.

EXERCISE 12

Use the adjective in parentheses or change it to an adverb to fill in
the blanks.

I have two friends who are complete opposites. My friend Paula

complains _____*constantly*_____ about everything. I always tell her
             (example: constant)

that she is a _____ person and that is the most important
          (1 healthy)

thing in life. But she is never _____. She says that
             (2 happy)

everyone is _____. When she drives, she behaves
　　　　　　　　　(3 impolite)

_____ to other drivers. She says they're all
　　(4 rude)

_____, but I think Paula is the crazy one. She doesn't
　　(5 crazy)

make changes _____. She had to move two months
　　　　　　　　　(6 easy)

ago and she hates her _____ apartment. I think it's a
　　　　　　　　　　　　　(7 new)

_____ apartment, but she finds something wrong with
　　(8 nice)

everyone.

everything.
　　I have another friend, Karla. Karla is handicapped, in a wheelchair,

but she has a _____ attitude about life. She's also an
　　　　　　　　(9 positive)

_____ person. She swims _____.
　　(10 active)　　　　　　　　　　　　　　　(11 good)

She's always learning new things. She's studying French and can speak

it _____ now. She learns _____
　　(12 fluent)　　　　　　　　　　　　　(13 quick)

and is _____ about everything. She goes to museums
　　　　(14 curious)

_____ and knows a lot about art. She is a good role
　　(15 frequent)

model for her friends.

Before You Read

1. Do you know of any old people who have a healthy, good life?

2. Who is the oldest member of your family? Is he or she in good health?

The Old Oaken Bucket in Winter by Grandma Moses

Read the following article. Pay special attention to *very* and *too*.

They say you can't teach an old dog new tricks. But is this really true? Anna Mary Moses proved that even elderly people can start a new career or take up a new hobby.

Anna Mary Moses was born in 1860. She had a **very** hard life working as a farmer's wife in New York state. She was always interested in art, but she was **too** busy working on the farm and raising her five children to paint. In her 70s, she became **too** weak to do hard farm work. She liked to do embroidery, but as she became older, she couldn't because of arthritis. It was easier for her to hold a paintbrush than a needle, so she started to paint. She painted pictures of farm life. A New York City art collector saw her paintings in a drugstore window and bought them. Today, some of her paintings are in major art museums.

When she was 92, she wrote her autobiography. At the age of 100, she illustrated a book. She was still painting when she died at age 101. Better known as "Grandma Moses," she created 1,600 pictures.

11.6 | *Too* vs. *Very*

Examples	Explanation
Grandma Moses was **very** old when she wrote her autobiography. Her paintings became **very** popular.	*Very* shows a large degree. It doesn't indicate any problems.
She was **too** busy working on the farm to paint. She became **too** weak to do farm work.	*Too* shows that there is a problem. We often use an infinitive after *too*.

EXERCISE 13 Fill in the blanks with *very* or *too*.

EXAMPLES   Basketball players are _____*very*_____ tall.

I'm _____*too*_____ short to touch the ceiling.

1. In December, it's _____ cold to go swimming outside.

2. June is usually a _____ nice month.

3. Some elderly people are in _____ good health.

4. Some elderly people are _____ sick to take care of themselves.

5. It's _____ important to know English.

6. This textbook is _____ long to finish in three weeks.

7. The president has a _____ important job.

8. The president is _____ busy to answer all his letters.

9. Some Americans speak English _____ fast for me. I can't understand them.

10. I can speak my own language _____ well.

11. When you buy a used car, you should inspect it _____ carefully.

12. A turtle moves _____ slowly.

13. If you drive _____ slowly on the highway, you might get a ticket.

11.7 | *Too* and *Enough*

	Examples	Explanation
Too + Adjective/Adverb	In her 70s, Grandma Moses was **too weak** to do farm work. When she was younger, she worked **too hard** to have time for painting.	Use *too* **before** adjectives and adverbs. **Be careful:** Don't use *too much* before adjectives and adverbs. 　*Wrong:* She worked *too much* hard.
Adjective/Adverb + *Enough*	She was **talented enough** to get the attention of an art collector. She painted **skillfully enough** to get her pictures in art museums.	Use *enough* **after** adjectives and adverbs.
Enough + Noun	When she was younger, she didn't have **enough time** to paint.	Use *enough* **before** nouns.

EXERCISE 14   Fill in the blanks with *too* or *enough* plus the word in parentheses ( ).

EXAMPLES   Your son is four years old. He's _____*too young*_____ to go to first grade.
                                                  (young)

My sister is 18 years old. She's _____*old enough*_____ to get a driver's
                                               (old)

license.

1. I can't read Shakespeare in English. It's _____ for me.
                                            (hard)

2. My brother is 21 years old. He's _____ to get married.
                                            (old)

3. My grandfather is 90 years old and in bad health. My family takes

   care of him. He's _____ to take care of himself.
                                        (sick)

4. I saved $5,000. I want to buy a used car. I think I have _____

   _____.
            (money)

5. I'd like to get a good job, but I don't have _____.
                                            (experience)

6. She wants to move that piano, but she can't do it alone. She's not

   _____.
           (strong)

7. The piano is _____ for one person to move.
                         (heavy)

8. I sit at my desk all day, and I don't get_____.
                                            (exercise)

EXERCISE 15   *Combination Exercise.* Find the mistakes with the underlined words and correct them. Not all underlined words have a mistake.

We just read a story about Grandma Moses. We learned that you are never too ~~much~~ old to learn something new. I always thought I was
        (example)

too old to learn another language, but now that I'm in the U.S. I have no
 (1)

choice. Most of the students in class are young and learn very quick.
                                                              (2)

But I am 58 years old, and I'm not a fast learner at my age. I don't catch
                                                 (3)

on as quickly as my younger classmates. However, most of them have a

job so they don't have <u>enough time</u> to study. Some of them have small
(4)

children, so they are very <u>busily</u> and don't always have <u>enough energy</u>
(5)   (6)

to do their homework. I'm not working and my children are <u>enough old</u>
(7)

to take care of themselves. In fact, they're in college also. So I have

<u>enough time</u> to do all my homework. My kids are <u>proudly</u> of me for going
(8)   (9)

to college at my age. My teacher always tells me I'm doing <u>too well</u> in her
(10)

class. After learning English, I'm planning to get a degree in history. I am

<u>too</u> interested in this subject. It was my favorite subject when I was in high
(11)

school. When I finish my degree, I'll be in my 60s. It will probably be

<u>too late</u> for me to find a job in this field, but I don't care. I just have a <u>very</u>
(12)   (13)

great love of this subject. My kids think it will be <u>too much</u> hard for me
(14)

because history books are <u>hardly</u> to read. But I am <u>too</u> motivated, so I know
(15)   (16)

I can do it. Besides, if Grandma Moses could learn to paint in her 70s and
write a book when she was 92, I can certainly study history at my age.

Grandma Moses is a very <u>well</u> role model. Who says you can't teach an
(17)

old dog <u>news</u> tricks?
(18)

1. Adjectives and Adverbs:

ADJECTIVES	ADVERBS
She has a **beautiful** voice.	She sings **beautifully.**
She is **careful.**	She drives **carefully.**
She has a **late** class.	She arrived **late.**
She is a **good** driver.	She drives **well.**

2. Adjective Modifiers and Noun Modifiers:

ADJECTIVE MODIFIER	NOUN MODIFIER
a clean window	a store window
a new store	a shoe store
warm coats	winter coats
a new license	a driver's license

3. *Very/Too/Enough:*

He's **very** healthy.
He's **too** young to retire. He's only 55.
He's old **enough** to understand life.
He has **enough** money to take a vacation.

EDITING ADVICE

1. Don't make adjectives plural.

   Those are importants ideas.

2. Put the specific noun before the general noun.

   truck driver
   He is a ~~driver truck~~.

3. Some adjectives end in *-ed.* Don't omit the *-ed.*

   ed
   I'm finish with my project.
   ^

4. If the adjective ends in *-ed,* don't forget to include the verb *be.*

   is
   He married.
   ^

5. A noun modifier is always singular.

   She is a letters carrier.

6. Put the adjective before the noun.

          very important
    He had a meeting ~~very important~~.

7. Don't use an article before an adjective if there is no noun.

    Your house is ~~a~~ beautiful.

8. Use *one(s)* after an adjective to substitute for a noun.

                                          one
    He wanted a big wedding, and she wanted a small.

9. Don't confuse *too* and *very*. *Too* indicates a problem.

                very
    My father is ~~too~~ healthy.

10. Don't confuse *too much* and *too*. *Too much* is followed by a noun. *Too* is followed by an adjective or adverb.

    It's too ~~much~~ hot today. Let's stay inside.

11. Put *enough* after the adjective.

          old
    He's enough ~~old~~ to drive.

12. Don't use *very* before a verb. *Very* is used only with adjectives and adverbs.

    He ~~very~~ likes the U.S. *very much*.

13. Put the adverb at the end of the verb phrase.

            late
    He ~~late~~ came home.
                      slowly
    He opened ~~slowly~~ the door.

14. Use an adverb to describe a verb. Use an adjective to describe a noun.

                 ly
    He drives careful.

    That man is very nice~~ly~~.
                        well
    You speak English very ~~good~~.

PART 1 Find the mistakes with the underlined words and correct them. Not every sentence has a mistake. If the sentence is correct, write *C*.

> **EXAMPLES** She is very <u>carefully</u> about money.
>
> She drives very <u>carefully</u>.   *C*

1. I took my <u>olds</u> shoes to a <u>shoes</u> repair shop.
2. It's <u>too much</u> cold outside. Let's stay inside today.
3. Basketball players are <u>too</u> tall.
4. The <u>very rich</u> woman bought <u>an expensive birthday present</u> for her <u>beautiful daughter</u>.
5. She is only 16 years old. She's <u>too young</u> to get married.
6. I found a <u>wonderful job</u>. I'm <u>too</u> happy.
7. My father is only 50 years old. He is <u>too much</u> young to retire.
8. He speaks English very <u>good</u>.
9. You came home late last night. I was very <u>worry</u> about you.
10. He worked <u>very hard</u> last night.
11. He counted the money <u>very carefully</u>.
12. My sister is <u>marry</u>.
13. I prefer a <u>small car</u>. My wife prefers <u>a large</u>.
14. He won a prize. He seems very <u>happily</u>.
15. I <u>very</u> like my new apartment.
16. Those sisters are very <u>differents</u> from each other.
17. This class is <u>a</u> big.

PART 2 Find the mistakes in word order and correct them. Not every sentence has a mistake. If the sentence is correct, write *C*.

> **EXAMPLES** He writes (very carefully) his compositions.
>
> He has enough time to do his homework.   *C*

1. I got my license driver's last year.
2. My brother is only 15 years old. He's not enough old to drive.
3. He early ate breakfast.

4. She opened slowly the door.

5. She speaks English very fluently.

6. They are too young to retire.

7. He bought a car very expensive.

PART 3 Fill in the blanks with the correct form, adjective or adverb, of the word in parentheses ( ).

EXAMPLE   Sue is a _patient_ person. Don does everything _impatiently_.
(patient)   (impatient)

1. Sue has _____ handwriting. Don writes _____. I can't
(neat)   (sloppy)

   even read what he wrote.

2. She likes to drive _____. He likes to drive _____.
(careful)   (fast)

3. She speaks English _____. He has a _____ time with
(fluent)   (hard)

   English.

4. She learns languages _____. Learning a new
(easy)

   language is _____ for Don.
(difficult)

5. She types _____. He makes a lot of mistakes.
(accurate)

   He needs someone to check his work _____.
(careful)

6. She has a very _____ voice. He speaks _____.
(soft)   (loud)

7. She sings _____. He sings like a _____ chicken.
(beautiful)   (sick)

8. She is always very _____. He sometimes
(responsible)

   behaves _____.
(childish)

9. She saves her money _____. He buys things
(careful)

   he doesn't need. He spends his money _____.
(foolish)

10. She exercises _____. He's very _____
(regular)   (lazy)

    about exercising.

Classroom Activities

Hello Hello

1. Circle the words that best describe your actions. Find a partner and compare your personality to your partner's personality. How many characteristics do you have in common?

a.	I usually spend my money	carefully	foolishly
b.	I do my homework	willingly	unwillingly
c.	I write compositions	carefully	carelessly
d.	I usually walk	slowly	quickly
e.	I write	neatly	sloppily
f.	I like to drive	fast	slowly
g.	I write my language	well	poorly
h.	Before a test, I study	hard	a little
i.	I exercise	regularly	infrequently
j.	I play tennis	well	poorly
k.	I like to live	dangerously	carefully
l.	I make important decisions	quickly	slowly and methodically
m.	I learn languages	easily	with difficulty
n.	I learn math	easily	with difficulty
o.	I make judgments	logically	intuitively

2. Game: "In the manner of"

Teacher: Write these adverbs on separate pieces of paper or on index cards: gladly, suddenly, slowly, comfortably, simply, steadily, foolishly, efficiently, accurately, quietly, surprisingly, excitedly, promptly, fearlessly, fearfully, indecisively, carefully, carelessly, neatly, smoothly, repeatedly. Make sure the students know the meaning of each of these adverbs. Ask one student to leave the room. The other students pick one adverb. When the student returns to the room, he/she asks individuals to do something by giving imperatives. The others do this task in the manner of the adverb that was chosen. The student tries to guess the adverb.

EXAMPLE Edgar, write your name on the blackboard.
Sofia, take off one shoe.
Maria, open the door.
Nora, give me your book.

3. Name something.

EXAMPLE Name some things you do well.

I speak my native language well.
I swim well.

a. Name some things you do well.
b. Name some things you don't do well.

c. Name some things you do quickly.
d. Name some things you do slowly.
e. Name something you learned to do easily.

Talk
About it

1. In a small group or with the entire class, discuss the situation of older people in your native culture. Who takes care of them when they are too old or too sick to take care of themselves? How does your family take care of its older members?

2. In a small group or with the entire class, discuss the situation of handicapped people in the U.S. or in another country. Are there special schools? Are there special facilities, such as parking, public washrooms, elevators?

3. Discuss the meaning of this quote by Grandma Moses:

"What a strange thing is memory, and hope. One looks backward, the other forward; one is of today, the other of tomorrow. Memory is history recorded in our brain. Memory is a painter. It paints pictures of the past and of the day."

Write
About it

1. Write about a famous person you know about who accomplished something in spite of a handicap or age.

2. Write about a man or woman whom you admire very much. You may write about a famous person or any person you know (family member, teacher, doctor, etc).

Outside
Activity

Rent the movie *The Miracle Worker*. It's the story of Helen Keller and Anne Sullivan.

Internet
Activities

1. Use the Internet to find information about the following people. Who are they and what extraordinary things did they do?

- Erik Weihenmayer
- Sherman Bull
- Enrique Oliu
- Lance Armstrong

2. Use the Internet to find the American Sign Language finger alphabet. Try to make the letters with your hand.

3. Use the Internet to find some paintings by Grandma Moses.

Additional Activities at http://elt.heinle.com/gic

LESSON

12

GRAMMAR

Comparatives

Superlatives

CONTEXT: U.S. Geography

U.S. Geography

A Tale of Two Cities

The Sears Tower, Chicago

The Empire State Building, New York

The Space Needle, Seattle

Before You
Read

1. What is the tallest building in this city?

2. In your opinion, what is the most interesting city? Why is it interesting?

3. What cities or regions have the best climate?

The United States of America

 Read the following information. Pay special attention to comparative and superlative forms.

Did You
Know?

Before 1849, the population of California was very small. In 1849, gold was found in California and about 100,000 people rushed there to try to get rich.

1. In area, the United States is the third **largest** country in the world (after Russia and Canada). In population, the U.S. is the third **largest** country in the world (after China and India).

2. The **biggest** city in the U.S. in population is New York. It has about 8 million people.

3. The **tallest** building in the U.S. is the Sears Tower in Chicago (442 meters or 1,450 feet tall). But it is not the **tallest** building in the world. That building is in Kuala Lumpur (452 meters or 1,483 feet tall).

4. New York City has the **highest** cost of living. But the cost of living in Tokyo is much **higher** than in New York.

5. Hispanics are the **fastest** growing minority in the U.S. In 2003, Hispanics passed African Americans as the **largest** minority.

6. Rhode Island is the **smallest** state in area (1,145 square miles or 2,700 square kilometers).

7. Alaska is the **largest** state in area. Alaska is even **larger** than Colombia, South America.

8. The **least populated** state is Wyoming. It has **less** than half a million people.
9. California is the **most populated** state. It has about 34 million people. There are **more** people in California than in Peru.
10. Juneau, Alaska gets the **most** snow, about 101 inches per year.
11. Phoenix, Arizona, gets the **most** sunshine. Eight-five percent of the days are sunny.
12. Mount McKinley is the **highest** mountain in the U.S. (20,320 feet or 6,193 meters). It is in Alaska.
13. There are five great lakes in the U.S. The **biggest** is Lake Superior. The others are Lake Huron, Lake Michigan, Lake Erie, and Lake Ontario.
14. The **tallest** waterfall in the U.S. is in California. But Niagara Falls in New York and Ontario, Canada, is **more famous**. It is one of the **most popular** tourist attractions. Twelve million tourists a year visit Niagara Falls. It has the **greatest** volume of water.
15. The state that is the **farthest** north is Alaska. The state that is the **farthest** south is Hawaii.
16. The **most recent** state to join the U.S. is Hawaii. It joined in 1959.
17. The **oldest** state is Delaware. It became a state in 1787.

Niagara Falls

12.1 | Comparatives and Superlatives—An Overview

Examples	Explanation
New York City is the **biggest** city in the U.S. California is the **most populated** state in the U.S.	We use the superlative form to point out the number-one item in a group of three or more.
Los Angeles is **bigger** than Chicago. There are **more** people in California than in Peru.	We use the comparative form to compare two items.

EXERCISE 1   Circle the correct word to complete the statement.

EXAMPLE   Chicago is *bigger* / *smaller* than Los Angeles.

1. The tallest building in the world *is* / *isn't* in the U.S.

2. The most populated state is *Alaska* / *California*.

3. The U.S. *is* / *isn't* the largest country in the world in area.

4. *Alaska* / *California* has the largest area.

5. The fastest growing minority is *Hispanics* / *African Americans*.

12.2 | Comparative and Superlative Forms of Adjectives and Adverbs

	Simple	Comparative	Superlative
One-syllable adjectives and adverbs*	tall	taller	the tallest
	fast	faster	the fastest
Two-syllable adjectives that end in -y	easy	easier	the easiest
	happy	happier	the happiest
Other two-syllable adjectives	frequent	more frequent	the most frequent
	active	more active	the most active
Some two-syllable adjectives have two forms.**	simple	simpler	the simplest
		more simple	the most simple
	common	commoner	the commonest
		more common	the most common
Adjectives with three or more syllables	important	more important	the most important
	difficult	more difficult	the most difficult
-ly adverbs	quickly	more quickly	the most quickly
	brightly	more brightly	the most brightly
Irregular adjectives and adverbs	good/well	better	the best
	bad/badly	worse	the worst
	far	farther	the farthest
	little	less	the least
	a lot	more	the most

Language Notes:
1. *Exceptions to one-syllable adjectives:

bored	more bored	the most bored
tired	more tired	the most tired

2. **Other two-syllable adjectives that have two forms:
   handsome, quiet, gentle, narrow, clever, friendly, angry, polite, stupid

Spelling Rules for Short Adjectives and Adverbs

Rule	Simple	Comparative	Superlative
Add -er and -est to short adjectives and adverbs.	tall fast	taller faster	tallest fastest
For adjectives that end in e, add -r and -st.	nice late	nicer later	nicest latest
For adjectives that end in y, change y to i and add -er and -est.	easy happy	easier happier	easiest happiest
For words ending in consonant-vowel-consonant, double the final consonant, then add -er and -est. **Exception:** Do not double final w. new—newer—newest	big sad	bigger sadder	biggest saddest

EXERCISE 2 Give the comparative and superlative forms of the word.

EXAMPLES   fat   *fatter*   *the fattest*

important   *more important*   *the most important*

1. interesting _____   _____

2. young   _____   _____

3. beautiful   _____   _____

4. good   _____   _____

5. common   _____   _____

6. thin   _____   _____

7. carefully   _____   _____

8. pretty   _____   _____

9. bad   _____   _____

10. famous   _____   _____

11. lucky   _____   _____

12. simple   _____   _____

13. high   _____   _____

14. delicious   _____   _____

15. far   _____   _____

16. foolishly   _____   _____

12.3 | Superlative Adjectives

Examples	Explanation

New York is **the biggest** city in the U.S.
California is **the most populated** state in the U.S.
China has **the largest** population in the world.
	We use the superlative form to point out the number-one item of a group of three or more. Use *the* before a superlative form.
	We often put a prepositional phrase at the end of a superlative sentence:
	    in the world in my family
	    in my class in my country

Niagara Falls is **one of the most popular** tourist attraction**s** in the U.S. The Sears Tower is **one of the tallest** building**s** in the world.	We often put "one of the" before a superlative form. Then we use a plural noun.

EXERCISE 3 Fill in the blanks with the superlative form of the word in parentheses ( ). Include *the* before the superlative form.

EXAMPLE Alaska is _____ *the largest* _____ state in area.
(large)

1. _____ lake in the U.S. is Lake Superior.
(big)

2. _____ river in the U.S. is the Missouri.
(long)

3. _____ mountain in the U.S. is Mount McKinley.
(high)

4. Johnson is one of _____ last names in the U.S.
(common)

5. Niagara Falls is one of _____ tourist attractions.
(popular)

6. San Francisco is one of _____ cities in the U.S.
(expensive)

7. San Francisco is one of _____ American cities.
(beautiful)

8. Harvard is one of _____ universities in the U.S.
(good)

9. The Sears Tower is _____ building in the U.S.
(tall)

10. Crime is one of _____ problems in the U.S.
(bad)

11. Boston is one of _____ cities in the U.S.
(old)

EXERCISE 4 ABOUT YOU Talk about the number-one person in your family for each of these adjectives.

EXAMPLES interesting
My aunt Rosa is the most interesting person in my family.

tall
The tallest person in my family is my brother Carlos.

1. intelligent
2. kind
3. handsome/beautiful
4. stubborn
5. lazy
6. tall

7. serious
8. nervous
9. strong
10. funny
11. responsible
12. neat

EXERCISE 5 Write a superlative sentence, giving your opinion about each of the following items. (You may use "one of the . . ." plus a plural noun.)

EXAMPLE big problem today
The biggest problem in the U.S. today is crime.
OR
One of the biggest problems in my country today is the economy.

1. exciting sport

2. bad war

3. bad tragedy in the world or in the U.S.

4. important invention of the last 100 years

5. interesting city in the world

6. big problem in the U.S. today

7. bad job

8. good job

_____

9. hard teacher at this school

_____

10. popular movie star

_____

12.4 | Word Order with Superlatives

Examples	Explanation
What is *the biggest* lake? California is *the most populated* state.	A superlative adjective comes **before** a noun.
The Sears Tower is **the tallest building** in the U.S. OR **The tallest building** in the U.S. is the Sears Tower.	When the verb *be* connects a noun to a superlative adjective + noun, there are two possible word orders.
The Hispanic population **is growing** *the most quickly* in the U.S. The population of India **is increasing** *the most rapidly* in the world.	We put superlative adverbs **after** the verb (phrase).
It **rains** *the most* in Hawaii. It **snows** *the most* in Alaska.	We put *the most, the least, the best, the worst* **after** a verb.
Phoenix gets *the most* sunshine. Alaska has *the least* sunshine in the winter.	We put *the most, the least, the best, the worst* **before** a noun.

EXERCISE 6   Name the person in your family who is the superlative in each of the following activities. (Put the superlative form after the verb phrase.)

EXAMPLES   cook well
My mother cooks the best in the family.

eat a lot
My brother eats the most in my family.

1. talk a lot
2. drive well
3. walk fast

4. speak English well
5. stay up late
6. get up early

7. speak softly
8. eat a lot

EXERCISE 7 ABOUT YOU Name the person in your family who is the superlative in each of the following activities. (Put the superlative form before the noun.)

EXAMPLE
watch a lot of TV
My brother watches the most TV. He watches TV four hours a day.

1. spend a lot of money

2. get a lot of mail

3. drink a lot of coffee

4. spend a lot of time in the bathroom

5. spend a lot of time on the telephone

6. have a bad temper

7. use a lot of makeup

A TALE OF TWO CITIES[1]

Before You **Read**

1. Compare this city to another city.

2. Do you have any friends or relatives in American cities? Do you visit them?

San Francisco

Chicago

[1]These statistics are from 2001.

Look at the following chart. Then read the sentences that follow. Pay special attention to comparative forms.

	San Francisco	Chicago
Population	777,000	2,900,000
Cost of home*	$604,000	$260,000
Unemployment	2.5%	4%
Cost of living (100 = national average)	208	96
Average family income	$40,561	$30,707
High school graduates	78% of population	66% of population
Average temperature in July	59 degrees	75 degrees
Average temperature in January	51 degrees	22 degrees
Rainfall (inches annually)	20	37
Number of clear days (no clouds) per year	162	94
Air pollution (amount of ozone in air; US average = 100)	42	79
Crime (per 100,000 people)	7,595	9,454

*Cost of home is based on 2,000 square feet in 2001.

- Chicago has a **larger** population **than** San Francisco.
- A house in San Francisco is **more expensive than** a house in Chicago.
- Unemployment in Chicago is **higher than** in San Francisco.
- The average family income is **more** in San Francisco **than** in Chicago, but San Francisco has a **higher** cost of living.
- San Francisco has **more** high school graduates **than** Chicago.
- San Francisco has a **better** climate **than** Chicago. Chicago gets **more** rain **than** San Francisco. San Francisco is **sunnier than** Chicago.
- Chicago is **warmer** in the summer.
- Chicago is **colder** in the winter.
- Chicago has **more** air pollution **than** San Francisco.
- Chicago has **more** crime.

12.5 | Comparisons

Examples	Explanation
Chicago has a **larger** population **than** San Francisco. San Francisco is **more expensive than** Chicago.	We use the comparative form to compare two items. We use *than* before the second item of comparison.
Chicago is **colder than** San Francisco in the winter, but it is **warmer** in the summer.	Omit *than* if the second item of comparison is not included.
The cost of living in San Francisco is **much higher than** in Chicago. Unemployment is **a little higher** in Chicago.	*Much* or *a little* can come before a comparative form.
Formal: You know more about American cities than **I do.** **Informal:** You know more about American cities than **me.** **Formal:** I can speak English better than **he can.** **Informal:** I can speak English better than **him.**	When a pronoun follows *than*, the correct form is the subject pronoun (*he, she, I, etc.*) Usually an auxiliary verb follows (*is, do, did, can, etc.*). Informally, many Americans use the object pronoun (*him, her, me, etc.*) after *than*. An auxiliary verb does not follow.

EXERCISE 8 Circle the correct words to complete the statement.

EXAMPLE Chicago has *more* / *less* crime than San Francisco.

1. Chicago has a *larger* / *smaller* population than San Francisco.

2. Chicago is a *safer* / *more dangerous* place to live than San Francisco.

3. Houses in Chicago are *more expensive* / *less expensive* than houses in San Francisco.

4. Winter in Chicago is *better* / *worse* than winter in San Francisco.

5. Chicago has *more* / *less* rain than San Francisco.

EXERCISE 9 ABOUT YOU Compare yourself to another person, or compare two people you know using these adjectives.

EXAMPLES tall
My father is taller than I am. (OR than me.)

talkative
My mother is more talkative than my father.

1. tall	5. thin	9. successful
2. educated	6. quiet	10. strong
3. friendly	7. stubborn	11. nervous
4. lazy	8. patient	12. polite

EXERCISE 10 Compare men and women. Give your own opinion. Talk in general terms. Discuss your answers.

EXAMPLE intelligent
In my opinion, women are more intelligent than men.
OR
In my opinion, men are more intelligent than women.

1. polite	7. talkative
2. strong	8. patient
3. tall	9. romantic
4. intelligent	10. sensitive
5. kind	11. logical
6. friendly	12. responsible

EXERCISE 11 Compare this city to another city you know.

EXAMPLES big
Tokyo is bigger than Boston.

crowded
Tokyo is more crowded than Boston.

1. crowded	4. noisy	7. cold in winter
2. modern	5. beautiful	8. dirty
3. big	6. interesting	9. sunny

12.6 | Word Order with Comparisons

Examples	Explanation
Houses in San Francisco **are more expensive** than houses in Chicago. I want to move to a **warmer climate.**	Put comparative adjectives **after** the verb *be* or before a noun.
The Hispanic population **is growing more quickly** than the African American population.	We put comparative adverbs **after** the verb (phrase).
It **rains more** in Chicago. It **snows more** in Chicago.	We put *more, less, better, worse* **after** a verb.
San Francisco has **more sunshine** than Chicago. San Francisco has **less pollution.**	We put *more, less, fewer, better, worse* **before** a noun.

EXERCISE 12   Compare men and women. Give your own opinion. Talk in general terms. Discuss your answers.

EXAMPLES   work hard
In my opinion, women work harder than men.

talk a lot
In my opinion, women talk more than men.

1. run fast
2. gossip a lot
3. take care of children well
4. worry a lot
5. drive foolishly
6. work hard

7. drive fast
8. spend a lot on clothes
9. think fast
10. live long
11. get old fast
12. make decisions quickly

EXERCISE 13   Compare this city to another city you know. Use *better, worse,* or *more.*

EXAMPLES   factories
Chicago has more factories than Ponce.

public transportation
Moscow has better public transportation than Chicago.

1. traffic
2. climate
3. rain
4. crime

5. pollution
6. job opportunities
7. factories
8. tall buildings

9. people
10. sunshine
11. snow
12. homeless people

EXERCISE 14 Make comparisons with the following words. Give your opinion and reasons. You may work with a partner or in a small group.

EXAMPLE   men / women—have an easy life

In my opinion, men have an easier life than women. Women have to

work two jobs—in the office and at home.

1. men / women—have responsibilities

   _____

2. men / women—live long

   _____

3. American women / women in my native culture—have an easy life

   _____

4. American couples / couples in my native culture—have children

   _____

5. married men / single men—are responsible

   _____

6. American teenagers / teenagers in my native culture—have freedom

   _____

7. American teenagers / teenagers in my native culture—have responsibilities

   _____

8. American children / children in my native culture—have toys

   _____

9. American children / children in my native culture—have a good education

   _____

10. American teachers / teachers in my native culture—have high salaries

    _____

11. American teachers / teachers in my native culture—get respect

    _____

EXERCISE 15 Fill in the blanks with the comparative or superlative form of the word in parentheses ( ). Include *than* or *the* where necessary.

EXAMPLES August is usually ___*hotter than*___ May in Chicago.
(hot)

January is usually ___*the coldest*___ month of the year in Chicago.
(cold)

1. Los Angeles is _____ San Francisco.
(warm)

2. Seattle is _____ city in Washington.
(big)

3. The state of Hawaii is _____ south in the U.S.
(far)

4. Mexico City is _____ New York.
(crowded)

5. New York is _____ Los Angeles.
(crowded)

6. Mexico City is one of _____ cities in the world.
(crowded)

7. New York is a crowded city, but Tokyo is _____.
(crowded)

8. San Francisco is one of _____ cities in the U.S.
(beautiful)

9. _____ building in the world is not in the U.S.
(tall)

10. The population of India is growing _____
(rapidly)
the population of the U.S.

Seattle Space Needle

EXERCISE 16 Two students in Seattle are talking. Fill in the blanks with appropriate words to make comparatives and superlatives.

A: I'm planning to visit Chicago.

B: You're going to love it. It's a beautiful city. In fact, it's one of
___*the most beautiful*___ cities in the U.S.
(example)

A: It's the second largest city, isn't it?

B: Not anymore. Los Angeles is now _____ Chicago.
(1)

A: What should I see while I'm there?

B: You can visit the Sears Tower. It's _____ building in
(2)
the U.S. It has 110 stories. On a clear day, you can see many miles.

A: Did you go to the top when you were there?

B: When I was there, the weather was bad. It was raining. I hope you have _____ weather than I had. When are you going?
    (3)

A: In August.

B: Ugh! August is the _____ month of the year. It's
    (4)
often 90 degrees or more. If you get hot, you can always go to the beach and cool off.

A: Is Chicago near an ocean?

B: Of course not. It's near Lake Michigan.

A: Is it big like Lake Washington?

B: It's much _____ than Lake Washington. In fact, it's
    (5)
one of the _____ lakes in the U.S.
    (6)

A: Is Chicago very rainy?

B: Not in the summer. It's sunny. In fact, it's much

_____ than Seattle.
    (7)

A: What do you suggest that I see?

B: You should see the famous architecture downtown. The

_____ architects in the U.S. built buildings in
    (8)
Chicago.

A: Do I need to take taxis everywhere or does Chicago have a good public transportation system?

B: Taxis are so expensive! They're much _____ than
    (9)

Lake Michigan

the buses and trains. You should use the public transportation. But remember there's a lot of crime in Chicago, so it's not safe to travel alone at night. It's

_____ in the daytime.
    (10)

A: Does Chicago have _____ crime
    (11)
than Seattle?

B: Yes. But if you're careful, you'll be OK. I'm sure you'll enjoy it. It's an interesting place because it has people from all over the world. In fact, I

think it's one of the _____
    (12)

cities in the U.S.

1. Comparison of Adjectives

SHORT ADJECTIVES
Chicago is a **big** city.
Chicago is **bigger than** Boston.
New York is **the biggest** city in the U.S.

LONG ADJECTIVES
Houston is a **populated** city.
Chicago is **more populated than** Houston.
New York is **the most populated** city in the U.S.

2. Comparison of Adverbs

SHORT ADVERBS
She drives **fast.**
She drives **faster than** her husband.
Her son drives **the fastest** in the family.

-LY ADVERBS
You speak English **fluently.**
You speak English **more fluently than** your brother.
Your sister speaks English **the most fluently** in your family.

3. Word Order

VERB (PHRASE) + COMPARATIVE ADVERB
She **speaks English more fluently** than her husband.
She **talks more** than her husband.

COMPARATIVE ADJECTIVE + NOUN
She has **more experience** than her husband.
She has a **better accent** than her sister.

EDITING ADVICE

1. Don't use a comparison word when there is no comparison.

California is a big~~ger~~ state.

2. Don't use *more* and *-er* together.

My new car is ~~more~~ better than my old one.

3. Use *than* before the second item in a comparison.

than
He is younger ~~that~~ his wife.

4. Use *the* before a superlative form.

    the
China has ᴧ biggest population in the world.

5. Use a plural noun after the phrase "one of the."

    s
Jim is one of the tallest boy ᴧ in the class.

6. Use the correct word order.

    drives faster
She ~~faster drives~~ than her husband.

    more
I have ᴧ responsibilities ~~more~~ than you.

                          country
The U.S. is the ~~country~~ most powerful ᴧ in the world.

7. Don't use *the* with a possessive form.

My ~~the~~ best friend lives in London.

8. Use correct spelling.

    happier
She is ~~happyer~~ than her friend.

LESSON 12 TEST/REVIEW

PART 1 Find the mistakes with the underlined words and correct them. Not every sentence has a mistake. If the sentence is correct, write *C*.

                than
EXAMPLES I am taller ᴧ my father.
            I am tall, but my brother is <u>taller</u>.   *C*

1. Paul is one of <u>the youngest student</u> in this class.

2. She is <u>more older than</u> her husband.

3. I'm <u>the most tall</u> person in my family.

4. My father is <u>more educated</u> my mother.

5. She is <u>the most intelligent</u> person in her family.

6. New York City is <u>biggest</u> city in the U.S.

7. My sister's <u>the oldest</u> son got married last month.

8. Houston is a very <u>big</u> city.

9. He is <u>much older</u> than his wife.

10. New York is <u>biger</u> than Los Angeles.

11. I speak English <u>more better than</u> I did a year ago.

12. Book One is <u>easyer</u> than Book Two.

PART 2 Find the mistakes with word order and correct them. Not every sentence has a mistake. If the sentence is correct, write *C*.

EXAMPLES You more (know) about the U.S. than I do.

Soccer is more interesting than football for me. *C*

1. I have problems more than you.

2. I earlier woke up than you.

3. Paris is the city most beautiful in the world.

4. She speaks English more fluently than her brother.

5. You faster type than I do.

6. My father is the most intelligent person in the family.

7. Your car is expensive more than my car.

8. You sing more beautifully than I do.

9. I travel more than my friend does.

10. You have more money than I do.

PART 3 Fill in the blanks with the comparative or the superlative of the word in parentheses ( ). Add *the* or *than* if necessary.

EXAMPLES New York is _____*bigger than*_____ Chicago.
                                 (big)

          New York is _____*the biggest*_____ city in the U.S.
                                   (big)

1. Mount Everest is _____ mountain in the world.
                                 (high)

2. A D grade is _____ a C grade.
                          (bad)

3. Johnson is one of _____ last names in the U.S.
   (common)

4. Tokyo is _____ Miami.
   (populated)

5. June 21 is _____ day of the year.
   (long)

6. The teacher speaks English _____ I do.
   (well)

7. Lake Superior is _____ lake in the U.S.
   (large)

8. Children learn a foreign language _____ adults.
   (quickly)

9. Do you think that Japanese cars are _____
   (good)

   American cars?

10. A dog is _____ a cat.
    (friendly)

11. Women drive _____ men.
    (carefully)

12. Who is _____ student in this class?
    (good)

13. The teacher speaks English _____ I do.
    (fluently)

14. A dog is intelligent, but a monkey is _____ .
    (intelligent)

EXPANSION ACTIVITIES

Classroom *Activities*

1. Form a small group of three to five students. Fill in the blanks to give information about yourself. Compare your list with the lists of other members of your group to make superlative statements.

   EXAMPLE Susana has the most relatives in this city.

   a. Number of relatives I have in this city _____

   b. My height _____

   c. Number of letters in my last name _____

   d. Number of children I have _____

   e. Number of sisters and brothers I have _____

   f. Age of my car _____

g. Number of hours I watch TV per week _____

h. Number of hours I exercise per week _____

i. Money I spent today _____

j. Distance I travel to come to this school _____

k. Cups of coffee I drank today _____

l. Number of miles I usually drive or walk per day _____

m. Number of movies I usually see per year _____

2. Work with a partner from the same native culture, if possible. Compare American men and men from your native culture. Compare American women and women from your native culture. Report some of your ideas to the class.

3. The manager of a company is interviewing two people for the same job: a younger woman (24 years old) and an older woman (55 years old). He can't decide which one to hire. Find a partner. One person (the manager) will make a statement. The partner will say, "Yes, but . . ." and follow with another statement.

EXAMPLES A: Older people are wiser.
B: Yes, but younger people are quicker.
A: Older people have more experience.
B: Yes, but younger people are more flexible.

4. Find a partner. Choose one of the following pairs and decide which of the two is better. Write five reasons why it is better. One person will make a statement saying that one is better than the other. The other person will follow with, "Yes, but . . ." and give another point of view.

EXAMPLE A: I think dogs are better pets than cats. They are more loyal.
B: Yes, but dogs need more attention.

- cats and dogs
- big cities and small towns
- travel by train and travel by plane
- houses and condos
- spring and fall
- voice mail and answering machines

1. Choose one of the topics below to write a comparison:

a. Compare your present car with your last car.
b. Compare two cities you know well.

    c. Compare American women and women in your native culture.

    d. Compare American men and men in your native culture.

    e. Compare soccer and football.

    f. Compare your life in the U.S. and your life in your native country.

    g. Compare a place where you lived before with the place where you live now.

2. Write about the biggest problem in the world (or in your native country, or in the U.S.) today. Why is this a problem? How can we solve the problem?

Outside Activity

Interview a native speaker of English. Get his or her opinion about the superlative of each of the following items. Share your findings with the class.

EXAMPLE good car
What do you think is the best car?

    a. good car

    b. beautiful actress

    c. good president in the last 25 years

    d. beautiful city in the U.S.

    e. good university in the U.S.

    f. popular movie at this time

    g. terrible tragedy in American history

    h. big problem in the U.S. today

    i. popular singer in the U.S.

    j. best athlete

    h. handsome actor

Internet Activities

1. Using the Internet, find a site that compares cities. Compare any two American cities that interest you.

2. Using the Internet, find out about the city where you live. Find out:

- the name of the mayor
- the population
- the annual rainfall
- the coldest month
- interesting places to visit

 Additional Activities at http://elt.heinle.com/gic

GRAMMAR

Auxiliary Verbs with *Too* and *Either*
Auxiliary Verbs in Tag Questions

CONTEXT: Dating and Marriage

Dating and Marriage
Saturday with Meg and Don

Before You Read

1. How is dating different from marriage?

2. Do American married couples spend more or less time together than couples in your native culture?

 Read the following article. Pay special attention to auxiliary verbs and *too* and *either*.

Most married couples want to spend time together, but the busy American lifestyle often doesn't allow it. Meg and Don are a typical American couple.

Before Meg and Don met, they were both lonely. Meg wanted to get married, and Don **did too.** They both wanted to get married. Meg believed that marriage would mean a lot of togetherness, and Don **did too.** When they were dating, they spent all their free time together. They discovered they had a lot in common. A year after they met, they decided to get married. As they planned their wedding, they discovered their first differences in making plans for their wedding: Meg wanted a big wedding, but Don **didn't.** Meg wanted an outdoor wedding, but Don **didn't.** They solved their differences by having a big indoor wedding.

As a married couple, they are now facing the realities of busy schedules and different interests. Don works hard, and Meg **does too.** They often have to work overtime. Don likes to cook, and Meg **does too,** but they rarely have time to do it. They often bring home carry-out dinners or eat in fast-food restaurants. On weekends, Don likes to go fishing, but Meg **doesn't.** So Don takes fishing trips with his friends, and Meg stays home. Meg likes to go to movies, but Don **doesn't.** He prefers to stay home and watch TV when he comes home from work. Both of them are planning to take college courses soon, which will give them even less time together.

So how do they solve these differences and stay close as a married couple? Once a month, they invite friends over on weekends to have dinner and watch a movie or a football game on TV. When Don goes on a fishing trip, Meg gets together with her best friend and they go to a movie. That way, Don enjoys himself, and Meg **does too.**

Even though the realities of marriage are different from the romance of dating, Meg and Don are finding ways to adjust to married life.

13.1 | Auxiliary Verbs with *Too* and *Either*

The auxiliary verbs are *do, does, did,* the modals, and *be.* We use auxiliary verbs with *too* and *either* to show similarity and avoid repetition of the same verb phrase.

Examples	Explanation
Don is busy, and Meg **is too.** Don likes to cook, and Meg **does too.** Don was lonely, and Meg **was too.** Don lived alone, and Meg **did too.**	For affirmative statements, use the auxiliary verb + *too.*
Don doesn't have much free time, and Meg **doesn't either.** Don can't see his friends very often, and Meg **can't either.**	For negative statements, use the auxiliary verb + *either.*
Don: I like to cook. *Meg*: **Me too.** *Don*: I don't have much time. *Meg*: **Me neither.**	In informal speech, we often say *me too* and *me neither.*
American: Meg has a hard job, and Don **does too.** **British:** Meg has a hard job, and Don **has too.**	When *have* is the main verb, Americans usually use *do, does, did* as a substitute. The British often use *have.*

EXERCISE 1 Fill in the blanks with an auxiliary verb + *too* to show what Meg and Don have in common. Make sure you use the same tense as the main verb.

EXAMPLE Don likes to cook, and Meg _____*does too*_____ .

1. Don has a hard job, and Meg _____ .

2. Don is a hard worker, and Meg _____ .

3. Don will take some college courses next semester, and Meg

    _____ .

4. Don was lonely before, and Meg _____ .

5. Don worked last Saturday, and Meg _____ .

EXERCISE 2 Fill in the blanks with an auxiliary verb + *either* to show what Meg and Don have in common. Make sure you use the same tense as the main verb.

EXAMPLE Don doesn't like fast food, and Meg _____*doesn't either*_____ .

1. Don didn't finish college, and Meg _____ .

2. Don isn't interested in baseball, and Meg _____ .

3. Don doesn't have much free time, and Meg _____.

4. Don can't find time to cook, and Meg _____.

5. Don doesn't have any brothers or sisters, and Meg

_____.

13.2 | Auxiliary Verbs with Opposite Statements

We can use auxiliary verbs with *but* to show contrast and avoid repetition of the same verb phrase.

Examples	Explanation
Don likes to go fishing, **but** Meg **doesn't**. Don is happy watching TV, **but** Meg **isn't**. Don doesn't like to go to movies, **but** Meg **does**. Don didn't want to have a big wedding, **but** Meg **did**.	We can use **but** to connect opposite statements. We often put a comma before *but*.
Meg: I want a big wedding. *Don*: I **don't**.	In conversation, we don't need *but* when one person says the opposite of another.

EXERCISE 3   Fill in the blanks with an auxiliary verb to show what Meg and Don don't have in common.

EXAMPLE   Don likes to go fishing, but Meg _____*doesn't*_____.

1. Meg likes to go to movies, but Don _____.

2. Meg doesn't like to watch football on TV, but Don

_____.

3. Meg reads when she has free time, but Don _____.

4. Don wanted to have a small wedding, but Meg _____.

5. Meg is interested in politics, but Don _____.

6. Meg isn't interested in cars, but Don _____.

7. Meg can play the piano, but Don _____.

EXERCISE 4   Fill in the blanks to compare the U.S. and another country you know. Use *and . . . too* or *and . . . either* for similarities between the U.S. and the other country. Use *but* for differences. Use an auxiliary verb in all cases.

EXAMPLE   The U.S. is a big country, _____*and Russia is too.*_____
          OR
          The U.S. is a big country, _____*but Cuba isn't.*_____

1. The U.S. has more than 290 million people, _____

2. The U.S. is in North America, _____

3. The U.S. has a president, _____

4. The U.S. doesn't have a socialist government, _____

5. The U.S. fought in World War II, _____

6. The U.S. was a colony of England, _____

7. Americans like football, _____

8. Americans don't celebrate Labor Day in May, _____

9. American public schools are closed on December 25, _____

_____

10. The U.S. has a presidential election every four years, _____

_____

EXERCISE 5 ABOUT YOU Check (✓) *yes* or *no* to tell what is true for you. Exchange your book with another student. Make statements about you and the other student.

EXAMPLE I don't speak Spanish, but Luis does.

	Yes	No
1. I speak Spanish.		✓
2. I'm interested in football.		
3. I'm interested in soccer.		
4. I have a car.		
5. I use the Internet.		
6. I can drive.		
7. I plan to move to another city.		
8. I'm going to buy a computer this year.		
9. I would like to live in a small American town.		
10. I exercise every day.		
11. I'm studying math this semester.		
12. I studied English when I was in elementary school.		
13. I finished high school.		
14. I'm a vegetarian.		
15. I have a cell phone.		

EXERCISE 6 Fill in the blanks in the conversation below. Use an auxiliary verb and *too* or *either* when necessary.

A: I'm moving on Saturday. Maybe you and your brother can help me. Are you working on Saturday?

B: My brother is working on Saturday, but I ___*'m not*_____.
(example)

I can help you.

A: I need a van. Do you have one?

B: I don't have one, but my brother _____. I'll ask him
(1)

if we can use it. By the way, why are you moving?

A: There are a couple of reasons. I got married recently. I like the

apartment, but my wife _____. She says it's too
(2)

small for two people.

B: How many rooms does your new apartment have?

A: The old apartment has two bedrooms, and the new one

_____. But the rooms are much bigger in the new
(3)

one, and there are more closets. Also, we'd like to live near the lake.

B: I _____, but apartments there are very expensive.
(4)

A: We found a nice apartment that isn't so expensive. Also, I'd like to own a dog, but my present landlord doesn't permit pets.

B: Mine doesn't _____. What kind of dog do you plan
(5)

to get?

A: I like big watchdogs. Maybe a German shepherd or a doberman. I

don't like small dogs, but my wife _____.
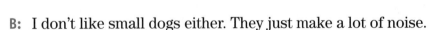
(6)

B: I don't like small dogs either. They just make a lot of noise.

A: So now you know my reasons for moving. Can I count on you for Saturday?

B: Of course you can.

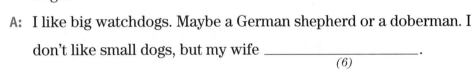

13.3 | Tag Questions

Examples	Explanation
Married life is hard, **isn't it?** You don't like to go fishing, **do you?** Meg and Don work hard, **don't they?** Americans don't have much free time, **do they?**	A tag question is a short question that we put at the end of a statement. Use a tag question to ask if your statement is correct of if the listener agrees with you. The tag question uses an auxiliary verb in the same tense as the main verb.

SATURDAY WITH MEG AND DON

Before You **Read**

1. When families talk about "quality time," what do you think they mean?

2. What do you like to do with your free time?

 Read the following conversation between Meg (M) and Don (D). Pay special attention to tag questions.

M: Would you like to go out to a movie tonight?

D: Not really.

M: Before we got married, you always wanted to go to movies, **didn't you?**

D: I suppose so. But I'm tired now. I'd rather stay home and watch TV or rent a movie.

M: You're always tired, **aren't you?**

D: Well, actually, yes. I work hard all week, and now I just want to relax.

M: When we got married, we planned to spend a lot of time together, **didn't we?**

D: I know. But married life is hard. Besides, we spend a lot of time together on weekends, **don't we?**

M: Yes, we do. We go shopping, we do the laundry, we visit your parents, we cut the grass, we clean the house. But we don't have any fun together anymore, **do we?**

D: Fishing is fun for me. Next weekend I'm going fishing with my buddies. But you don't like fishing, **do you?**

M: Not really.

D: Before we got married, you said you'd try fishing with me, **didn't you?**

M: Yes, I did. But I was just trying to please you then. I realize I like to eat fish, but I don't like to catch them.

D: Well, somebody has to catch them if you want to eat them.

M: But we never eat them because we don't have time to cook. Now that it's Saturday, we're both too tired to cook. What are we going to do for dinner tonight?

D: We can get some carry-out from that new Chinese place nearby, **can't we?**

M: I suppose so.

D: You're not happy, **are you?**

M: That's not true! I love you, but I just want to spend more "quality time" with you.

D: I have an idea. Let's invite some friends over next weekend, and we can make our special fish recipe for them. That will be fun, **won't it?**

M: That's a great idea.

Auxiliary Verbs with *Too* and *Either*; Auxiliary Verbs in Tag Questions

13.4 | Auxiliary Verbs in Tag Questions

Affirmative Statements	Negative Tag Questions	Explanation
Don likes fishing,	**doesn't** he?	An affirmative statement has a negative tag question. Make a contraction with the auxiliary verb + *not* and then use a subject pronoun.
You're always tired,	**aren't** you?	
We can eat out,	**can't** we?	
We planned to spend time together,	**didn't** we?	
Meg is unhappy,	**isn't** she?	

Negative Statements	Affirmative Tag Questions	Explanation
You aren't happy,	**are you?**	A negative statement has an affirmative tag question. Use the auxiliary verb + a subject pronoun.
You don't like fishing,	**do you?**	
We never have fun together anymore,	**do we?**	

Using Tag Questions

Examples	Explanation
There isn't a lot of free time, **is there?** There are a lot of things to do, **aren't there?**	If the sentence begins with *there is* or *there are*, use *there* in the tag.
This is a typical marriage, **isn't it?** That will be fun, **won't it?**	If the sentence begins with *this* or *that*, use *it* in the tag.
These are normal problems, **aren't they?** Those romantic days are over, **aren't they?**	If the sentence begins with *these* or *those*, use *they* in the tag.
Informal: I'm right, **aren't I?** **Formal:** I'm right, **am I not?**	*Am I not?* is a very formal tag. Informally, we usually say *aren't I?*

EXERCISE 7 Add a tag question. All the statements are affirmative and have an auxiliary verb.

EXAMPLE   This class is large, _*isn't it?*_

1. You're a foreign student, _____

2. You can understand English, _____

3. We'll have a test soon, _____

4. We should study, _____

5. There's a library at this school, _____

6. You'd like to improve your English, _____

7. This is an easy lesson, _____

8. I'm asking too many questions, _____

EXERCISE 8 Add a tag question. All the statements are negative and have an auxiliary verb.

EXAMPLE You can't speak Italian, _____*can you?*_____

1. You aren't an American citizen, _____

2. The teacher can't speak your language, _____

3. We shouldn't talk in the library, _____

4. You weren't absent yesterday, _____

5. There aren't any Japanese students in this class,

_____

6. This exercise isn't hard, _____

EXERCISE 9 Add a tag question. All the statements are affirmative. Substitute the main verb with an auxiliary verb in the tag question.

EXAMPLE You have the textbook, _____*don't you?*_____

1. English has a lot of irregular verbs, _____

2. You want to speak English well, _____

3. You understood the explanation, _____

4. You have a cell phone, _____

5. They bought a laptop last week, _____

6. We had a test last week, _____

Auxiliary Verbs with *Too* and *Either*; Auxiliary Verbs in Tag Questions

EXERCISE 10 Add a tag question. All the statements are negative.

EXAMPLE We don't have class on Saturday, _____*do we?*_____

1. The teacher doesn't pronounce your name correctly,

   _____

2. Your brother didn't take the last test, _____

3. You didn't bring your dictionary today, _____

4. We don't always have homework, _____

5. I don't have your phone number, _____

6. Your mother doesn't speak English, _____

EXERCISE 11 This is a conversation between two acquaintances,[1] Bob (B) and Sam (S). Sam can't remember where he met Bob. Fill in the blanks with a tag question.

B: Hi, Sam.

S: Uh, hi. . . .

B: You don't remember me, _____*do you?*_____
    (example)

S: You look familiar, but I can't remember your name. We were in the

    same chemistry class last semester, _____
    (1)

B: No.

S: Then we probably met in math class, _____
    (2)

B: Wrong again. I'm Meg Wilson's brother.

S: Now I remember you. Meg introduced us at a party

    last summer, _____. And your name
    (3)

    is Bob, _____
    (4)

B: That's right.

S: How are you, Bob? You graduated last year,

    _____
    (5)

[1]An *acquaintance* is a person you don't know well.

B: Yes. And I've got a good job now.

S: You majored in computers, _____
(6)

B: Yes. But I decided to go into real estate.

S: And how's your sister Meg? I never see her anymore. She moved back to California, _____
(7)

B: No. She's still here. But she's married now, and she's very busy.

S: Who did she marry?

B: Don Tripton. You met him, _____
(8)

S: Yes, I think so. Say hello to Meg when you see her. It was great seeing you again, Bob.

EXERCISE 12 A mother (M) is talking to her daughter (D). Fill in the blanks with a tag question.

M: You didn't get your scholarship, _____*did you?*_____
(example)

D: How did you know?

M: Well, you look very disappointed. You can apply again next year,

_____?
(1)

D: Yes. But what will I do this year?

M: There are government loans, _____?
(2)

D: Yes.

M: And you don't have to pay them back until you graduate,

_____?
(3)

D: No.

M: And your professors will give you letters of recommendation,

_____?
(4)

D: I'm sure they will.

M: So don't worry. Just try to get a loan, and you can apply again next year for a scholarship.

13.5 | Answering a Tag Question

Statement with Tag Question	Short Answer	Explanation
Meg and Don are married now, **aren't they?** They work hard, **don't they?**	**Yes,** they are. **Yes,** they do.	When we use a negative tag, we expect the answer to be *yes*.
They don't have much free time, **do they?** Meg doesn't like to go fishing, **does she?**	**No,** they don't. **No,** she doesn't.	When we use an affirmative tag, we expect the answer to be *no*.
Don: You aren't happy, **are you?** *Meg:* You like to go to movies, **don't you?**	*Meg:* **Yes,** I am. I love you. *Don:* **No,** I don't. I like to watch movies at home on TV.	Answering *yes* to an affirmative tag shows disagreement. Answering *no* to a negative tag shows disagreement.

EXERCISE 13 Complete the answer in the left column. Then check the meaning of the answer in the right column. (You may work with a partner.)

A: You don't have a car, do you? **B:** Yes, _____ *I do.* _____	✓ Person B has a car. Person B doesn't have a car.
A: You aren't married, are you? **B:** No, I _____	Person B is married. Person B isn't married.
A: You don't like this city, do you? **B:** No, _____	Person B likes this city. Person B doesn't like this city.
A: The U.S. is the best country in the world, isn't it? **B:** No, _____	Person B agrees with the statement. Person B doesn't agree with the statement.
A: You don't speak Russian, do you? **B:** No, _____	Person B speaks Russian. Person B doesn't speak Russian.
A: You can drive, can't you? **B:** No, _____	Person B can drive. Person B can't drive.
A: You don't have a watch, do you? **B:** Yes, _____	Person B has a watch. Person B doesn't have a watch.
A: You work on Saturday, don't you? **B:** Yes, _____	Person B works on Saturday. Person B doesn't work on Saturday.

Read a statement to another student and add a tag question.
The other student will tell you if this information is correct or not.

EXAMPLES   You speak Polish, _____*don't you?*_____
No, I don't. I speak Ukrainian.

You aren't from Poland, _____*are you?*_____
No, I'm not. I'm from Ukraine.

You came to the U.S. two years ago, _____*didn't you?*_____
Yes, I did.

1. You're married, _____

2. You have children, _____

3. You didn't study English in elementary school,

   _____

4. You have a car, _____

5. You don't live alone, _____

6. You'll take another English course next semester,

   _____

7. You won't graduate this year, _____

8. You took the last test, _____

9. You have to work on Saturday, _____

10. The teacher doesn't speak your language, _____

11. You can type, _____

12. This class isn't too hard for you, _____

13. There was a test last Friday, _____

14. You don't speak German, _____

15. I'm asking you a lot of personal questions, _____

EXERCISE 15   Fill in the blanks with a tag question and an answer that tells if the
information is true or not.

A: You come from Russia, _____*don't you?*_____
                                    (example)

B: _____. I come from Ukraine.
        (1)

A: They speak Polish in Ukraine, _____
                                         (2)

B: _____. They speak Ukrainian and Russian.
        (3)

A: Ukraine isn't part of Russia, _____
(4)

B: _____. Ukraine and Russia are different. They were
(5)

both part of the former Soviet Union.

A: You come from a big city, _____
(6)

B: _____. I come from Kiev. It's the capital of Ukraine.
(7)

It's very big.

A: Your parents aren't here, _____
(8)

B: _____. We came together two years ago. I live with
(9)

my parents.

A: You studied English in your country, _____
(10)

B: _____. I only studied Russian and German. I never
(11)

studied English there.

A: You're not going to go back to live in your country,

_____
(12)

B: _____. I'm an immigrant here. I plan to become an
(13)

American citizen.

EXERCISE 16 This is a conversation between Meg (M) and her best friend,
Lydia (L). Fill in the blanks with tag questions and answers.

M: Hello?
L: Hi, Meg. This is Lydia.
M: Oh, hi, Lydia.
L: Can you talk? I hear the TV in the background. Don's home,

___*isn't he?*___
(example)

M: _____, he _____. He's watching
(1)   (2)

TV, as usual.

L: Are you busy?

M: I'm always busy, _____(3)_____?

L: Well, _____(4)_____, you _____(5)_____.

M: But I can make some time for you. What's up?

L: I have a new boyfriend. His name is Peter.

M: But you're dating Michael, _____(6)_____?

L: _____(7)_____. Not anymore. We broke up a month ago.

The last time I talked to you was over a month ago,

_____(8)_____?

M: Over a month ago? That's terrible. We used to talk every day.

L: Now that you're married, you don't have much free time anymore,

_____(9)_____?

M: _____(10)_____, I _____(11)_____. I almost never have time for myself anymore. Or for my friends. Tell me about your new boyfriend.

L: We have so much in common. We both like sports, the same kind of music, the same kind of food . . . If we get married, we'll have the rest of our lives to have fun together.

M: You're not thinking of getting married, _____(12)_____?

L: _____(13)_____. Not yet. I'm just dreaming.

M: Dating is so much fun, _____(14)_____?

L: _____(15)_____, it _____(16)_____. But marriage isn't, _____(17)_____?

M: "Fun" is not a word that describes marriage.

L: But you had a lot of fun with Don before you got married,

_____?
(18)

M: _____, we _____. But things
(19)   (20)

changed after the wedding. Now all we do together is laundry,
shopping, and cleaning.

L: That doesn't sound very interesting. But there are good things about

being married, _____?
(21)

M: Of course. Don's my best friend. We help each other with all our
problems.

L: Before you got married, I was your best friend,

_____? But now I almost never see you.
(22)

M: You're right, Lydia. I'll try harder to call you more often.

SUMMARY OF LESSON 13

1. Use auxiliary verbs to avoid repetition of the same verb phrase.

Affirmative	and	Shortened Affirmative + *Too*
Meg has a job,	and	Don does too.
Meg is busy,	and	Don is too.

Negative	and	Shortened Negative + *Either*
Meg doesn't work on Saturdays,	and	Don doesn't either.
Meg can't find free time,	and	Don can't either.

Affirmative	but	Shortened Negative
Meg finished college,	but	Don didn't.
Don likes fishing,	but	Meg doesn't.

Negative	but	Shortened Affirmative
Don doesn't like movies,	but	Meg does.
Don didn't want a big wedding,	but	Meg did.

2. Use auxiliary verbs in tag questions.

Affirmative	Negative Tag
You're busy now,	aren't you?
We have a hard life,	don't we?
There are a lot of things to do,	aren't there?

Negative	Affirmative Tag
You don't like fishing,	do you?
I can't go fishing alone,	can I?
We never have time together,	do we?

EDITING ADVICE

1. Don't omit the auxiliary from a shortened sentence with *too* or *either*.

                      do
My brother has a new house, and I too.

                    didn't
John didn't take the test, and I either.

2. Don't confuse *too* and *either*.

                         either
Jack doesn't speak French, and his wife doesn't ~~too~~.

3. If half your sentence is negative and half is affirmative, the connecting word is *but*, not *and*.

                    but
He doesn't speak French, ~~and~~ his wife does.

4. Be careful to answer a tag question correctly.

                         No
New York isn't the capital of the U.S., is it? ~~Yes~~, it isn't.

5. Use a pronoun (or *there*) in the tag question.

                    it
That's your hat, isn't ~~that~~?

                        there
There's some milk in the refrigerator, isn't ~~it~~?

6. Be careful to use the correct auxiliary verb and the correct tense.

                    did
Her sister didn't go to the party, ~~does~~ she?

                    will
She won't go back to her country, ~~does~~ she?

PART 1 Find the mistakes with the underlined words and correct them. Not every sentence has a mistake. If the sentence is correct, write *C*.

EXAMPLES   Today is Friday, isn't ~~today~~? *it*

My friend doesn't like soccer, and I don't either.   *C*

1. My mother speaks English well, <u>and</u> my father doesn't.

2. My mother speaks English well, and my brother <u>does too</u>.

3. The vice president doesn't live in the White House, does he? <u>Yes</u>, he doesn't.

4. A soccer team has 11 players, and a football team <u>too</u>.

5. Bob doesn't have a car, and Mary doesn't <u>too</u>.

6. You're not an American citizen, <u>do</u> you?

7. You didn't finish your dinner, <u>do</u> you?

8. There will be a test next week, <u>won't there</u>?

9. Your father can't come to the U.S., <u>can he</u>?

10. This is the last question, <u>isn't this</u>?

PART 2 This is a conversation between two students who meet for the first time. Fill in the blanks with an auxiliary verb to complete this conversation. Use *either* or *too* when necessary.

C: Hi. My name is Carlos. I'm a new student.

E: I _____*am too*_____. My name is Elena.
    (example)

C: I come from Mexico.

E: Oh, really? I _____. I come from a small town in the
    (1)

northern part of Mexico.

C: I come from Mexico City. I love big cities.

E: I _____. I prefer small towns.
    (2)

C: How do you like living here in Los Angeles?

E: I don't like it much, but my sister _____. She has a
    (3)

good job, but I _____. I miss my job back home.
    (4)

C: I love it here, and my family _____. The climate is
(5)

similar to the climate of Mexico City.

E: What about the air quality? Mexico City doesn't have clean air, and Los

Angeles _____, so you probably feel right at home.
(6)

C: Ha! You're right about the air quality, but there are many nice things
about Los Angeles. Do you want to get a cup of coffee and continue
this conversation? I don't have any more classes today.

E: I _____, but I have to go home now. I enjoyed our talk.
(7)

C: I _____. Maybe we can continue it some other time.
(8)

Well, see you in class tomorrow.

PART 3 In this conversation, a new student is trying to find out
information about the school and class. Add a tag question.

A: There's a parking lot at the school, ___*isn't there?*___
(example)

B: Yes. It's east of the building.

A: The teacher's American, _____
(1)

B: Yes, she is.

A: She doesn't give hard tests, _____
(2)

B: Not too easy, not too hard.

A: We'll have a day off for Christmas, _____
(3)

B: We'll have a whole week off.

A: We have to write compositions, _____
(4)

B: A few.

A: And we can't use a dictionary when we write a composition,

_____
(5)

B: Who told you that? Of course we can. You're very nervous about

school, _____
(6)

A: Yes, I am. It isn't easy to learn a new language, _____
(7)

B: No.

A: And I should ask questions about things I want to know,

_____
(8)

B: Yes, of course. You don't have any more questions,

_____
(9)

A: No.

B: Well, I'll see you in the next class. Bye.

EXPANSION ACTIVITIES

Classroom _Activities_

1. Complete each statement. Then find a partner and compare yourself to your partner by using an auxiliary verb.

EXAMPLES **A:** I speak _____ _Chinese_ _____.

B: I do too. OR I don't.

A: I don't speak _____ _Spanish_ _____.

B: I don't either. OR I do.

a. I speak _____.

b. I don't speak _____.

c. I can _____.

d. I have _____.

e. I don't have _____.

f. I'm _____.

g. I usually drink _____ every day.

h. I'm going to _____ next week.

i. I come from _____.

j. I'm wearing _____ today.

k. I bought _____ last week.

l. I went _____ last week.

m. I don't like _____.

n. I brought _____ to the U.S.

o. I don't like to eat _____.

p. I can't _____ very well.

q. I should _____ more.

2. Find a partner. Tell your partner some things that you think you know about him or her and about his or her native culture or country. Your partner will tell you if you are right or wrong.

EXAMPLES   The capital of your country is New Delhi, isn't it?
Hindus don't eat beef, do they?
You're studying engineering, aren't you?

3. Work with a partner to match Column A with Column B. (Alternate activity: Teacher, copy this page. Cut the copied page along the lines. Give half the class statements from Column A and half the class tag questions from Column B. The students walk around the room to match the statement to the tag question.)

Column A	Column B
Washington is the capital of the U.S.,	is it?
Los Angeles isn't the biggest city,	isn't there?
Puerto Ricans are American citizens,	don't they?
Americans have freedom of speech,	does it?
There's an election every four years,	are you?
Americans fought in World War II,	wasn't she?
There will be a presidential election in 2012,	isn't it?
The president lives in the White House,	doesn't he?
George Washington was the first American president,	won't there?
You're not an American citizen,	did she?
Amelia Earhart didn't come back from her last flight,	aren't they?
Florida doesn't have cold winters,	wasn't he?
Helen Keller was a great woman,	didn't they?

4. The teacher will read each statement. If the statement is true for you, stand up. Students will take turns making statements about two people.

EXAMPLE   Teacher: Stand up if you drank coffee this morning.

Student: I drank coffee this morning, and Tom did too.
Mario didn't drink coffee this morning, and Sofia didn't either.
I drank coffee this morning, but Lisa didn't.

Stand up if you . . .
• have more than five sisters and brothers
• walked to class today
• will buy a house in the next two years

- are wearing running shoes
- have a photo of a family member in your pocket or bag
- want to review this lesson
- went to a movie last week
- can't swim
- plan to buy a car soon
- are tired now
- aren't married
- ate pizza today
- speak Polish
- don't like this game
- can understand American TV
- didn't take the last test

5. Tell the teacher what you think you know about the U.S. or Americans. You may work with a partner. The teacher will tell you if you're right or wrong.

   EXAMPLES Most Americans don't speak a foreign language, do they?
   Alaska is the largest state, isn't it?

6. Discuss what makes a strong marriage.

Write About it

1. Choose two sports, religions, countries, people, or stores and write sentences comparing them.

   EXAMPLE my mother and my father

   My father speaks English well, but my mother doesn't.

   My father isn't an American citizen, and my mother isn't either.

   My father was born in 1938, and my mother was too.

2. Find a partner. Write a list of some things you have in common and some differences you have.

   EXAMPLES *Alex plays the violin, and I do too.*

   Alex is majoring in chemistry, but I'm not.

   Alex doesn't have a computer, and I don't either.

   _____

   _____

   _____

Internet Activity

Find a Web site that gives marriage, dating, or relationship advice. Bring an article to class and discuss the advice.

Additional Activities at **http://elt.heinle.com/gic**

GRAMMAR
Verb Review

CONTEXT: Washington Interns

Washington Interns

The Supreme Court, Washington, D.C.

Before You Read

1. How can a college student get work experience?

2. What do most college students do during their summer break?

Read the information and letter that follows it. Pay special attention to verb tenses.

Some college students **want** to find interesting work and **gain** valuable experience in the summer. One way **is** to work as an intern in Washington, D.C. Interns **don't get** paid; the reward **comes** from the experience and knowledge they **gain**. Interns **learn** about the U.S. government and politics.

Lena Rosen **decided** to work in Washington last summer as an intern. Here **is** a letter she **wrote** to her parents.

Dear Mom and Dad,

I **can't** believe it! I**'m working** at the Supreme Court. I**'m gaining** so much experience here. When I **go** to law school next year, I **will have** a much greater understanding of American law. And when I **apply** for a job, this internship **will look** really good on my résumé.

At first, I **felt** a little lost and lonely because I **didn't know** anyone. But that soon **changed**. Through my classes and job, I **meet** new and interesting people every day.

Besides my work, I**'m taking** classes at Georgetown University. My professors are great! I**'m learning** so much. My knowledge about American law **is increasing** greatly.

I **have** an interesting roommate, too. She**'s** from California. Her name **is** Nicole. She**'s working** at the Department of Education. She**'s planning** to become a teacher. We **have** a small but comfortable apartment. We **have to shop** and **make** our own meals. So besides learning about the Supreme Court, I**'m learning** how to cook. I**'m becoming** much more responsible. **Are** you surprised?

Whenever Nicole and I **have** free time, we **go** to see the interesting places in Washington. But we rarely **have** free time because of our jobs and our classes. We **might go** to the art museum this weekend if we have enough time.

There **is** one thing I **don't like:** I **have to wear** formal clothes every day. I **can't wear** blue jeans at my job. We **must look** very professional for our jobs. I **didn't have** the right kind of clothes when I **arrived,** so I **went** shopping and **spent** about $500 on new clothes. I **hope** you **don't mind.** I **put** the charges on your credit card. As you know, I**'m not making** any money here. But **don't worry.** I**'m not going to spend** any more money.

When I **get** home, I**'ll tell** you much more about my experience this summer. I **know** I **should write** more often, but I just **don't have** the time.

Love,
Lena

**FAQs (Frequently Asked Questions)
About Washington Internships:**

- How **does** a student **get** an internship?
  Students **should contact** their senators or representatives to apply for an internship.

- What kind of work **do** interns **do?**
  They **work** in research, **help** plan events, **manage** databases, and **write** for newsletters.

- Where **do** they **live?**
  They **live** in on-campus apartments at Georgetown University.

- **Do** they **have to take** classes?
  Yes, they **do.** And they **must participate** in other activities.

- How busy **is** their schedule?
  It **is** *very* busy. Interns **learn** about education, politics, and government.

- **Will** they **receive** college credit for the internship?
  Yes. They **will receive** six hours of college credit.

14.1 | Verb Tenses

Simple Present Tense

Examples	Uses
Washington **is** the capital of the U.S. Some students **want** summer jobs. Washington interns **take** classes at Georgetown University.	• Facts
American students **have** vacation in the summer. Many American students **wear** blue jeans to class.	• Customs and habits
They **take** classes every day. When they **have** free time, they **go** to interesting places.	• Regular activities
I **have** a great roommate now. I **like** my job now.	• With nonaction verbs
When I **get** home, I'll show you my pictures.	• In a future time clause
If you **become** an intern in Washington, you will get valuable experience.	• In a future *if* clause
My roommate **is** from California. My roommate **comes** from San Diego.	• With place of origin

Present Continuous Tense

Examples	Explanation
Lena **is writing** a letter to her parents now.	• Actions that are happening now
Lena **is learning** how to cook. She **isn't making** any money this summer.	• Actions that are happening in a present time period

Future Tense

Examples	Explanation
They **are going to return** to college in the fall. Nicole **is going to become** a teacher.	• Plans for the future (use *be going to*)
I **will** never **forget** this experience. This experience **is going to help** me in my future.	• Predictions (use *will* or *be going to*)
I'll write more later.	• Promises (use *will*)

Simple Past Tense

Examples	Explanation
I **went** shopping because I **needed** clothes. I **spent** $500 on clothes. I **used** your credit card.	• Actions that happened at a specific time in the past

Be

Examples	Explanation
Washington **is** the capital of the U.S.	• To classify or define the subject
Washington **is** interesting.	• To describe the subject
The Supreme Court **is** in Washington.	• To tell the location of the subject
Nicole **is** from San Diego.	• With a place of origin
She **was born** in California.	• With *born*
There **are** many government buildings in Washington.	• With *there*

Modals

Examples	Explanation
Lena **can** wear jeans to class. Lena **can** study at night.	• Permission • Ability
She **should** write to her parents more often. If you want more information about internships, you **should** write to your senator.	• Advisability
She **must** look professional in her job. Interns **must** participate in activities.	• Necessity
They **might** go to the art museum this weekend. Lena **may** visit Nicole in California next year.	• Possibility

Language Notes:

1. An infinitive doesn't show tense.

    I **want to go** to Washington.

    She **wants to go** to Washington.

    They **wanted to go** to Washington.

2. The verb after a modal is always the base form.

    She **should study.**

    Wrong: She should to study.

    Wrong: She should studying.

EXERCISE 1 Fill in the blanks with the correct tense or form of the verb in parentheses ( ).

I can't _____believe_____ it! I _____ at
(example: believe)   (1 work)

the Supreme Court now. I _____ so much experience
                              (2 gain)

here. When I _____ to law school next year, I
              (3 go)

_____ a much greater understanding of American law.
   (4 have)

And when I _____ for a job, this internship
              (5 apply)

_____ really good on my résumé.
   (6 look)

At first, I _____ a little lost and lonely because I
                (7 feel)

_____ anyone. But that soon _____.
   (8 not/know)   (9 change)

Through my classes and job, I _____ new and
                                  (10 meet)

interesting people every day.

Besides my work, I _____ classes at Georgetown
                        (11 take)

University. My professors _____ great! I
                              (12 be)

_____ so much. My knowledge about American law
   (13 learn)

_____rapidly.
   (14 increase)

I _____ an interesting roommate, too. She
      (15 have)

_____ from California. Her name is Nicole. She
   (16 be)

_____ at the Department of Education. She's planning
   (17 work)

to _____ a teacher. We _____ a small
      (18 become)   (19 have)

but comfortable apartment. We have to _____ and
                                          (20 shop)

_____ our own meals. So besides learning about the
   (21 make)

Supreme Court, I _____ how to cook. I
(22 learn)

_____ much more responsible. Are you surprised?
(23 become)

Whenever Nicole and I _____ free time, we
(24 have)

_____ to see the interesting places in Washington. But
(25 go)

we rarely _____ free time because of our jobs and our
(26 have)

classes. We might _____ to the art museum this
(27 go)

weekend if we _____ enough time.
(28 have)

There is one thing I don't like: I have to wear formal clothes every day.

I can't _____ blue jeans at my job. We must
(29 wear)

_____ very professional for our jobs.
(30 look)

I _____ the right kind of clothes when I
(31 not/have)

_____, so I _____ shopping and
(32 arrive)   *(33 go)*

_____ about $500 on new clothes. I hope you
(34 spend)

_____. I _____ the charges on your
(35 not/mind)   *(36 put)*

credit card. As you know, I'm not making any money here. But don't

worry. I _____ any more money.
(37 not/spend)

When I _____ home, I _____ you
(38 get)   *(39 tell)*

much more about my experience this summer. I know I should

_____ more often, but I just don't have the time.
(40 write)

Love,
Lena

14.2 | Statements and Questions

Simple Present Tense

-s Form	Base Form
Lena **lives** with a roommate.	Interns **wear** formal clothes.
She **doesn't live** alone.	They **don't wear** jeans.
Does she **live** in a dorm?	**Do** they **wear** formal clothes to class?
No, she **doesn't.**	No, they **don't.**
Where **does** she **live?**	What **do** they **wear** to class?
Why **doesn't** she **live** in a dorm?	Why **don't** they **wear** jeans to work?
Who **lives** in a dorm?	How many students **wear** jeans?

Present Continuous Tense

Nicole **is planning** to become a teacher.	They **are taking** classes.
Lena **isn't planning** to become a teacher.	They **aren't taking** music classes.
Is she **planning** to teach in California?	**Are** they **taking** classes at Georgetown?
No, she **isn't.**	Yes, they **are.**
Where **is** she **planning** to teach?	What kind of classes **are** they **taking?**
Why **isn't** she **planning** to teach in California?	How many students **are taking** classes?
Who **is planning** to teach in California?	

Future Tense

Will	Be Going To
They **will go** home at the end of the summer.	Lena **is going to buy** books.
They **won't go** on vacation.	She **isn't going to buy** more clothes.
Will they **go** back to college?	**Is** she **going to buy** a computer?
Yes, they **will.**	No, she **isn't.**
When **will** they **go** back to college?	What **is** she **going to buy?**
Why **won't** they **go** on vacation?	Why **isn't** she **going to buy** a computer?
Who **will go** back to college?	Who **is going to buy** a computer?

Simple Past Tense

Regular Verb	Irregular Verb
She **used** her parents' credit card.	She **bought** new clothes.
She **didn't use** cash.	She **didn't buy** jeans.
Did she **use** their card a lot?	**Did** she **buy** formal clothes?
No, she **didn't.**	Yes, she **did.**
Why **did** she **use** their card?	Why **did** she **buy** formal clothes?
Why **didn't** she **use** cash?	Why **didn't** she **buy** jeans?
Who **used** the card?	Who **bought** formal clothes?

Be	
Present	**Past**
They **are** in Washington. They **aren't** at college. **Are** they at Georgetown? Yes, they **are.** Why **are** they in Washington? Why **aren't** they at college? Who **is** at college?	Lena **was** lost at first. She **wasn't** happy. **Was** she alone? Yes, she **was.** Why **was** she alone? Why **wasn't** she happy? Who **was** alone?

Modals	
Can	**Should**
She **can** wear jeans to class. She **can't** wear jeans to work. **Can** she wear jeans at college? Yes, she **can.** What **can** she wear? Why **can't** she wear jeans to work? Who **can** wear jeans?	She **should** study every day. She **shouldn't** go to parties every day. **Should** she study about American government? Yes, she **should.** What else **should** she study? Who **should** study?

EXERCISE 2   Fill in the blanks with the negative form of the underlined verb.

EXAMPLE   Lena <u>is</u> in Washington this summer. She ____*isn't*____ at home.

1. She's <u>getting</u> experience. She _____ money for her work.

2. She <u>bought</u> new clothes. She _____ jeans.

3. She <u>writes</u> a lot for her classes. She _____ _____ a lot of letters.

4. She'll <u>finish</u> college next year. She _____ _____ college this summer.

5. She's <u>going to return</u> to college in the fall. She _____ _____ to Washington next summer.

6. She <u>can wear</u> jeans to class. She _____ jeans to work.

7. She <u>must look</u> professional at work. She _____ _____ informal at work.

Verb Review   **409**

Fill in the blanks with a question about interns.

Do interns get money for their work?

No, they don't. They get experience, not money.

Will the internship end in September?

No, it won't. The internship will end in August.

1. _____

Yes, they do. They have to take classes.

2. _____

No, they don't live in dorms. They live in apartments.

3. _____

Yes, they are. They are very busy with classes, work, and activities.

4. _____

Yes, they will. They will receive six hours of college credit.

5. _____

No, she can't. She can't wear jeans to work.

6. _____

Yes, she is. She's learning how to cook.

7. _____

No, she didn't. She didn't know anyone when she arrived in Washington.

8. _____

Yes, she does. She works in the Supreme Court.

9. _____

Yes, she did. She bought some new clothes.

Write a question with the *wh-* word given. Use the same tense. (An answer is not necessary.)

Lena is calling her mother. Why *is she calling her mother?*

1. Lena will go home soon. When _____

_____

2. Her mother doesn't remember the roommate's name. Why _____

_____

3. Lena can't go home for a weekend. Why _____

_____

4. Lena doesn't have much money. How much money _____

_____

5. Lena is learning a lot this summer. What _____

_____

6. She doesn't have time to write letters. Why _____

_____

7. Lena went to Virginia last weekend. Who(m) _____

_____ with?

8. Nicole comes from a different state. Where _____

_____ from?

9. Lena didn't cook before this summer. Why _____

_____

10. Someone went to Virginia. Who _____

_____

11. The internship will help Lena in the future. How _____

_____

12. She is working in a government department. In which department

_____

13. Lena felt lonely at first. Why _____

_____

14. She can't wear jeans to work. Why _____

_____

15. She must take classes. How many classes _____

_____

16. She is going to get college credits for her internship. How many

credits _____

17. Lena should call her parents more often. How often _____

_____

EXERCISE 5 Lena (L) is talking to her mother (M) on the phone. She is calling from Washington. Fill in the blanks with the correct form of the words in parentheses ( ).

M: Hello?

L: Hi, Mom. This is Lena.

M: Hi, Lena. I _____*am*_____ happy to _____ your voice.
_____(example: be)_____ _____(1 hear)_____

You _____.
_____(2 never/write)_____

L: I'm sorry, Mom. I _____ much time.
_____(3 not/have)_____

M: Why _____ time?
_____(4 you/not/have)_____

L: I have to work, go to classes, and participate in activities all day.

Last weekend we _____ to Virginia.
_____(5 go)_____

M: Who _____?
_____(6 drive)_____

L: No one. We _____ by metro. Public transportation
_____(7 go)_____

is really good here.

M: _____ enough to eat this summer? Who
_____(8 you/get)_____

_____ for you?
_____(9 cook)_____

L: I _____ to _____ this summer.
_____(10 learn)_____ _____(11 cook)_____

_____ surprised?
_____(12 be/you)_____

M: Yes, I am. When you were home, you never _____.
_____(13 cook)_____

You _____ it.
_____(14 hate)_____

L: Not anymore. Nicole and I often _____, and
_____(15 cook)_____

_____ our friends for dinner on the weekends.
_____(16 invite)_____

M: Who _____ Nicole?
_____(17 be)_____

L: I _____ in my last letter. She's my roommate.
(18 tell)

_____?
(19 you/not/remember)

M: Yes, of course. Now I _____. How could I forget?
(20 remember)

L: She's the same age as I am—19. She _____ from
(21 come)

California.

M: How _____? _____ it?
(22 be/your job)   (23 you/like)

L: It's great! I _____ so much this summer.
(24 learn)

M: _____ you in the future?
(25 this internship/help)

L: Yes, it will. It will be great on my résumé.

M: _____ enough money?
(26 you/have)

L: No, I don't. I _____ most of the money you
(27 spend)

_____ me when I got here.
(28 give)

M: You _____ my credit card. But don't spend money
(29 can/use)

on foolish things.

L: I won't.

M: I _____ you. _____ home for a
(30 miss)   (31 can/you/come)

weekend? We _____ for your ticket.
(32 pay)

L: I can't, Mom. We _____ activities on weekends, too.
(33 have)

M: _____ again next week?
(34 you/call)

L: If I _____ time, I _____.
(35 have)   (36 call)

But I _____ so little free time.
(37 have)

M: I'm sure you have enough time for a ten-minute phone call to your
mother.

L: You're right. I _____ you again next week. Give my
                    (38 call)

      love to Dad.
M: I will.

EDITING ADVICE

1. Use the correct word order for questions.

   your brother work?
   Where does ~~work your brother~~?

   can't you
   Why ~~you can't~~ find a job?

   is your brother
   How old ~~your brother is~~?

2. Do not forget to use *do* or *does* or *did* in a question.

   does your father live
   Where ~~lives your father~~?

   did   *give*
   When ^ the teacher ~~gave~~ a test?

3. Do not use *be* with a simple present-tense or past-tense verb.

   I ~~am~~ eat breakfast every morning.

   saw
   Yesterday, he ~~was see~~ a good movie.

4. Use the base form after *do*, *does*, and *did*.

   go
   I didn't ~~went~~ to the party.

   buy
   Did you ~~bought~~ a new car?

5. For the simple present tense, use the *-s* form when the subject is
   he, she, it, or a singular noun. Use the base form in all other cases.

   s
   Lisa never drink ^ coffee in the morning.

   My friends usually visit~~s~~ me on Saturday.

6. Use the correct past form for irregular verbs.

   left
   We ~~leaved~~ the party early.

   fell
   He ~~felt~~ down on the ice.

7. Use the base form after *to*.

   drive
   I wanted to ~~drove~~ to New York.

   He likes to eat~~s~~ popcorn.

8. Use the base form after a modal.

> *study*
> She should ~~studies~~ more.

> We must ~~to~~ drive under 55 miles per hour.

> I can't help~~ing~~ you now.

9. Connect two verbs with *to* (unless one is a modal).

> *to*
> I forgot ^ do the homework.

> *to*
> She needs ^ find a job.

10. Do not use the present continuous tense with nonaction verbs.

> I ~~am~~ know~~ing~~ the answer now.

> *s*
> He ~~is~~ hear~~ing~~ the noise in the next room.

11. Do not use *be* before a simple future verb.

> The doctor will ~~be~~ see you at 3:15.

12. Use the correct form of *be*.

> *were*
> They ~~was~~ late to the meeting.

> *are*
> You ~~is~~ always on time.

13. Use the correct negative form.

> *don't*
> They ~~not~~ know the answer.

> *don't*
> You ~~doesn't~~ need a pen.

14. Do not forget to include a form of *be* in a present continuous sentence.

> *is*
> She ^ washing the dishes now.

> *am*
> I ^ studying now.

15. Do not use the future tense in a time clause or an *if* clause. Use the simple present tense.

> When I ~~will~~ graduate, I will get a job.

> *are*
> You will fail the course if you ~~will be~~ absent more than five times.

16. Do not use the *-ing* form for the simple present tense.

> I drink~~ing~~ coffee every morning.

PART 1   Find the mistakes with the underlined words and correct them. Not every sentence has a mistake. If the sentence is correct, write *C.*

EXAMPLES   She <u>writing</u> a letter now.   *is*

               I <u>felt</u> sick yesterday.   *C*

1. We <u>taking</u> a test now.

2. Interns <u>doesn't</u> make money.

3. Lena <u>spended</u> a lot of money on clothes.

4. How <u>a student can</u> get an internship?

5. Where <u>live student interns</u>?

6. Lena <u>live</u> in an apartment.

7. She <u>can to cook</u>.

8. She <u>might needing</u> new clothes.

9. She <u>don't like</u> to wear formal clothes.

10. When I <u>will get</u> home, I <u>will show</u> you my pictures.

11. Lena <u>was bought</u> some new clothes for her job.

12. Where <u>did she went</u> last weekend?

13. I <u>will be never forget</u> my new friends.

14. I <u>am not knowing</u> all the other interns.

15. <u>Does Lena has</u> a car?

16. She <u>wanted to went</u> to a party last weekend.

17. She <u>should studying</u> now.

18. She <u>needs take</u> many courses.

19. They <u>was</u> in Virginia last week.

20. Lena <u>liking</u> her job.

PART **2** Fill in the blanks with the correct tense or form of the words in parentheses ( ).

I _____*come*_____ from India. I _____ to the
    (example: come)   *(1 decide/move)*

U.S. ten months ago. It was difficult _____ my friends
                                    (2 leave)

and family, but I _____ to the U.S. and have more
                  (3 want/come)

opportunities.

    When I _____ in India, I was a draftsman. When I
               (4 live)

_____ to the U.S. in July, I _____
    (5 come)   *(6 not/find)*

a job at first because my English wasn't good enough. Last September,

I _____ a job in a laundromat. I don't like my job at all.
    (7 find)

I _____ a better job soon. I know I _____
    (8 want/find)   *(9 get)*

a better job when I _____ English better. I
                (10 speak)

_____ my money now. When I _____
    (11 save)   *(12 have)*

enough money, I _____ engineering courses at the
           (13 begin/take)

university. My parents _____ proud of me when I
               (14 be)

_____ .
    (15 graduate)

    Right now, I _____ ESL courses at a college near my
               (16 take)

house. I _____ English in India, but it was different
       (17 study)

from American English. When I listen to Americans at my job or on TV, I

_____ a lot of things they say. Sometimes when I
  (18 can/not/understand)

_____ with Americans at my job, they _____
    (19 speak)   *(20 not/understand)*

me. They sometimes _____ at my pronunciation. They
              (21 laugh)

aren't bad people, but they _____ that it is hard
               (22 not/understand)

_____ another language and live in another country.
    (23 learn)

I usually _____ by myself at work. I _____
        (24 stay)   *(25 know)*

I _____ more, but I'm very shy.
  (26 should/practice)

When I _____ in India, I _____
(27 be)   (28 live)

in a big house with my parents, sisters and brothers, and grandparents.

Now I _____ a small apartment and live alone.
(29 have)

Sometimes I _____ lonely. I would like
(30 be)

_____ married someday, but first I want
(31 get)

_____ some money and _____
(32 earn)   (33 save)

for my future.

PART 3 Write the negative form of the underlined words.

EXAMPLE He <u>moved</u> to the U.S. He _____*didn't move*_____ to England.

1. He <u>studied</u> English in India. He _____ German.

2. He <u>wants to work</u> as an engineer. He _____ in a laundromat.

3. He <u>is going to study</u> engineering. He _____ art.

4. He <u>is taking</u> courses at a community college now. He _____ _____ courses at a university.

5. He's <u>saving</u> his money to get married. He _____ his money to go back to his country.

6. His coworkers <u>know</u> that he is a foreigner. They _____ _____ how difficult his life is.

7. He <u>should</u> practice English with Americans. He _____ _____ be shy.

8. He <u>can understand</u> some TV programs. He _____ _____ all TV programs.

PART 4 Read each statement. Then write a *yes/no* question about the words in parentheses ( ). Write a short answer.

EXAMPLE He <u>studied</u> English in India. (American English)
Did he study American English? No, he didn't.

1. He'll <u>study</u> engineering. (accounting)

_____

2. Americans don't understand him. (Indians)

_____

3. He's studying American English now. (American history)

_____

4. He lives in a small apartment. (with his family)

_____

5. He can understand British English. (American English)

_____

6. It is hard to learn another language. (live in another country)

_____

7. He wants to get married. (next year)

_____

8. He lived with his parents in India. (with his grandparents)

_____

PART 5 Read each statement. Then write a *wh-* question with the words in parentheses ( ). (An answer is not necessary.)

EXAMPLE He left India. (why)
Why did he leave India?

1. He is saving his money. (why)

_____

2. He is going to get married. (When)

_____

3. Some people laugh at him. (who)

_____

4. He is lonely. (why)

_____

5. His parents aren't in the U.S. (why)

_____

6. He didn't find a job at first. (why)

_____

7. He will graduate from the university. (when)

_____

8. He <u>came</u> to the U.S. alone. (why)

_____

9. His coworkers <u>don't understand</u> his accent. (why)

_____

10. He <u>lived</u> in a big house. (when)

_____

EXPANSION ACTIVITIES

Classroom Activities

1. Interview a student from another country. Use the words below to ask and answer questions. Practice the simple present, the present continuous, the future, and the simple past tenses.

EXAMPLES   you / from Asia

A: Are you from Asia?
B: Yes, I am. OR No, I'm not.

where / you / from

A: Where are you from?
B: I'm from Pakistan.

a. when / you / leave your country

b. how / you / come to the U.S.

c. you / come / to the U.S. alone

d. where / you / born

e. what language(s) / you speak

f. you / return to your country next year

g. you / have a job now

h. you / have a job in your country

i. how many brothers and sisters / you/ have

j. your country / big

k. your country / have a lot of petroleum

l. you / live in an apartment in your hometown

m. you / study English in your country

n. what / you / study this semester

o. what / you / study next semester

p. you / like this class

q. the teacher / speak your language

r. this class / hard for you

s. who / your teacher last semester

t. who / your teacher next semester

2. Write sentences in each category, if you can. Write one for the simple present, one for the present continuous, one for the future, and one for the simple past tense.

	Simple Present	Present Continuous	Future	Simple Past
Job	I work in a factory.	I'm looking for a new job.	Next week I'm going to have an interview.	In my country, I was a taxi driver.
School				
Family				
Weather				
Apartment				

Outside Activity

Use the words below to interview a native speaker of English at this school. Practice the simple present, the present continuous, the future, and the simple past tenses. Report something interesting to the class about this student.

EXAMPLE you have a car (what kind)

A: Do you have a car?
B: Yes, I do.
A: What kind of car do you have?
B: I have a Honda.

1. you / study another language now (what language)
2. you / live alone (who . . . with)
3. your family / live in this city
4. you / like this city (why / why not)
5. you / go to high school in this city (where)
6. what / your major
7. you / graduate soon (when)
8. what / you do / after / you / graduate
9. you / like to travel (when . . . your last vacation) (where . . . go)
10. you / own a computer (what kind) (when . . . buy it)
11. you / eat in a restaurant / last week (where)
12. you / buy something new / in the near future (what)
13. you / do something interesting / last weekend (what . . . do)
14. you / plan to do something interesting / next weekend (what . . . do)

Invite the native speaker to interview you. Write down the questions that he or she asks you.

Internet Activity

Using a search engine, look up "Washington internship" on the Internet. Find out what some students say about their experience as an intern.

Additional Activities at http://elt.heinle.com/gic

Appendices

The Verb *GET*

Get has many meanings. Here is a list of the most common ones:

- get something = receive
    I got a letter from my father.

- get + (to) place = arrive
    I got home at six. What time do you get to school?

- get + object + infinitive = persuade
    She got him to wash the dishes.

- get + past participle = become

get acquainted	get worried	get hurt
get engaged	get lost	get bored
get married	get accustomed to	get confused
get divorced	get used to	get scared
get tired	get dressed	

    They got married in 1989.

- get + adjective = become

get hungry	get sleepy
get rich	get dark
get nervous	get angry
get well	get old
get upset	get fat

    It gets dark at 6:30.

- get an illness = catch
    While she was traveling, she got malaria.

- get a joke or an idea = understand
    Everybody except Tom laughed at the joke. He didn't get it.
    The boss explained the project to us, but I didn't get it.

Continued

- get ahead = advance

  He works very hard because he wants to get ahead in his job.

- get along (well) (with someone) = have a good relationship

  She doesn't get along with her mother-in-law.

  Do you and your roommate get along well?

- get around to something = find the time to do something

  I wanted to write my brother a letter yesterday, but I didn't get around to it.

- get away = escape

  The police chased the thief, but he got away.

- get away with something = escape punishment

  He cheated on his taxes and got away with it.

- get back = return

  He got back from his vacation last Saturday.

- get back at someone = get revenge

  My brother wants to get back at me for stealing his girlfriend.

- get back to someone = communicate with someone at a later time

  The boss can't talk to you today. Can she get back to you tomorrow?

- get by = have just enough but nothing more

  On her salary, she's just getting by. She can't afford a car or a vacation.

- get in trouble = be caught and punished for doing something wrong

  They got in trouble for cheating on the test.

- get in(to) = enter a car

  She got in the car and drove away quickly.

- get out (of) = leave a car

  When the taxi arrived at the theater, everyone got out.

- get on = seat yourself on a bicycle, motorcycle, horse

  She got on the motorcycle and left.

- get on = enter a train, bus, airplane

  She got on the bus and took a seat in the back.

- get off = leave a bicycle, motorcycle, horse, train, bus, airplane

  They will get off the train at the next stop.

- get out of something = escape responsibility

  My boss wants me to help him on Saturday, but I'm going to try to get out of it.

- get over something = recover from an illness or disappointment

  She has the flu this weak. I hope she gets over it soon.

- get rid of someone or something = free oneself of someone or something undesirable

  My apartment has roaches, and I can't get rid of them.

Continued

- get through (to someone) = communicate, often by telephone
    She tried to explain the harm of eating fast food to her son, but she couldn't get through to him.
    I tried to call my mother many times, but her line was busy. I couldn't get through.

- get through (with something) = finish
    I can meet you after I get through with my homework.

- get together = meet with another person
    I'd like to see you again. When can we get together?

- get up = arise from bed
    He woke up at 6 o'clock, but he didn't get up until 6:30.

APPENDIX B

MAKE and *DO*

Some expressions use *make*. Others use *do*.	
Make	**Do**
make a date/an appointment	do (the) homework
make a plan	do an exercise
make a decision	do the dishes
make a telephone call	do the cleaning, laundry, ironing, washing, etc.
make a reservation	do the shopping
make a meal (breakfast, lunch, dinner)	do one's best
make a mistake	do a favor
make an effort	do the right/wrong thing
make an improvement	do a job
make a promise	do business
make money	What do you do for a living? (asks about a job)
make noise	How do you do? (said when you
make the bed	meet someone for the first time)

APPENDIX C

Question Formation

1. Statements and Related Questions with a Main Verb.

Wh- Word	Do/Does/Did (n't)	Subject	Verb	Complement
When	does	She / she	watches / watch	TV. / TV?
Where	do	My parents / your parents	live / live?	in Peru.
Who(m)	does	Your sister / she	likes / like?	someone.
Why	did	They / they	left / leave	early. / early?
How many books	did	She / she	found / find?	some books.
What kind of car	did	He / he	bought / buy?	a car.
Why	didn't	She / she	didn't go / go	home. / home?
Why	doesn't	He / he	doesn't like / like	tomatoes. / tomatoes?

Subject	Verb (base form or -s form or past form)	Complement
Someone / Who	has / has	my book. / my book?
Someone / Who	needs / needs	help. / help?
Someone / Who	took / took	my pen. / my pen?
One teacher / Which teacher	speaks / speaks	Spanish. / Spanish?
Some men / Which men	have / have	a car. / a car?
Some boys / How many boys	saw / saw	the movie. / the movie?
Something / What	happened. / happened?	

2. Statements and Related Questions with the Verb *Be*.

Wh- Word	Be	Subject	Be	Complement	AP5
Where	is	She she?	is	in California.	
Why	were	They they	were	hungry. hungry?	
Why	isn't	He he	isn't	tired. tired?	
When	was	He he	was	born in England. born?	
		One student Who Which student	was was was	late. late? late?	
		Some kids How many kids Which kids	were were were	afraid. afraid? afraid?	

3. Statements and Related Questions with an Auxiliary (Aux) Verb and a Main Verb.

Wh- Word	Aux	Subject	Aux	Main Verb	Complement
Where	is	She she	is	running. running?	
When	will	They they	will	go go	on a vacation. on a vacation?
What	should	He he	should	do do?	something.
How many pills	can	You you	can	take take?	a pill.
Why	can't	You you	can't	drive drive	a car. a car?
		Someone Who	should should	answer answer	the question. the question?

Alphabetical List of Irregular Past Forms

Base Form	Past Form	Base Form	Past Form
arise	arose	forget	forgot
awake	awoke	forgive	forgave
be	was/were	freeze	froze
bear	bore	get	got
beat	beat	give	gave
become	became	go	went
begin	began	grind	ground
bend	bent	grow	grew
bet	bet	hang	hung[1]
bind	bound	have	had
bite	bit	hear	heard
bleed	bled	hide	hid
blow	blew	hit	hit
break	broke	hold	held
breed	bred	hurt	hurt
bring	brought	keep	kept
broadcast	broadcast	kneel	knelt (or kneeled)
build	built	know	knew
burst	burst	lay	laid
buy	bought	lead	led
cast	cast	leave	left
catch	caught	lend	lent
choose	chose	let	let
cling	clung	lie	lay
come	came	light	lit (or lighted)
cost	cost	lose	lost
creep	crept	make	made
cut	cut	mean	meant
deal	dealt	meet	met
dig	dug	mistake	mistook
do	did	pay	paid
draw	drew	put	put
drink	drank	quit	quit
drive	drove	read	read
eat	ate	ride	rode
fall	fell	ring	rang
feed	fed	rise	rose
feel	felt	run	ran
fight	fought	say	said
find	found	see	saw
fit	fit	seek	sought
flee	fled	sell	sold
fly	flew	send	sent

Continued

[1]*Hanged* is used as the past form to refer to punishment by death. *Hung* is used in other situations. She *hung* the picture on the wall.

Base Form	Past Form	Base Form	Past Form
forbid	forbade	set	set
shake	shook	stink	stank
shed	shed	strike	struck
shine	shone (or shined)	strive	strove
shoot	shot	swear	swore
shrink	shrank	sweep	swept
shut	shut	swim	swam
sing	sang	swing	swung
sink	sank	take	took
sit	sat	teach	taught
sleep	slept	tear	tore
slide	slid	tell	told
slit	slit	think	thought
speak	spoke	throw	threw
speed	sped	understand	understood
spend	spent	upset	upset
spin	spun	wake	woke
spit	spit	wear	wore
split	split	weave	wove
spread	spread	weep	wept
spring	sprang	win	won
stand	stood	wind	wound
steal	stole	withdraw	withdrew
stick	stuck	wring	wrung
sting	stung	write	wrote

APPENDIX E

Meanings of Modals and Related Words

- Ability, Possibility

  Can you drive a truck?

  You **can** get a ticket for speeding.

- Necessity, Obligation

  A driver **must** have a license (legal obligation)

  I **have** *to* buy a new car. (personal obligation)

- Permission

  You **can** park at a meter.

  You **can't** park at a bus stop.

- Possibility

  I **may** buy a new car soon.

  I **might** buy a Japanese car.

- Advice

  You **should** buy a new car. Your old car is in terrible condition.

- Permission Request

    May I borrow your car?

    Can I have the keys, please?

    Could I have the keys, please?

- Polite Request

    Would you teach me to drive?

    Could you show me your new car?

- Want

    What **would** you **like** to eat?

    I'd like a turkey sandwich.

Capitalization Rules

- The first word in a sentence: **My** friends are helpful.

- The word "I": My sister and **I** took a trip together.

- Names of people: **J**ulia **R**oberts; **G**eorge **W**ashington

- Titles preceding names of people: **D**octor (**D**r.) **S**mith; **P**resident **L**incoln; **Q**ueen **E**lizabeth; **M**r. **R**ogers; **M**rs. **C**arter

- Geographic names: the **U**nited **S**tates; **L**ake **S**uperior; **C**alifornia; the **R**ocky **M**ountains; the **M**ississippi **R**iver

    NOTE: The word "the" in a geographic name is not capitalized.

- Street names: **P**ennsylvania **A**venue (**A**ve.); **W**all **S**treet (**S**t.); **A**bbey **R**oad (**R**d.)

- Names of organizations, companies, colleges, buildings, stores, hotels: the **R**epublican **P**arty; **H**einle **T**homson; **D**artmouth **C**ollege; the **U**niversity of **W**isconsin; the **W**hite **H**ouse; **B**loomingdale's; the **H**ilton **H**otel

- Nationalities and ethnic groups: **M**exicans; **C**anadians; **S**paniards; **A**mericans; **J**ews; **K**urds; **E**skimos

- Languages: **E**nglish; **S**panish; **P**olish; **V**ietnamese; **R**ussian

- Months: **J**anuary; **F**ebruary

- Days: **S**unday; **M**onday

- Holidays: **C**hristmas; **I**ndependence **D**ay

- Important words in a title: **G**rammar in **C**ontext; **T**he **O**ld **M**an and the **S**ea; **R**omeo and **J**uliet; **T**he **S**ound of **M**usic

    NOTE: Capitalize "the" as the first word of a title.

Metric Conversion Chart

Length

When You Know	Symbol	Multiply by	To Find	Symbol
inches	in	2.54	centimeters	cm
feet	ft	30.5	centimeters	cm
feet	ft	0.3	meters	m
yards	yd	0.91	meters	m
miles	mi	1.6	kilometers	km
Metric:				
centimeters	cm	0.39	inches	in
centimeters	cm	0.03	feet	ft
meters	m	3.28	feet	ft
meters	m	1.09	yards	yd
kilometers	km	0.62	miles	mi

Note:

1 foot = 12 inches

1 yard = 3 feet or 36 inches

Area

When You Know	Symbol	Multiply by	To Find	Symbol
square inches	in^2	6.5	square centimeters	cm^2
square feet	ft^2	0.09	square meters	m^2
square yards	yd^2	0.8	square meters	m^2
square miles	mi^2	2.6	square kilometers	km^2
Metric:				
square centimeters	cm^2	0.16	square inches	in^2
square meters	m^2	10.76	square feet	ft^2
square meters	m^2	1.2	square yards	yd^2
square kilometers	km^2	0.39	square miles	mi^2

Continued

Weight (Mass)

When You Know	Symbol	Multiply by	To Find	Symbol
ounces	oz	28.35	grams	g
pounds	lb	0.45	kilograms	kg
Metric:				
grams	g	0.04	ounces	oz
kilograms	kg	2.2	pounds	lb
Note:				
1 pound = 16 ounces				

Volume

When You Know	Symbol	Multiply by	To Find	Symbol
fluid ounces	fl oz	30.0	milliliters	mL
pints	pt	0.47	liters	L
quarts	qt	0.95	liters	L
gallons	gal	3.8	liters	L
Metric:				
milliliters	mL	0.03	fluid ounces	fl oz
liters	L	2.11	pints	pt
liters	L	1.05	quarts	qt
liters	L	0.26	gallons	gal

Temperature

When You Know	Symbol	Do this	To Find	Symbol
degrees Fahrenheit	°F	Subtract 32, then multiply by $\frac{5}{9}$	degrees Celsius	°C
Metric:				
degrees Celsius	°C	Multiply by $\frac{9}{5}$, then add 32	degrees Fahrenheit	°F

Sample temperatures	
Fahrenheit	Celsius
0	– 18
10	– 12
20	– 7
30	– 1
40	4
50	10
60	16
70	21
80	27
90	32
100	38

APPENDIX H

Prepositions of Time

- **in** the morning: He takes a shower *in* the morning.
- **in** the afternoon: He takes a shower *in* the afternoon.
- **in** the evening: He takes a shower *in* the evening.
- **at** night: He takes a shower *at* night.
- **in** the summer, fall, winter, spring: He takes classes *in* the summer.
- **on** that/this day: October 10 is my birthday. I became a citizen *on* that day.
- **on** the weekend: He studies *on* the weekend.
- **on** a specific day: His birthday is *on* March 5.
- **in** a month: His birthday is *in* March.
- **in** a year: He was born *in* 1978.
- **in** a century: People didn't use cars *in* the 19th century.
- **on** a day: I don't have class *on* Monday.
- **at** a specific time: My class begins *at* 12:30.
- **from** a time **to** another time: My class is *from* 12:30 *to* 3:30.
- **in** a number of hours, days, weeks, months, years: She will graduate *in* three weeks. (This means "after" three weeks.)

- **for** a number of hours, days, weeks, months, years: She was in Mexico *for* three weeks. (This means during the period of three weeks.)

- **by** a time: Please finish your test *by* 6 o'clock. (This means "no later than" 6 o'clock.)

- **until** a time: I lived with my parents *until* I came to the U.S. (This means "all the time before.")

- **during** the movie, class, meeting: He slept *during* the meeting.

- **about/around** 6 o'clock: The movie will begin *about* 6 o'clock. People will arrive *around* 5:45.

- **in** the past/future: *In* the past, she never exercised.

- **at** present: *At* present, the days are getting longer.

- **in** the beginning/end: *In* the beginning, she didn't understand the teacher at all.

- **at** the beginning/end of something: The semester beings *at* the beginning of September. My birthday is *at* the end of June.

- **before/after** a time: You should finish the job *before* Friday. The library will be closed *after* 6:00.

- **before/after** an action takes place: Turn off the lights *before* you leave. Wash the dishes *after* you finish dinner.

APPENDIX I

Glossary of Grammatical Terms

- **Adjective** An adjective gives a description of a noun.

    It's a *tall* tree.   He's an *old* man.   My neighbors are *nice*.

- **Adverb** An adverb describes the action of a sentence or an adjective or another adverb.

    She speaks English *fluently*.   I drive *carefully*.
    She speaks English *extremely* well.   She is *very* intelligent.

- **Adverb of Frequency** An adverb of frequency tells how often the action happens.

    I *never* drink coffee.   They *usually* take the bus.

- **Affirmative** means *yes*.

- **Apostrophe** ' We use the apostrophe for possession and contractions.

    My *sister's* friend is beautiful.   Today *isn't* Sunday.

- **Article** The definite article is *the*. The indefinite articles are *a* and *an*.

    I have *a* cat.   I ate *an* apple.   *The* president was in
                                                New York last weekend.

- **Auxiliary Verb** Some verbs have two parts: an auxiliary verb and a main verb.

    He *can't* study.   We *will* return.

- **Base Form** The base form, sometimes called the "simple" form, of the verb has no tense. It has no ending (-*s* or -*ed*): *be, go, eat, take, write.*

    I didn't *go* out.   He doesn't *know* the answer.

    You shouldn't *talk* loudly.

- **Capital Letter** A B C D E F G . . .

- **Clause** A clause is a group of words that has a subject and a verb. Some sentences have only one clause.

    She speaks Spanish.

    Some sentences have **a main clause** and a **dependent clause.**

MAIN CLAUSE	DEPENDENT CLAUSE (**reason clause**)
She found a good job	because she has computer skills.
MAIN CLAUSE	DEPENDENT CLAUSE (**time clause**)
She'll turn off the light	before she goes to bed.
MAIN CLAUSE	DEPENDENT CLAUSE (***if* clause**)
I'll take you to the doctor	if you don't have your car on Saturday.

- **Colon :**

- **Comma ,**

- **Comparative Form** A comparative form of an adjective or adverb is used to compare two things.

    My house is *bigger* than your house.

    Her husband drives *faster* than she does.

- **Complement** The complement of the sentence is the information after the verb. It completes the verb phrase.

    He works *hard*.   I slept *for five hours*.   They are *late*.

- **Consonant** The following letters are consonants: *b, c, d, f, g, h, j, k, l, m, n, p, q, r, s, t, v, w, x, y, z.*

    NOTE: *y* is sometimes considered a vowel, as in the world *syllable.*

- **Contraction** A contraction is made up of two words put together with an apostrophe.

    He's my brother.   *You're* late.   They *won't* talk to me.

    (*He's = he is*)   (*You're = you are*)   (*won't = will not*)

- **Count Noun** Count nouns are nouns that we can count. They have a singular and a plural form.

    1 pen — 3 pens   1 table — 4 tables

- **Dependent Clause** See **Clause.**

- **Direct Object** A direct object is a noun (phrase) or pronoun that receives the action of the verb.

    We saw *the movie.*   You have *a nice car.*   I love *you.*

- **Exclamation Mark** !

- **Frequency Words** Frequency words are *always, usually, often, sometimes, rarely, seldom, never.*

    I *never* drink coffee.   We *always* do our homework.

- **Hyphen** –

- **Imperative** An imperative sentence gives a command or instructions. An imperative sentence omits the word *you.*

    Come here.   *Don't be* late.   Please *sit* down.

- **Infinitive** An infinitive is *to* + base form.

    I want *to leave.*   You need *to be* here on time.

- **Linking Verb** A linking verb is a verb that links the subject to the noun or adjective after it. Linking verbs include *be, seem, feel, smell, sound, look, appear, taste.*

    She *is* a doctor.   She *seems* very intelligent.   She *looks* tired.

- **Modal** The modal verbs are *can, could, shall, should, will, would, may, might, must.*

    They *should* leave.   I *must* go.

- **Negative** means no.

- **Nonaction Verb** A nonaction verb has no action. We do not use a continuous tense (*be* + verb *-ing*) with a nonaction verb. The nonaction verbs are: *believe, cost, care, have, hear, know, like, love, matter, mean, need, own, prefer, remember, see, seem, think, understand, want.*

    She *has* a laptop.   We *love* our mother.

- **Noncount Noun** A noncount noun is a noun that we don't count. It has no plural form.

    She drank some *water.*   He prepared some *rice.*

    Do you need any *money*?

- **Noun** A noun is a person (*brother*), a place (*kitchen*), or a thing (*table*). Nouns can be either count (*1 table, 2 tables*) or noncount (*money, water*).

    My *brother* lives in California.   My *sisters* live in New York.

    I get *mail* from them.

- **Noun Modifier** A noun modifier makes a noun more specific.

    fire department   *Independence* Day   *can* opener

- **Noun Phrase** A noun phrase is a group of words that form the subject or object of the sentence.

    A very nice woman helped me at registration.

    I bought *a big box of candy.*

- **Object** The object of the sentence follows the verb. It receives the action of the verb.

   He bought *a car*.   I saw *a movie*.   I met *your brother*.

- **Object Pronoun** Use object pronouns (*me, you, him, her, it, us, them*) after the verb or preposition.

   He likes *her*.   I saw the movie. Let's talk about *it*.

- **Parentheses ( )**

- **Paragraph** A paragraph is a group of sentences about one topic.

- **Participle, Present** The present participle is verb + *-ing*.

   She is *sleeping*.   They were *laughing*.

- **Period .**

- **Phrase** A group of words that go together.

   Last month my sister came to visit.

   There is a strange car *in front of my house*.

- **Plural** Plural means more than one. A plural noun usually ends with *-s*.

   She has beautiful *eyes*.

- **Possessive Form** Possessive forms show ownership or relationship.

   Mary's coat is in the closet.   *My* brother lives in Miami.

- **Preposition** A preposition is a short connecting word: *about, above, across, after, around, as, at, away, back, before, behind, below, by, down, for, from, in, into, like, of, off, on, out, over, to, under, up with*.

   The book is *on* the table.

- **Pronoun** A pronoun takes the place of a noun.

   I have a new car. I bought *it* last week.

   John likes Mary, but *she* doesn't like *him*.

- **Punctuation** Period . Comma , Colon : Semicolon ; Question Mark ? Exclamation Mark !

- **Question Mark ?**

- **Quotation Marks " "**

- **Regular Verb** A regular verb forms its past tense with *-ed*.

   He *worked* yesterday.   I *laughed* at the joke.

- **s Form** A present tense verb that ends in *-s* or *-es*.

   He *lives* in New York.   She *watches* TV a lot.

- **Sense-Perception Verb** A sense-perception verb has no action. It describes a sense.

   She *feels* fine.   The coffee *smells* fresh.   The milk *tastes* sour.

- **Sentence** A sentence is a group of words that contains a subject[1] and a verb (at least) and gives a complete thought.

  SENTENCE: She came home.

  NOT A SENTENCE: When she came home

- **Simple Form of Verb** The simple form of the verb, also called the "base" form, has no tense; it never has an -s, -ed, or -ing ending.

  Did you *see* the movie?   I couldn't *find* your phone number.

- **Singular** Singular means one.

  She ate a *sandwich*.   I have one *television*.

- **Subject** The subject of the sentence tells who or what the sentence is about.

  My sister got married last April. *The wedding* was beautiful.

- **Subject Pronouns** Use subject pronouns (*I, you, he, she, it, we, you, they*) before a verb.

  They speak Japanese.   *We* speak Spanish.

- **Superlative Form** A superlative form of an adjective or adverb shows the number one item in a group of three or more.

  January is the *coldest* month of the year.

  My brother speaks English the *best* in my family.

- **Syllable** A syllable is a part of a word that has only one vowel sound. (Some words have only one syllable.)

  change (one syllable)   after (af·ter = 2 syllables)

  look (one syllable)   responsible (re·spon·si·ble = 4 syllables)

- **Tag Question** A tag question is a short question at the end of a sentence. It is used in conversation.

  You speak Spanish, *don't you?*   He's not happy, *is he?*

- **Tense** A verb has tense. Tense shows when the action of the sentence happened.

  SIMPLE PRESENT: She usually *works* hard.

  FUTURE: She *will work* tomorrow.

  PRESENT CONTINUOUS: She *is working* now.

  SIMPLE PAST: She *worked* yesterday.

- **Verb** A verb is the action of the sentence.

  He *runs* fast.   I *speak* English.

  Some verbs have no action. They are linking verbs. They connect the subject to the rest of the sentence.

  He *is* tall.   She *looks* beautiful.   You *seem* tired.

- **Vowel** The following letters are vowels: *a, e, i, o, u. Y* is sometimes considered a vowel (for example, in the word *syllable*).

---

[1] In an imperative sentence, the subject *you* is omitted: *Sit down. Come here.*

Verbs and Adjectives Followed by a Preposition

(be) accustomed to	forgive someone for	(be) proud of
(be) afraid of	(be) glad about	recover from
agree with	(be) good at	(be) related to
(be) angry about	(be) happy about	rely on/upon
(be) angry at/with	hear about	(be) responsible for
approve of	hear of	(be) sad about
argue about	hope for	(be) satisfied with
(be) ashamed of	(be) incapable of	(be) scared of
(be) aware of	insist on/upon	(be) sick of
believe in	(be) interested in	(be) sorry about
(be) bored with/by	(be) involved in	(be) sorry for
(be) capable of	(be) jealous of	speak about
care about/for	(be) known for	speak to/with
(be) compared to	(be) lazy about	succeed in
complain about	listen to	(be) sure of/about
(be) concerned about	look at	(be) surprised at
concentrate on	look for	take care of
consist of	look forward to	talk about
count on	(be) mad about	talk to/with
deal with	(be) mad at	thank someone for
decide on	(be) made from/of	(be) thankful to someone for
depend on/upon	(be) married to	think about/of
dream about/of	object to	(be) tired of
(be) engaged to	participate in	(be) upset about
(be) excited about	plan on	(be) upset with
(be) familiar with	pray to	(be) used to
(be) famous for	pray for	wait for
feel like	(be) prepared for	warn about
(be) fond of	prohibit from	(be) worried about
forget about	protect someone from	worry about

The United States of America: Major Cities

AL	Alabama	IN	Indiana	NE	Nebraska	SC	South Carolina
AK	Alaska	IA	Iowa	NV	Nevada	SD	South Dakota
AZ	Arizona	KS	Kansas	NH	New Hampshire	TN	Tennessee
AR	Arkansas	KY	Kentucky	NJ	New Jersey	TX	Texas
CA	California	LA	Louisiana	NM	New Mexico	UT	Utah
CO	Colorado	ME	Maine	NY	New York	VT	Vermont
CT	Connecticut	MD	Maryland	NC	North Carolina	VA	Virginia
DE	Delaware	MA	Massachusetts	ND	North Dakota	WA	Washington
FL	Florida	MI	Michigan	OH	Ohio	WV	West Virginia
GA	Georgia	MN	Minnesota	OK	Oklahoma	WI	Wisconsin
HI	Hawaii	MS	Mississippi	OR	Oregon	WY	Wyoming
ID	Idaho	MO	Missouri	PA	Pennsylvania	DC*	District of
IL	Illinois	MT	Montana	RI	Rhode Island		Columbia

*The District of Columbia is not a state. Washington, D.C., is the capital of the United States.
Note: Washington, D.C., and Washigton state are not the same.

Index